SALADIN AHMED   SAMI KIVELÄ   MATTIA IACONO

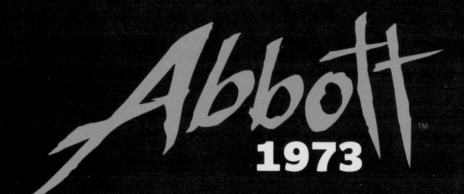

Published by

STUDIOS

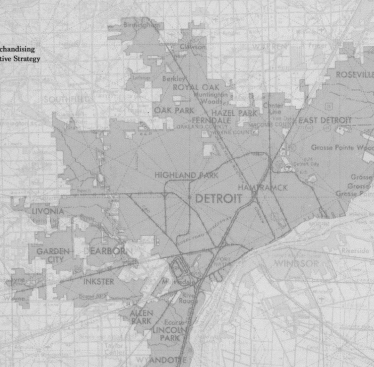

"JOURNA
THE FIRST R
OF HIS

ABBOTT: 1973, October 2021. Published by BOOM! Studios, a division of Boom Entertainment, Inc. Abbott is ™ & © 2021 Saladin Ahmed. Originally published in single magazine form as ABBOTT: 1973 No. 1-5. ™ & © 2021 Saladin Ahmed. All rights reserved. BOOM! Studios™ and the BOOM! Studios logo are trademarks of Boom Entertainment, Inc., registered in various countries and categories. All characters, events, and institutions depicted herein are fictional. Any similarity between any of the names, characters, persons, events, and/or institutions in this publication to actual names, characters, and persons, whether living or dead, events, and/or institutions is unintended and purely coincidental. BOOM! Studios does not read or accept unsolicited submissions of ideas, stories, or artwork.

BOOM! Studios, 5670 Wilshire Boulevard, Suite 400, Los Angeles, CA, 90036-5679. Printed in China. First Printing.

ISBN: 978-1-68415-651-1, eISBN: 978-1-64668-136-5

LISM IS OUGH DRAFT TORY"

Written by
Saladin Ahmed

Illustrated by
Sami Kivelä

Colored by
Mattia Iacono

Lettered by
Jim Campbell

Cover by
Taj Tenfold

Series Designer
Michelle Ankley

Collection Designer
Chelsea Roberts

Assistant Editor
Gavin Gronenthal

Editor
Jonathan Manning

Senior Editor
Eric Harburn

Abbott Created by
Saladin Ahmed

CHAPTER ONE

Issue One Cover by Taj Tenfold

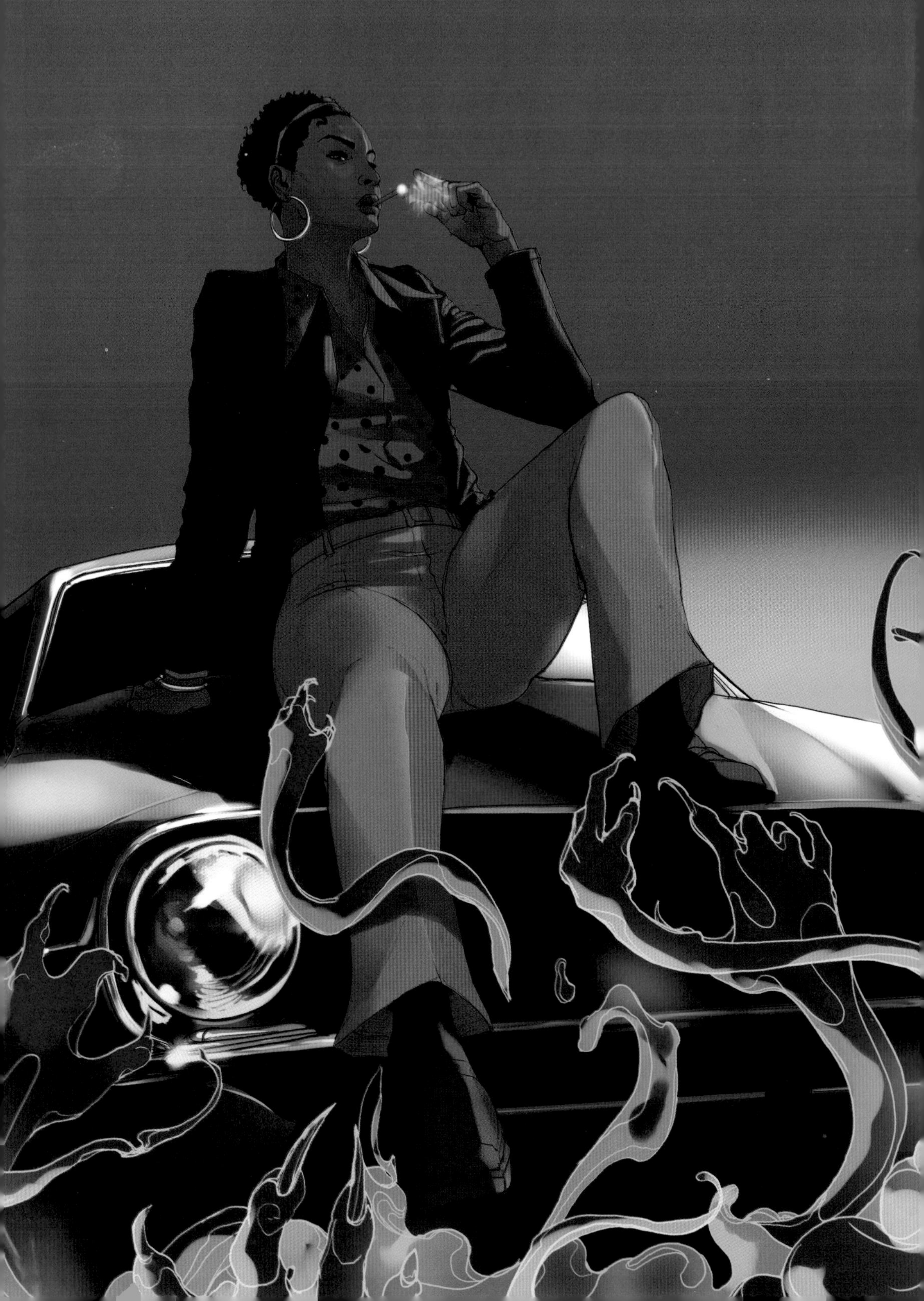

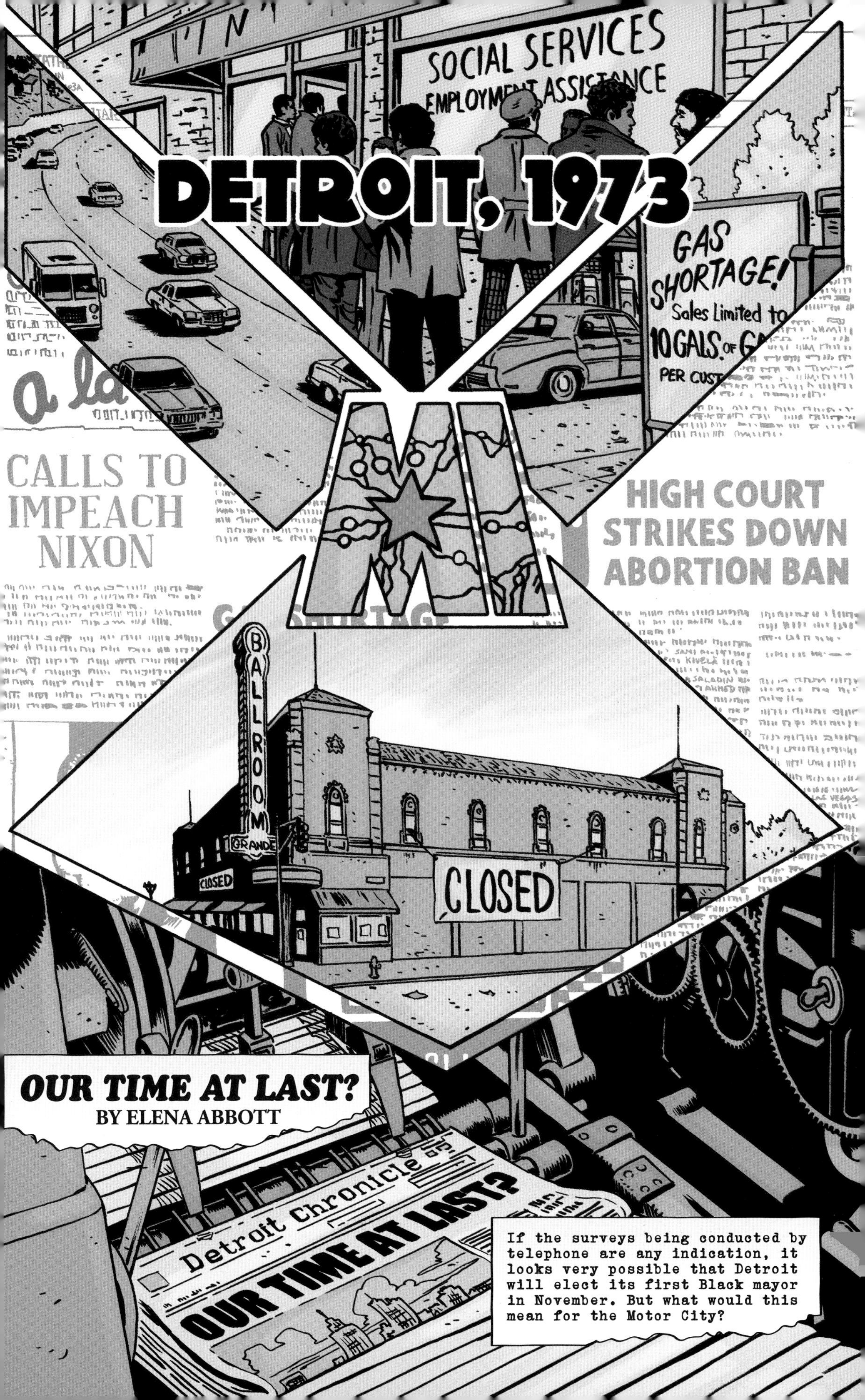
SOCIAL SERVICES
EMPLOYMENT ASSISTANCE
DETROIT, 1973
GAS SHORTAGE!
Sales Limited to
10 GALS. OF GA
PER CUST
CALLS TO IMPEACH NIXON
HIGH COURT STRIKES DOWN ABORTION BAN
BALLROOM
GRANDE
CLOSED
CLOSED
OUR TIME AT LAST?
BY ELENA ABBOTT
Detroit Chronicle
OUR TIME AT LAST?
If the surveys being conducted by telephone are any indication, it looks very possible that Detroit will elect its first Black mayor in November. But what would this mean for the Motor City?

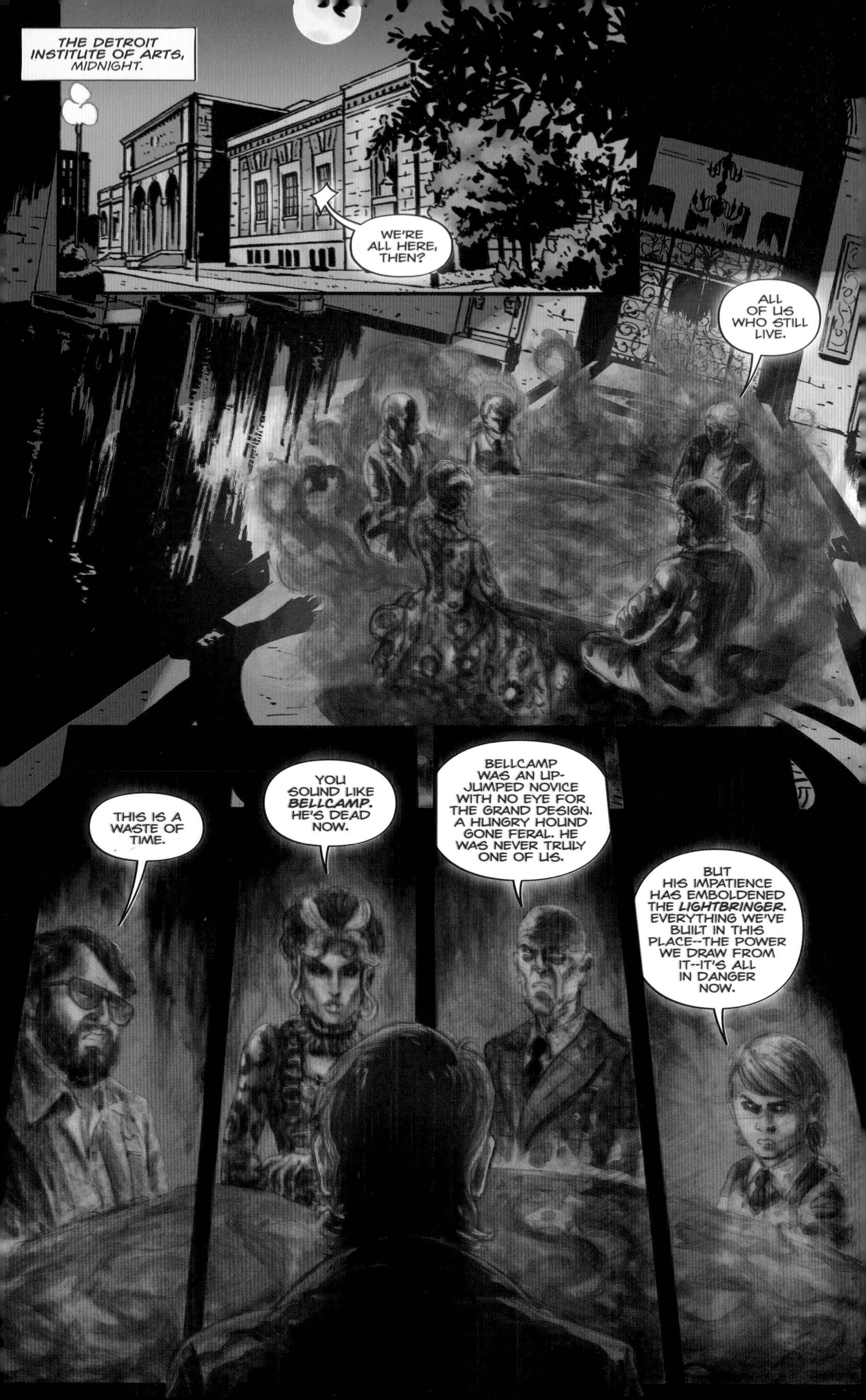
THE DETROIT INSTITUTE OF ARTS, MIDNIGHT.
WE'RE ALL HERE, THEN?
ALL OF US WHO STILL LIVE.
THIS IS A WASTE OF TIME.
YOU SOUND LIKE BELLCAMP. HE'S DEAD NOW.
BELLCAMP WAS AN UP-JUMPED NOVICE WITH NO EYE FOR THE GRAND DESIGN. A HUNGRY HOUND GONE FERAL. HE WAS NEVER TRULY ONE OF US.
BUT HIS IMPATIENCE HAS EMBOLDENED THE LIGHTBRINGER. EVERYTHING WE'VE BUILT IN THIS PLACE--THE POWER WE DRAW FROM IT--IT'S ALL IN DANGER NOW.

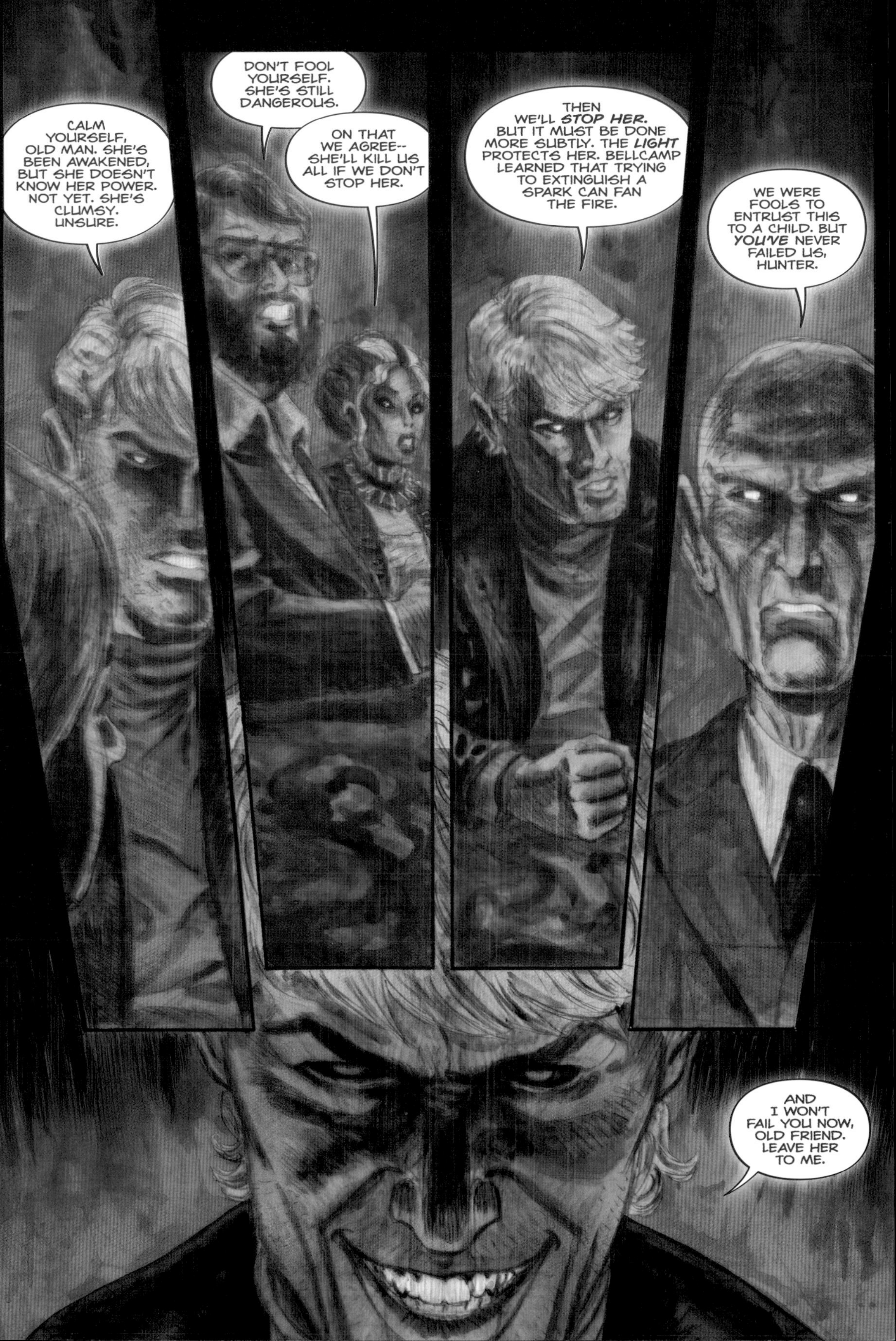
CALM YOURSELF, OLD MAN. SHE'S BEEN AWAKENED, BUT SHE DOESN'T KNOW HER POWER. NOT YET. SHE'S CLUMSY. UNSURE.
DON'T FOOL YOURSELF. SHE'S STILL DANGEROUS.
ON THAT WE AGREE-- SHE'LL KILL US ALL IF WE DON'T STOP HER.
THEN WE'LL *STOP HER.* BUT IT MUST BE DONE MORE SUBTLY. THE *LIGHT* PROTECTS HER. BELLCAMP LEARNED THAT TRYING TO EXTINGUISH A SPARK CAN FAN THE FIRE.
WE WERE FOOLS TO ENTRUST THIS TO A CHILD. BUT *YOU'VE* NEVER FAILED US, HUNTER.
AND I WON'T FAIL YOU NOW, OLD FRIEND. LEAVE HER TO ME.

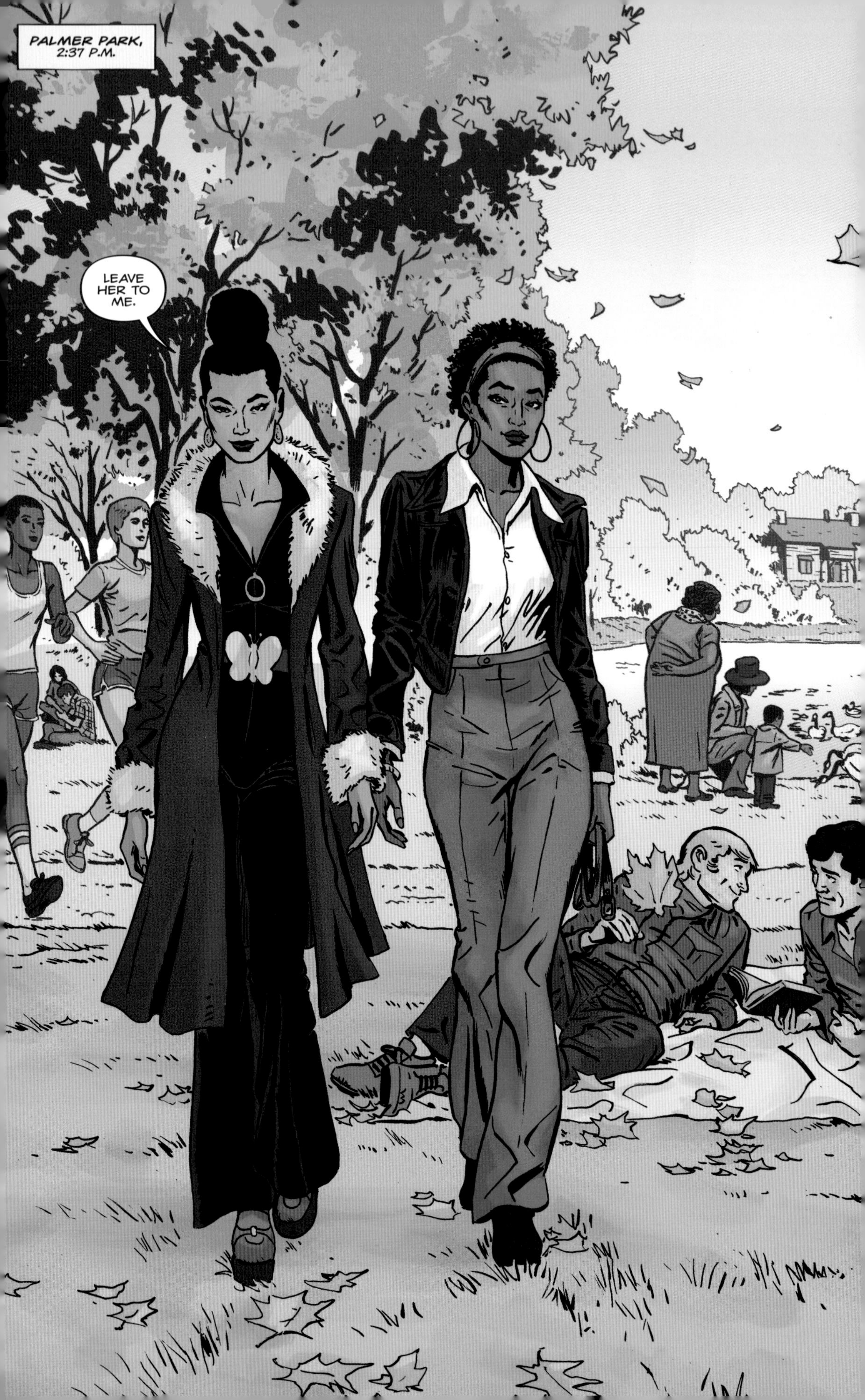
PALMER PARK, 2:37 P.M.
LEAVE HER TO ME.

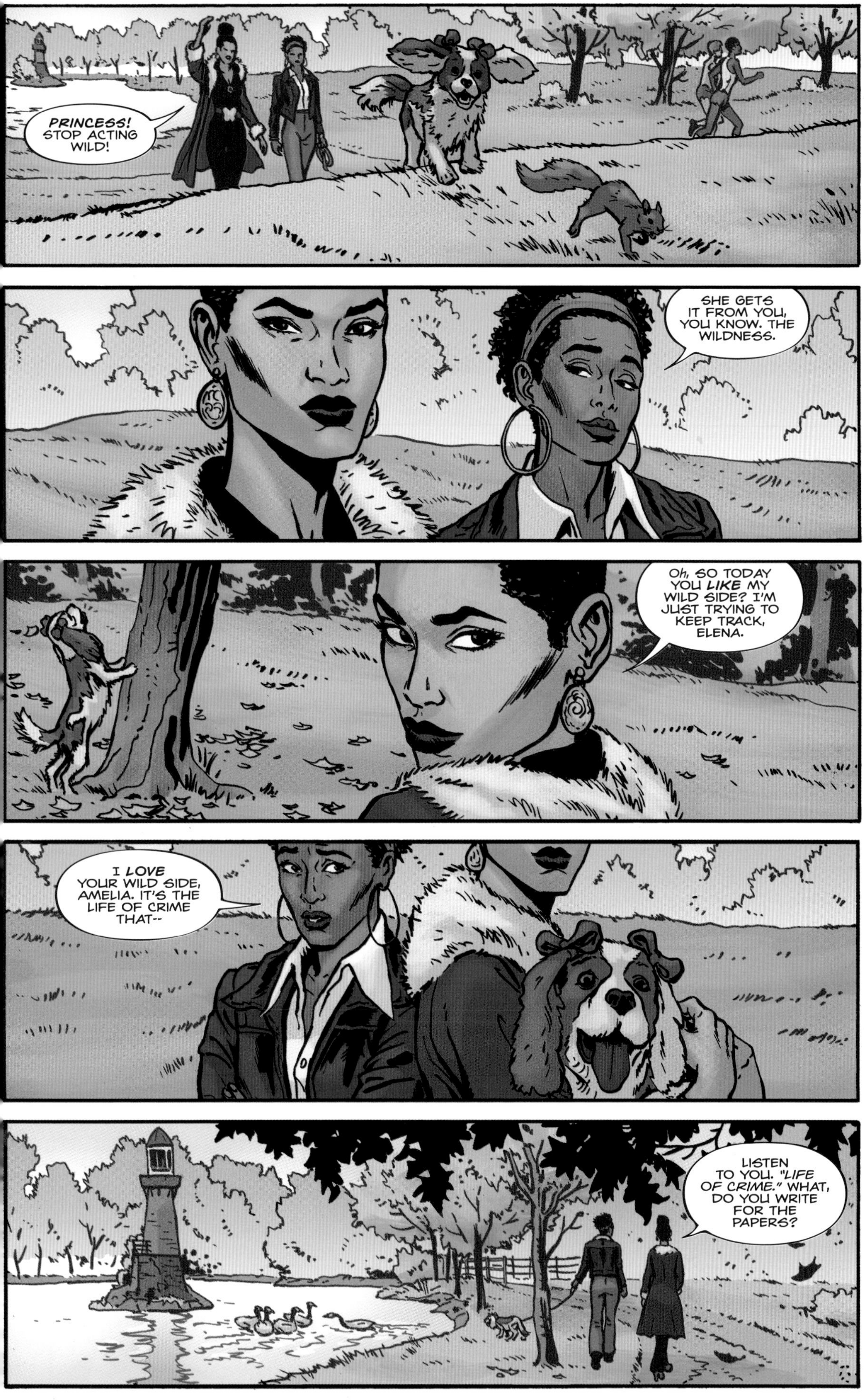
PRINCESS! STOP ACTING WILD!
SHE GETS IT FROM YOU, YOU KNOW. THE WILDNESS.
Oh, SO TODAY YOU LIKE MY WILD SIDE? I'M JUST TRYING TO KEEP TRACK, ELENA.
I LOVE YOUR WILD SIDE, AMELIA. IT'S THE LIFE OF CRIME THAT--
LISTEN TO YOU. "LIFE OF CRIME." WHAT, DO YOU WRITE FOR THE PAPERS?

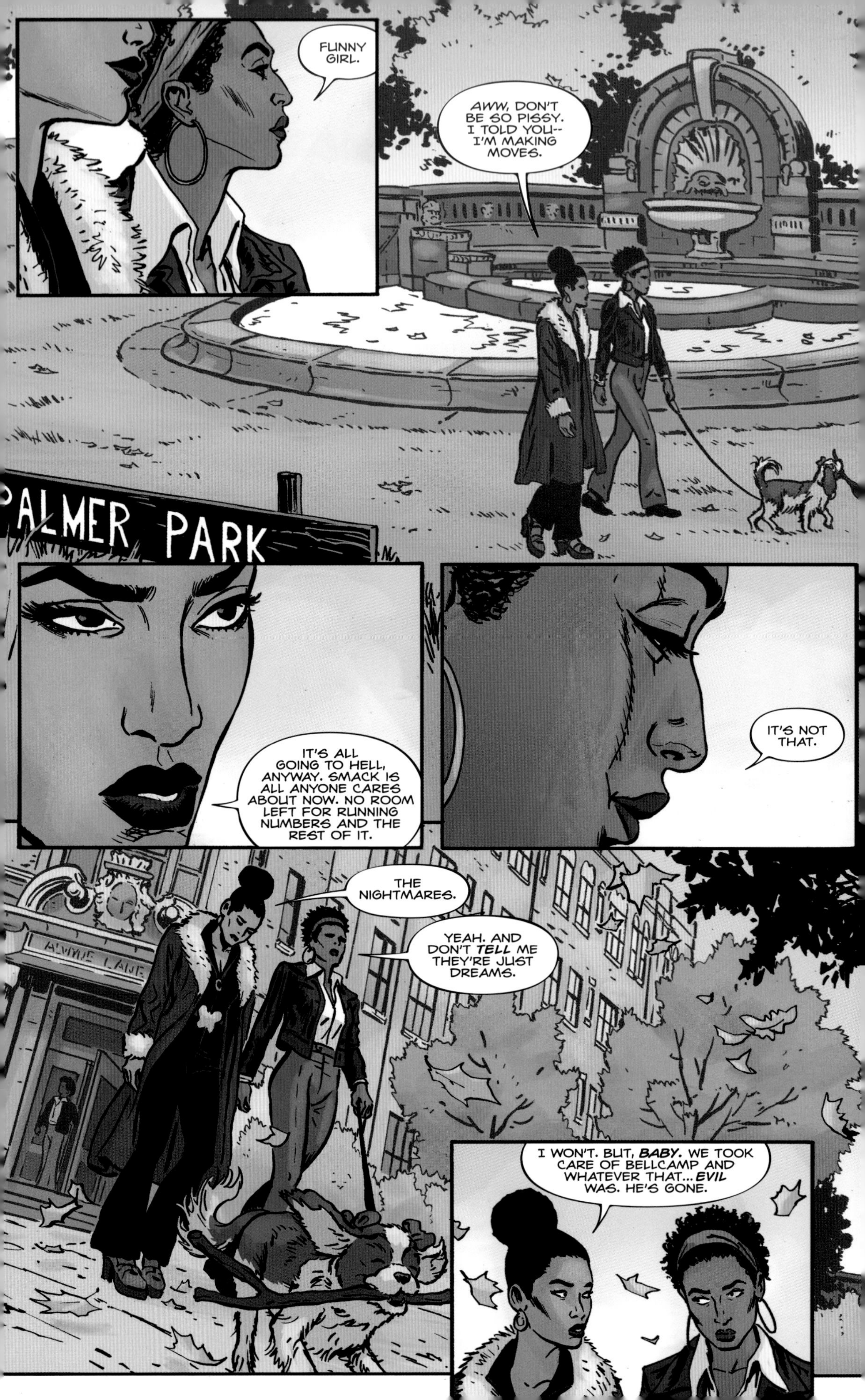
FUNNY GIRL.
AWW, DON'T BE SO PISSY. I TOLD YOU-- I'M MAKING MOVES.
PALMER PARK
IT'S ALL GOING TO HELL, ANYWAY. SMACK IS ALL ANYONE CARES ABOUT NOW. NO ROOM LEFT FOR RUNNING NUMBERS AND THE REST OF IT.
IT'S NOT THAT.
THE NIGHTMARES.
YEAH. AND DON'T ***TELL*** ME THEY'RE JUST DREAMS.
I WON'T. BUT, ***BABY.*** WE TOOK CARE OF BELLCAMP AND WHATEVER THAT... ***EVIL*** WAS. HE'S GONE.

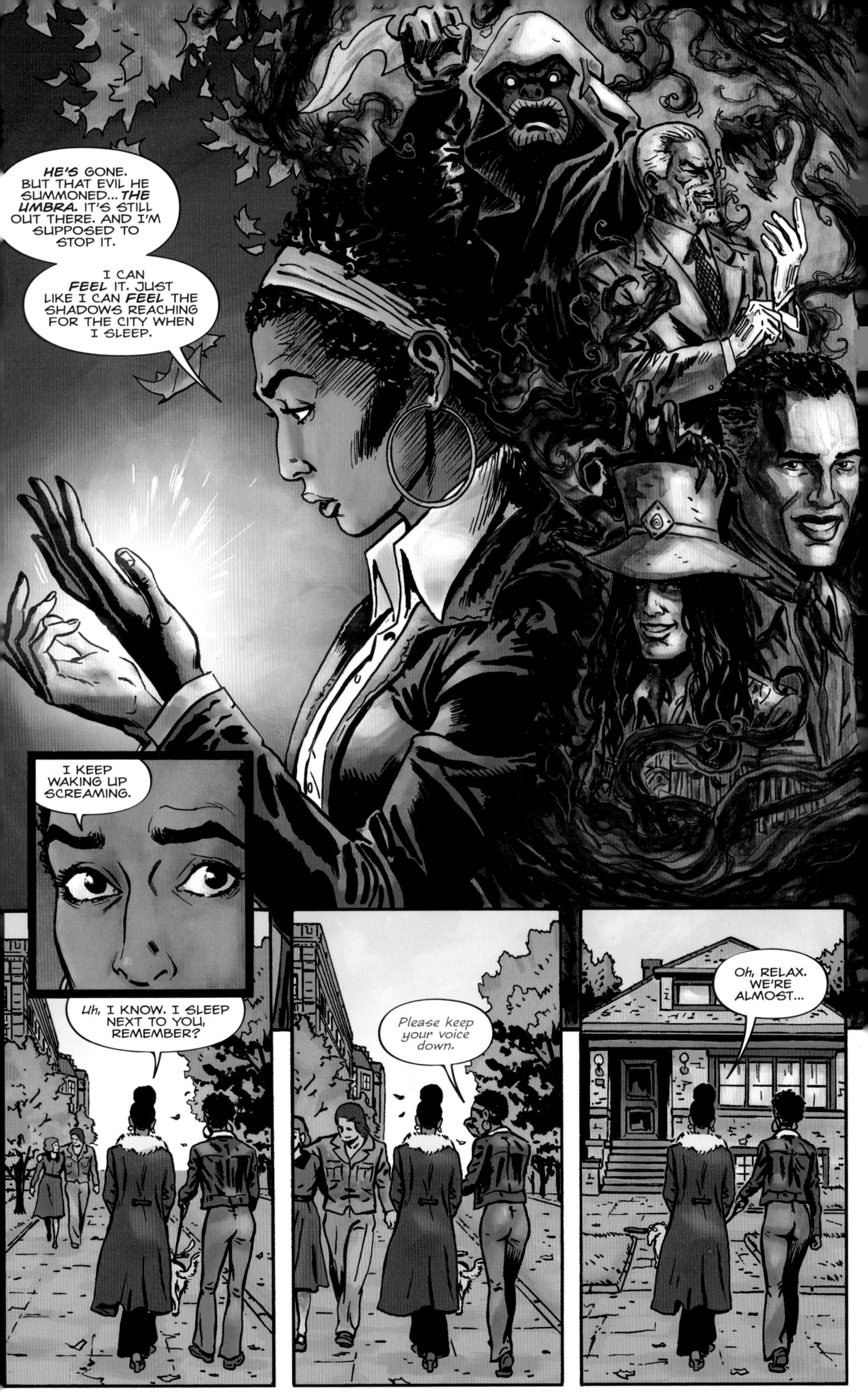
HE'S GONE. BUT THAT EVIL HE SUMMONED... THE UMBRA. IT'S STILL OUT THERE. AND I'M SUPPOSED TO STOP IT.
I CAN FEEL IT. JUST LIKE I CAN FEEL THE SHADOWS REACHING FOR THE CITY WHEN I SLEEP.
I KEEP WAKING UP SCREAMING.
Uh, I KNOW. I SLEEP NEXT TO YOU, REMEMBER?
Please keep your voice down.
Oh, RELAX. WE'RE ALMOST...

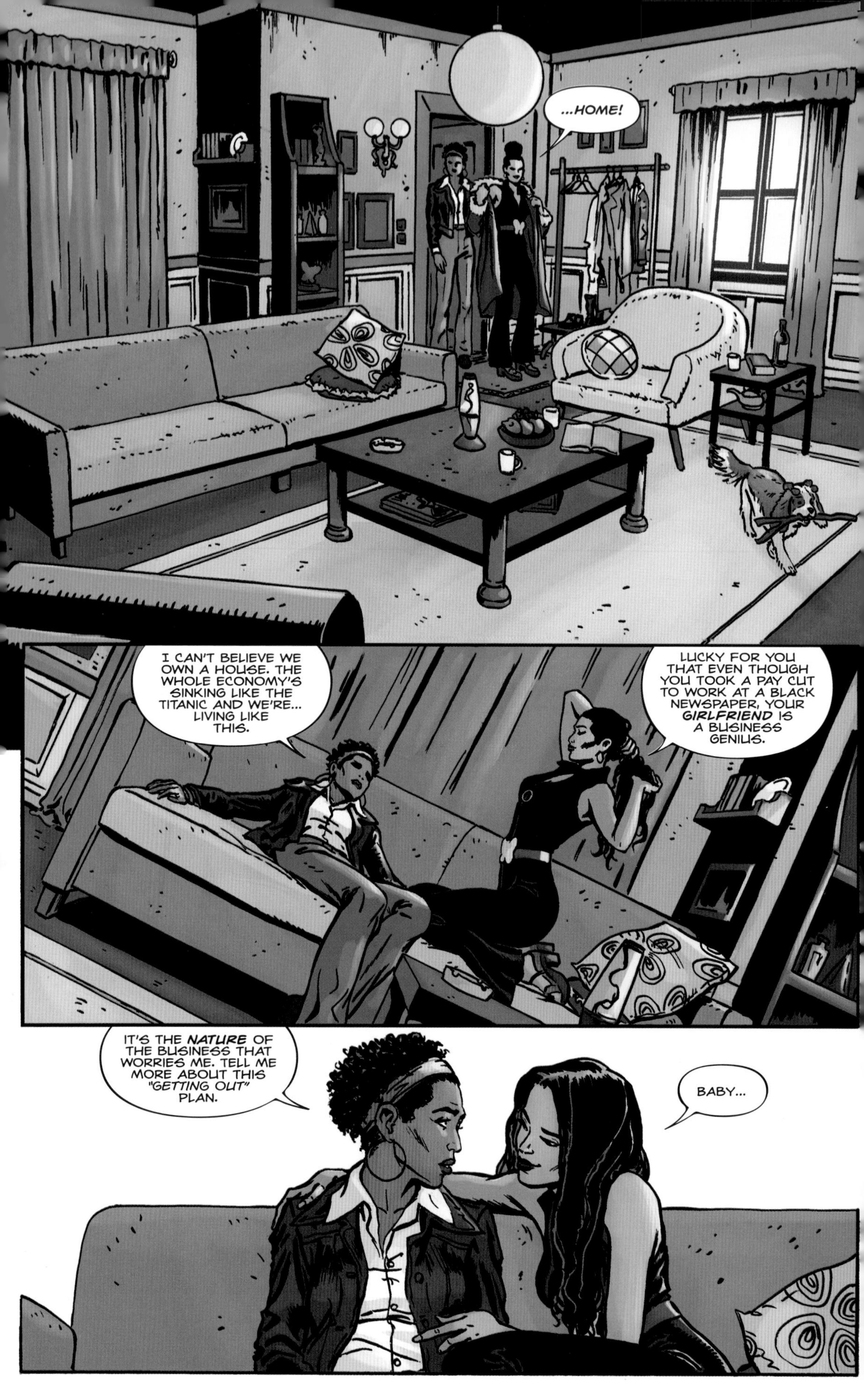
...HOME!
I CAN'T BELIEVE WE OWN A HOUSE. THE WHOLE ECONOMY'S SINKING LIKE THE TITANIC AND WE'RE... LIVING LIKE THIS.
LUCKY FOR YOU THAT EVEN THOUGH YOU TOOK A PAY CUT TO WORK AT A BLACK NEWSPAPER, YOUR GIRLFRIEND IS A BUSINESS GENIUS.
IT'S THE NATURE OF THE BUSINESS THAT WORRIES ME. TELL ME MORE ABOUT THIS "GETTING OUT" PLAN.
BABY...

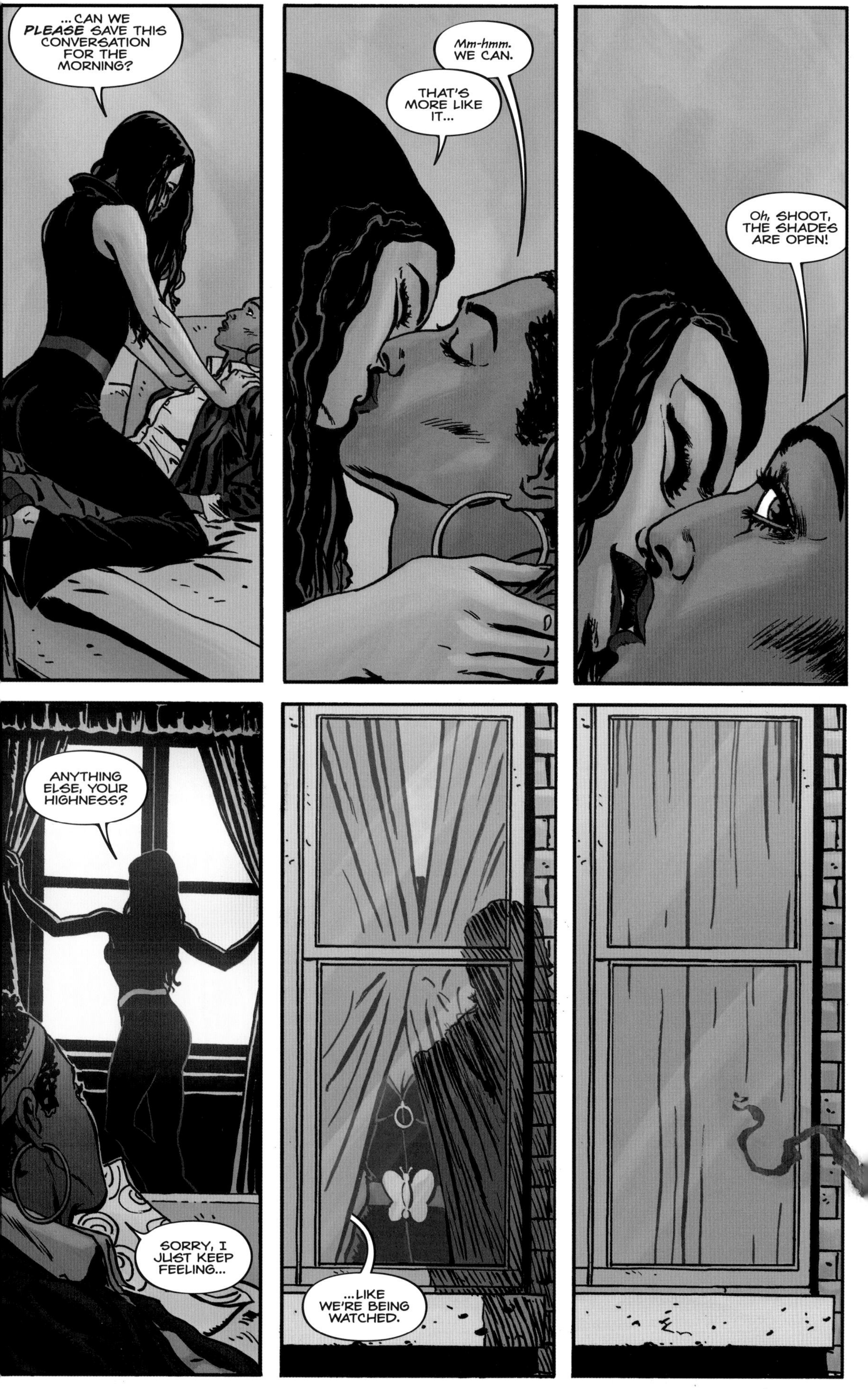
...CAN WE *PLEASE* SAVE THIS CONVERSATION FOR THE MORNING?
Mm-hmm. WE CAN.
THAT'S MORE LIKE IT...
Oh, SHOOT, THE SHADES ARE OPEN!
ANYTHING ELSE, YOUR HIGHNESS?
SORRY, I JUST KEEP FEELING...
...LIKE WE'RE BEING WATCHED.

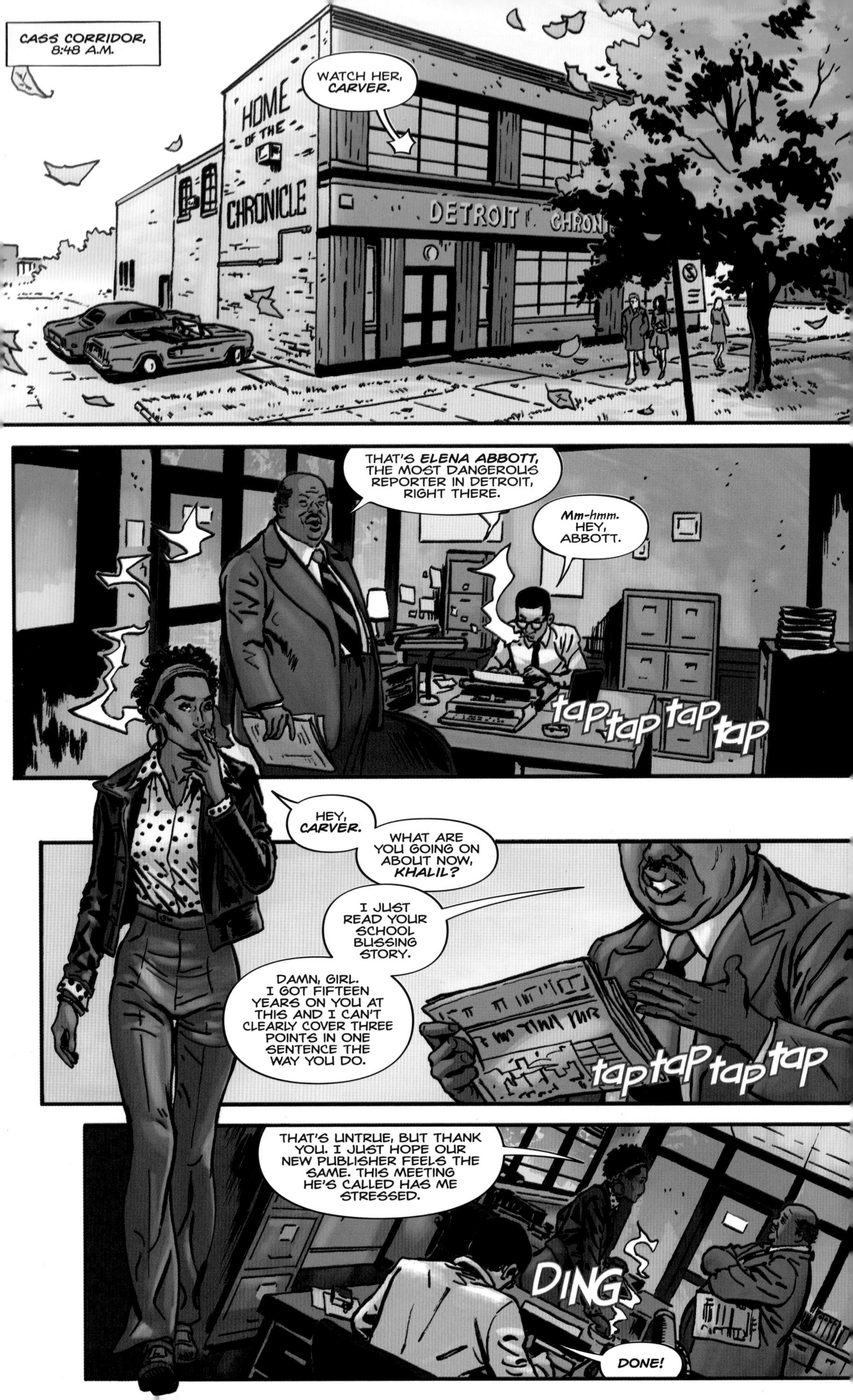
CASS CORRIDOR, 8:48 A.M.
WATCH HER, CARVER.
HOME OF THE CHRONICLE
DETROIT CHRON
THAT'S ELENA ABBOTT, THE MOST DANGEROUS REPORTER IN DETROIT, RIGHT THERE.
Mm-hmm. HEY, ABBOTT.
tap tap tap tap
HEY, CARVER.
WHAT ARE YOU GOING ON ABOUT NOW, KHALIL?
I JUST READ YOUR SCHOOL BUSSING STORY.
DAMN, GIRL. I GOT FIFTEEN YEARS ON YOU AT THIS AND I CAN'T CLEARLY COVER THREE POINTS IN ONE SENTENCE THE WAY YOU DO.
tap tap tap tap
THAT'S UNTRUE, BUT THANK YOU. I JUST HOPE OUR NEW PUBLISHER FEELS THE SAME. THIS MEETING HE'S CALLED HAS ME STRESSED.
DING
DONE!

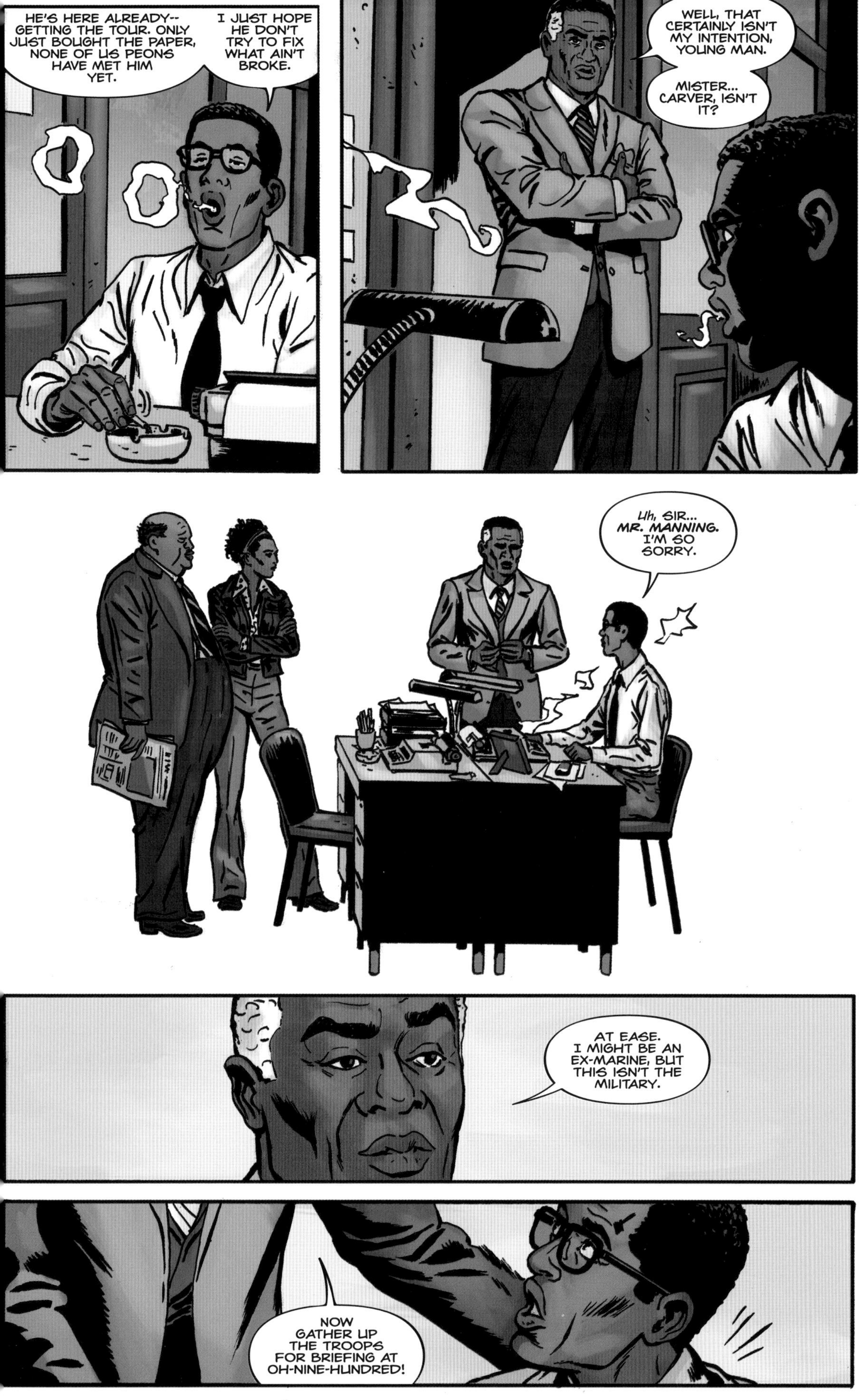
HE'S HERE ALREADY-- GETTING THE TOUR. ONLY JUST BOUGHT THE PAPER, NONE OF US PEONS HAVE MET HIM YET.
I JUST HOPE HE DON'T TRY TO FIX WHAT AIN'T BROKE.
WELL, THAT CERTAINLY ISN'T MY INTENTION, YOUNG MAN.
MISTER... CARVER, ISN'T IT?
UH, SIR... MR. MANNING. I'M SO SORRY.
AT EASE. I MIGHT BE AN EX-MARINE, BUT THIS ISN'T THE MILITARY.
NOW GATHER UP THE TROOPS FOR BRIEFING AT OH-NINE-HUNDRED!

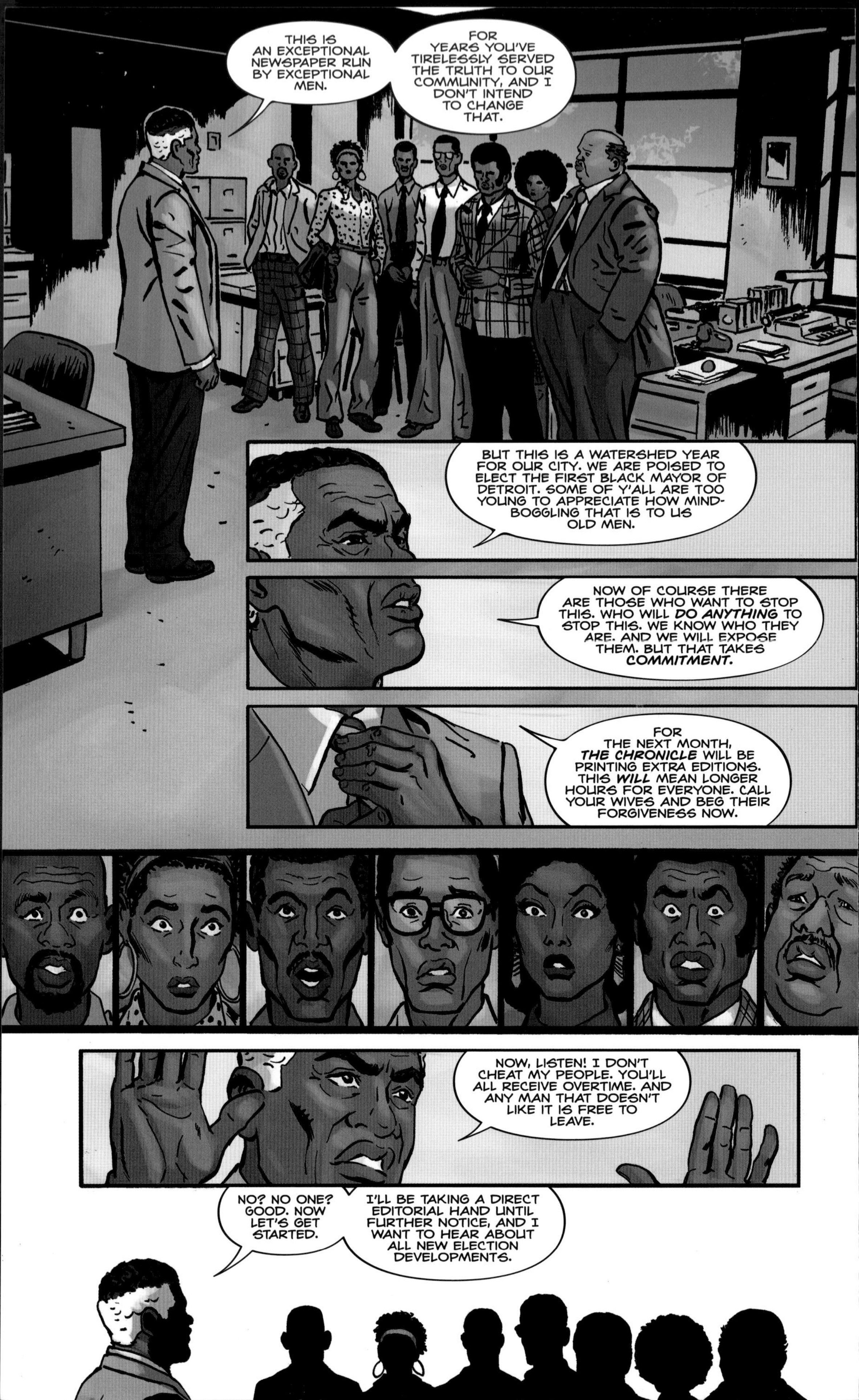
THIS IS AN EXCEPTIONAL NEWSPAPER RUN BY EXCEPTIONAL MEN.
FOR YEARS YOU'VE TIRELESSLY SERVED THE TRUTH TO OUR COMMUNITY, AND I DON'T INTEND TO CHANGE THAT.
BUT THIS IS A WATERSHED YEAR FOR OUR CITY. WE ARE POISED TO ELECT THE FIRST BLACK MAYOR OF DETROIT. SOME OF Y'ALL ARE TOO YOUNG TO APPRECIATE HOW MIND-BOGGLING THAT IS TO US OLD MEN.
NOW OF COURSE THERE ARE THOSE WHO WANT TO STOP THIS. WHO WILL *DO ANYTHING* TO STOP THIS. WE KNOW WHO THEY ARE. AND WE WILL EXPOSE THEM. BUT THAT TAKES ***COMMITMENT.***
FOR THE NEXT MONTH, ***THE CHRONICLE*** WILL BE PRINTING EXTRA EDITIONS. THIS ***WILL*** MEAN LONGER HOURS FOR EVERYONE. CALL YOUR WIVES AND BEG THEIR FORGIVENESS NOW.
NOW, LISTEN! I DON'T CHEAT MY PEOPLE. YOU'LL ALL RECEIVE OVERTIME. AND ANY MAN THAT DOESN'T LIKE IT IS FREE TO LEAVE.
NO? NO ONE? GOOD. NOW LET'S GET STARTED.
I'LL BE TAKING A DIRECT EDITORIAL HAND UNTIL FURTHER NOTICE, AND I WANT TO HEAR ABOUT ALL NEW ELECTION DEVELOPMENTS.

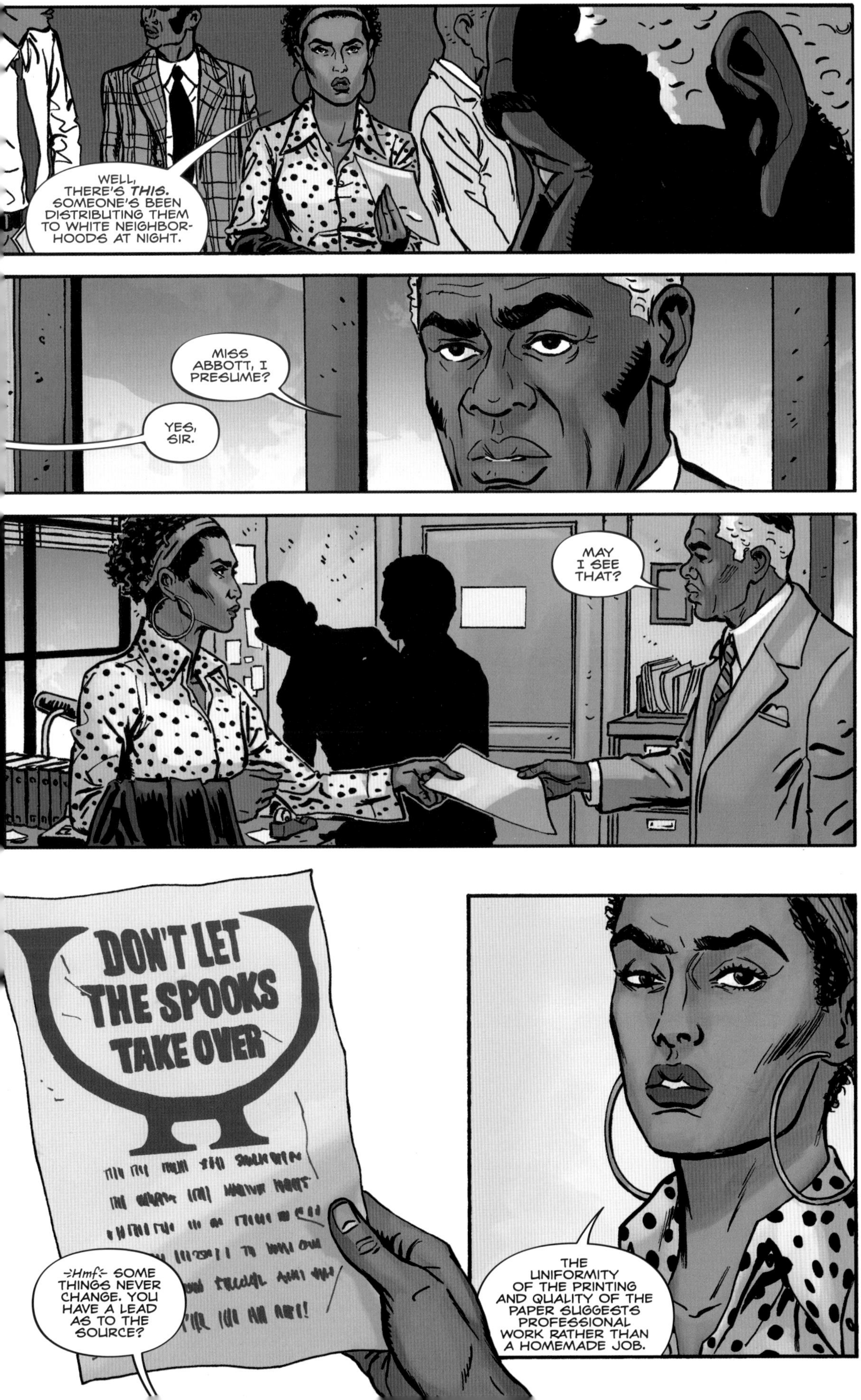
WELL, THERE'S *THIS.* SOMEONE'S BEEN DISTRIBUTING THEM TO WHITE NEIGHBOR-HOODS AT NIGHT.
MISS ABBOTT, I PRESUME?
YES, SIR.
MAY I SEE THAT?
DON'T LET THE SPOOKS TAKE OVER
Hmf SOME THINGS NEVER CHANGE. YOU HAVE A LEAD AS TO THE SOURCE?
THE UNIFORMITY OF THE PRINTING AND QUALITY OF THE PAPER SUGGESTS PROFESSIONAL WORK RATHER THAN A HOMEMADE JOB.

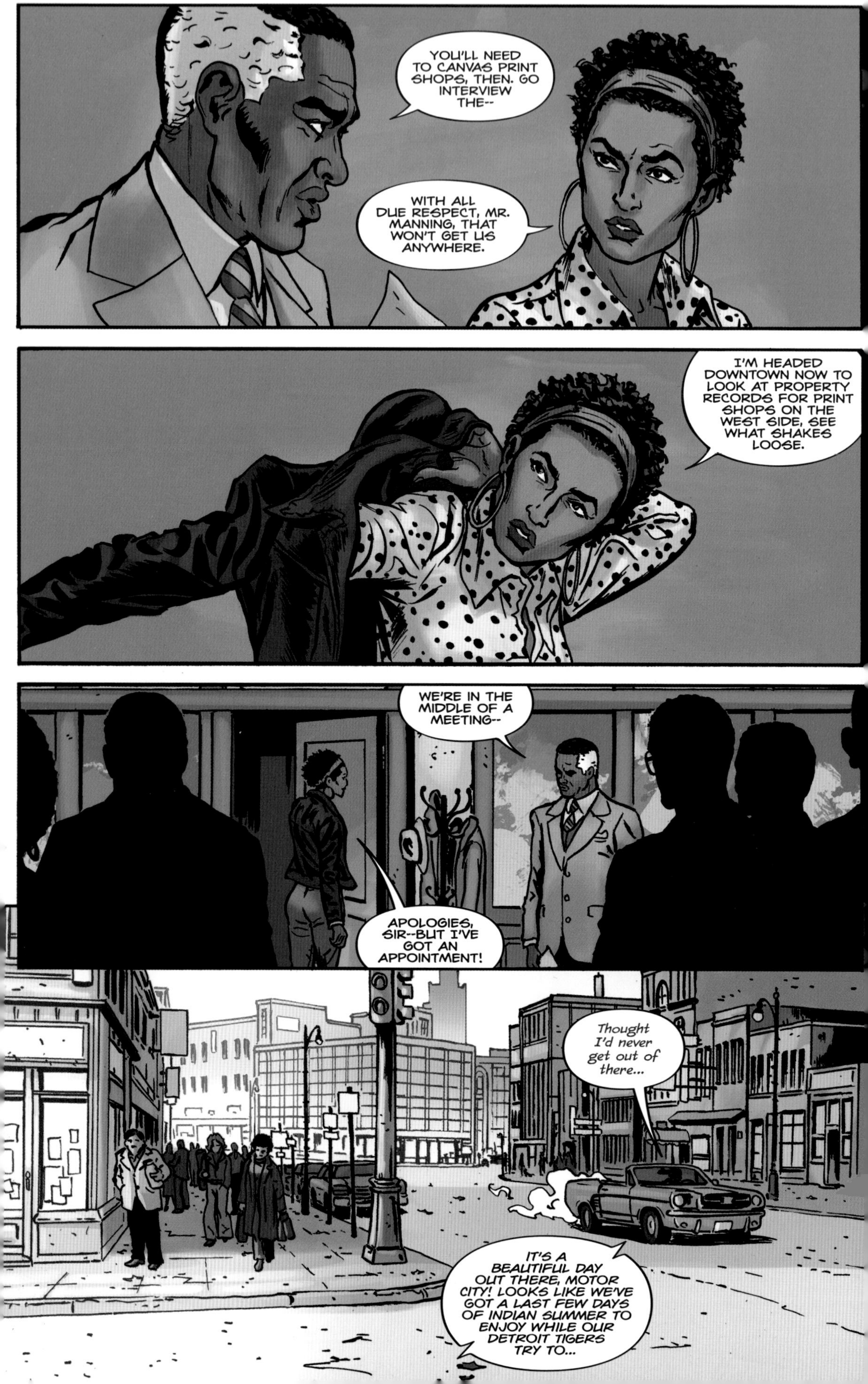
YOU'LL NEED TO CANVAS PRINT SHOPS, THEN. GO INTERVIEW THE--
WITH ALL DUE RESPECT, MR. MANNING, THAT WON'T GET US ANYWHERE.
I'M HEADED DOWNTOWN NOW TO LOOK AT PROPERTY RECORDS FOR PRINT SHOPS ON THE WEST SIDE, SEE WHAT SHAKES LOOSE.
WE'RE IN THE MIDDLE OF A MEETING--
APOLOGIES, SIR--BUT I'VE GOT AN APPOINTMENT!
Thought I'd never get out of there...
IT'S A BEAUTIFUL DAY OUT THERE, MOTOR CITY! LOOKS LIKE WE'VE GOT A LAST FEW DAYS OF INDIAN SUMMER TO ENJOY WHILE OUR DETROIT TIGERS TRY TO...

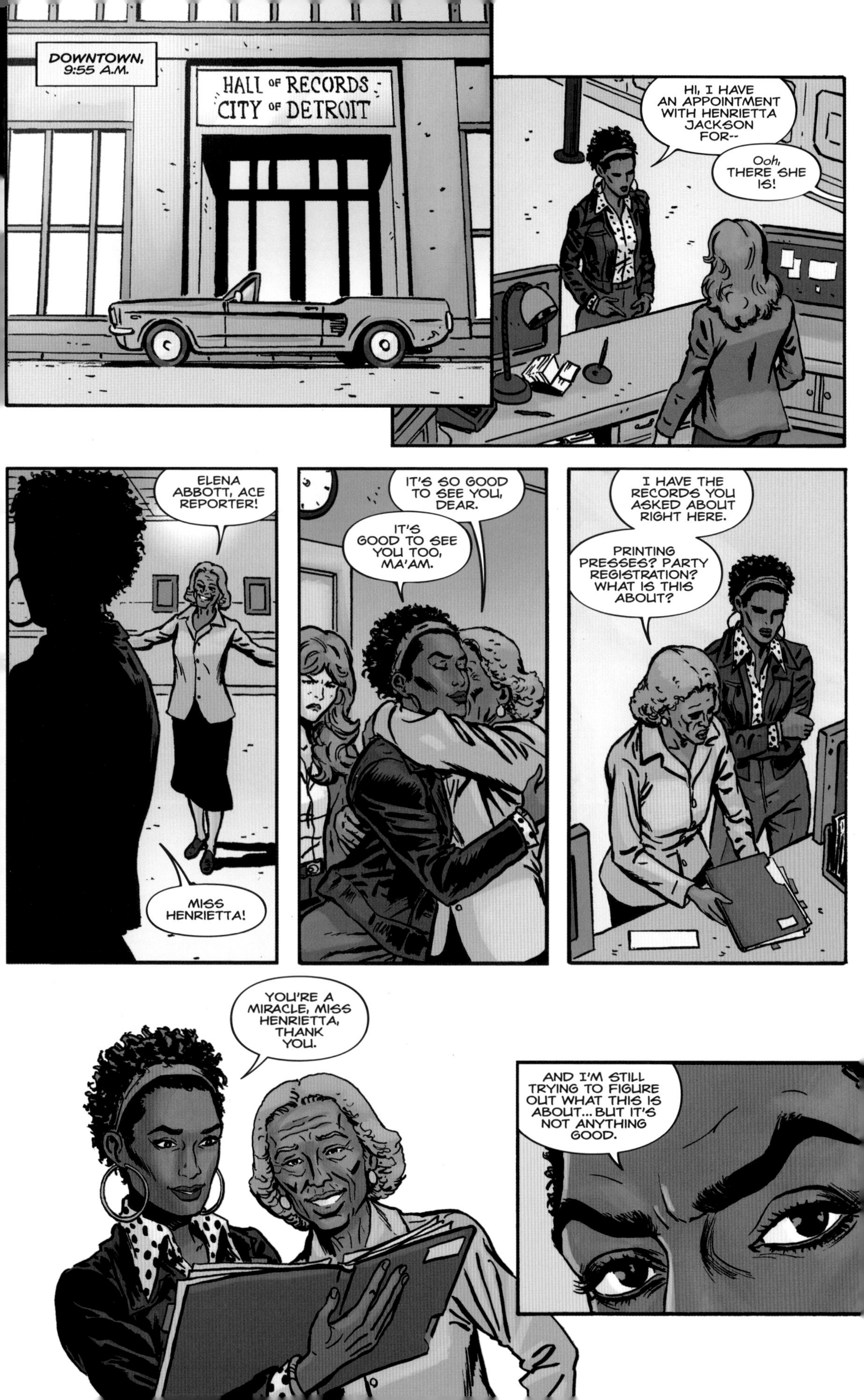
DOWNTOWN, 9:55 A.M.
HALL OF RECORDS CITY OF DETROIT
HI, I HAVE AN APPOINTMENT WITH HENRIETTA JACKSON FOR--
Ooh, THERE SHE IS!
ELENA ABBOTT, ACE REPORTER!
MISS HENRIETTA!
IT'S SO GOOD TO SEE YOU, DEAR.
IT'S GOOD TO SEE YOU TOO, MA'AM.
I HAVE THE RECORDS YOU ASKED ABOUT RIGHT HERE.
PRINTING PRESSES? PARTY REGISTRATION? WHAT IS THIS ABOUT?
YOU'RE A MIRACLE, MISS HENRIETTA, THANK YOU.
AND I'M STILL TRYING TO FIGURE OUT WHAT THIS IS ABOUT... BUT IT'S NOT ANYTHING GOOD.

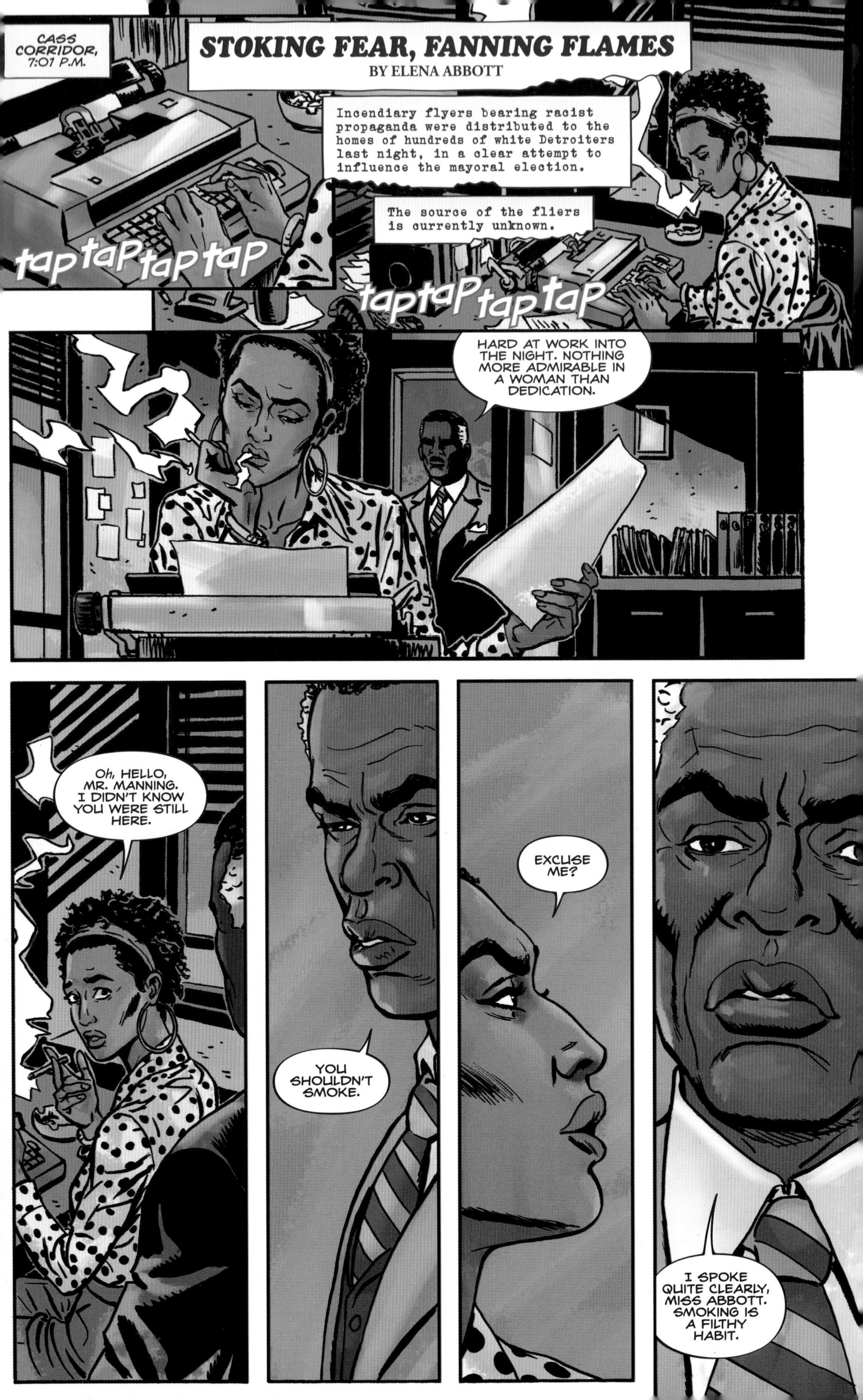
CASS CORRIDOR, 7:01 P.M.
STOKING FEAR, FANNING FLAMES
BY ELENA ABBOTT
Incendiary flyers bearing racist propaganda were distributed to the homes of hundreds of white Detroiters last night, in a clear attempt to influence the mayoral election.
tap tap tap tap
The source of the fliers is currently unknown.
tap tap tap tap
HARD AT WORK INTO THE NIGHT. NOTHING MORE ADMIRABLE IN A WOMAN THAN DEDICATION.
Oh, HELLO, MR. MANNING. I DIDN'T KNOW YOU WERE STILL HERE.
YOU SHOULDN'T SMOKE.
EXCUSE ME?
I SPOKE QUITE CLEARLY, MISS ABBOTT. SMOKING IS A FILTHY HABIT.

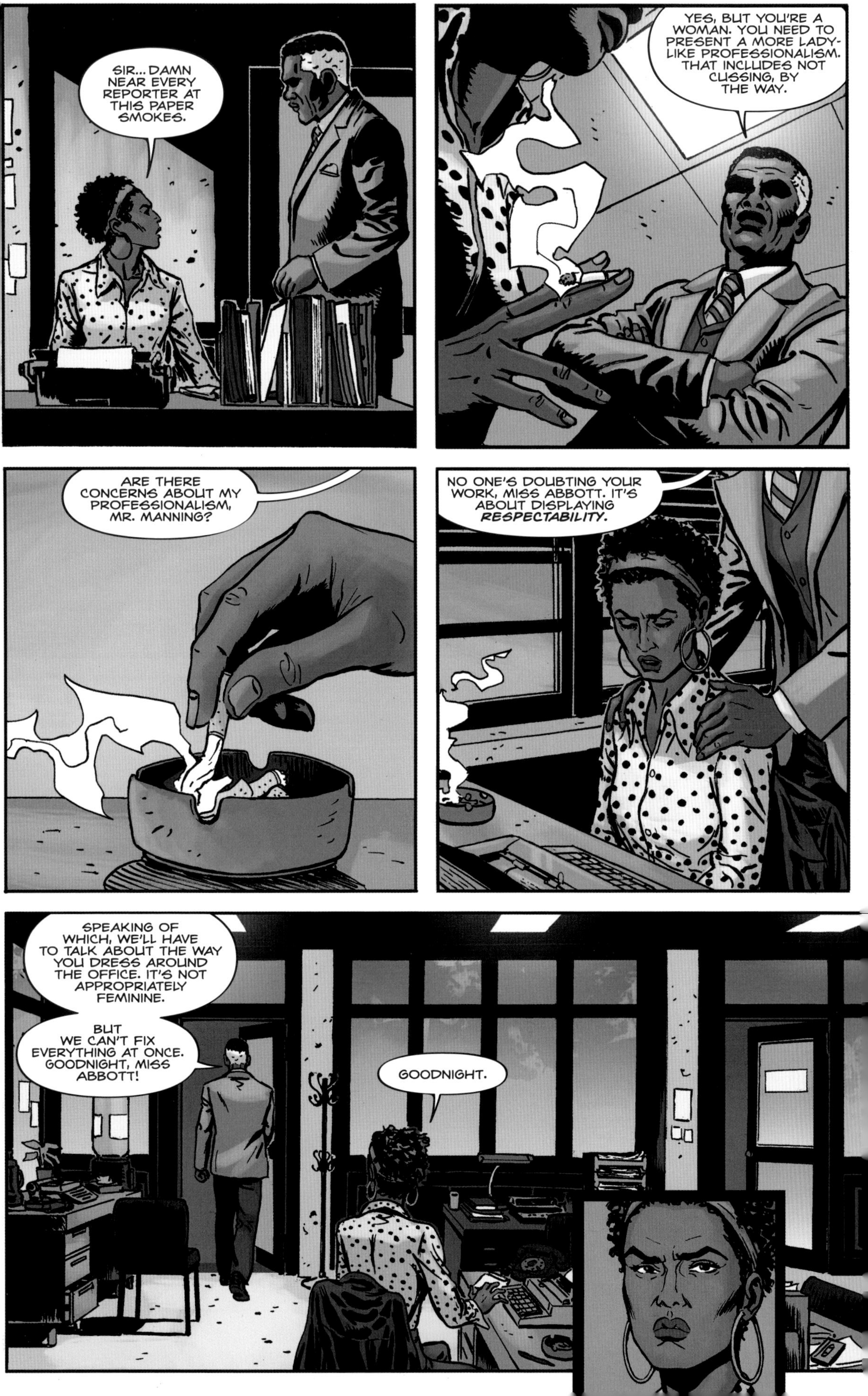
SIR... DAMN NEAR EVERY REPORTER AT THIS PAPER SMOKES.
YES, BUT YOU'RE A WOMAN. YOU NEED TO PRESENT A MORE LADY-LIKE PROFESSIONALISM. THAT INCLUDES NOT CUSSING, BY THE WAY.
ARE THERE CONCERNS ABOUT MY PROFESSIONALISM, MR. MANNING?
NO ONE'S DOUBTING YOUR WORK, MISS ABBOTT. IT'S ABOUT DISPLAYING *RESPECTABILITY.*
SPEAKING OF WHICH, WE'LL HAVE TO TALK ABOUT THE WAY YOU DRESS AROUND THE OFFICE. IT'S NOT APPROPRIATELY FEMININE.
BUT WE CAN'T FIX EVERYTHING AT ONCE. GOODNIGHT, MISS ABBOTT!
GOODNIGHT.

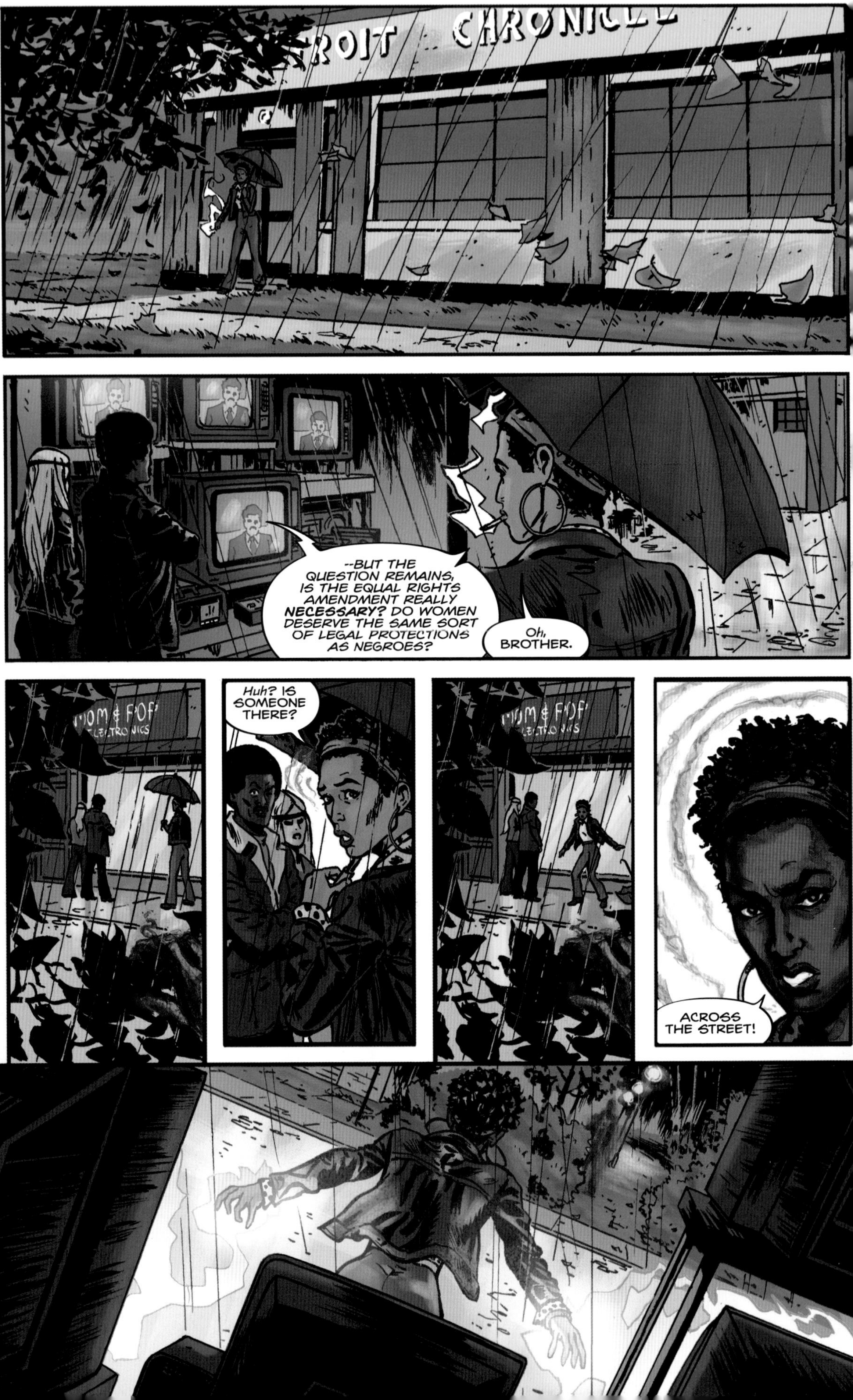
DETROIT CHRONICLE
--BUT THE QUESTION REMAINS, IS THE EQUAL RIGHTS AMENDMENT REALLY NECESSARY? DO WOMEN DESERVE THE SAME SORT OF LEGAL PROTECTIONS AS NEGROES?
Oh, BROTHER.
MOM & POP ELECTRONICS
Huh? IS SOMEONE THERE?
ACROSS THE STREET!

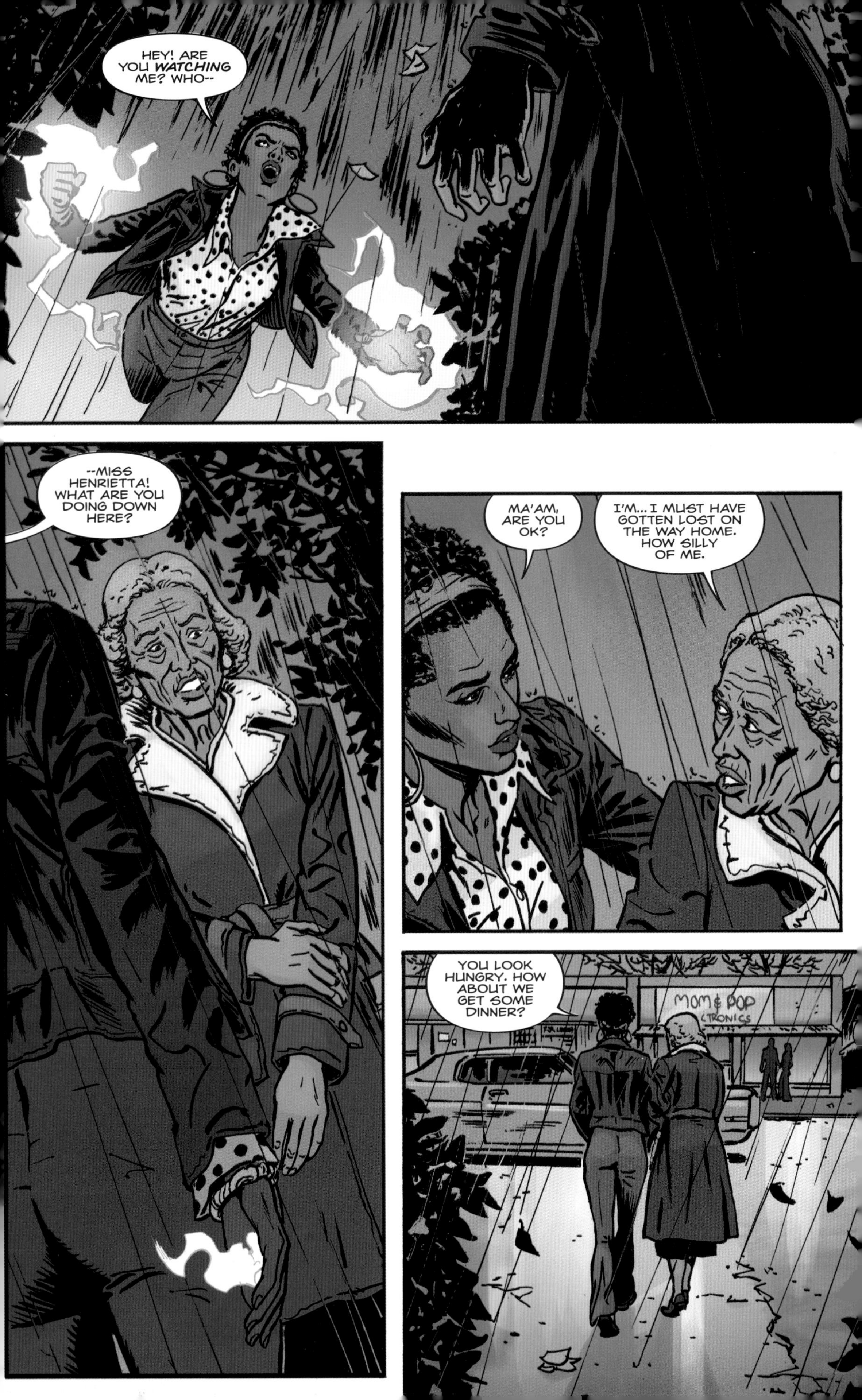
HEY! ARE YOU WATCHING ME? WHO--
--MISS HENRIETTA! WHAT ARE YOU DOING DOWN HERE?
MA'AM, ARE YOU OK?
I'M... I MUST HAVE GOTTEN LOST ON THE WAY HOME. HOW SILLY OF ME.
YOU LOOK HUNGRY. HOW ABOUT WE GET SOME DINNER?
MOM & POP
CTRONICS

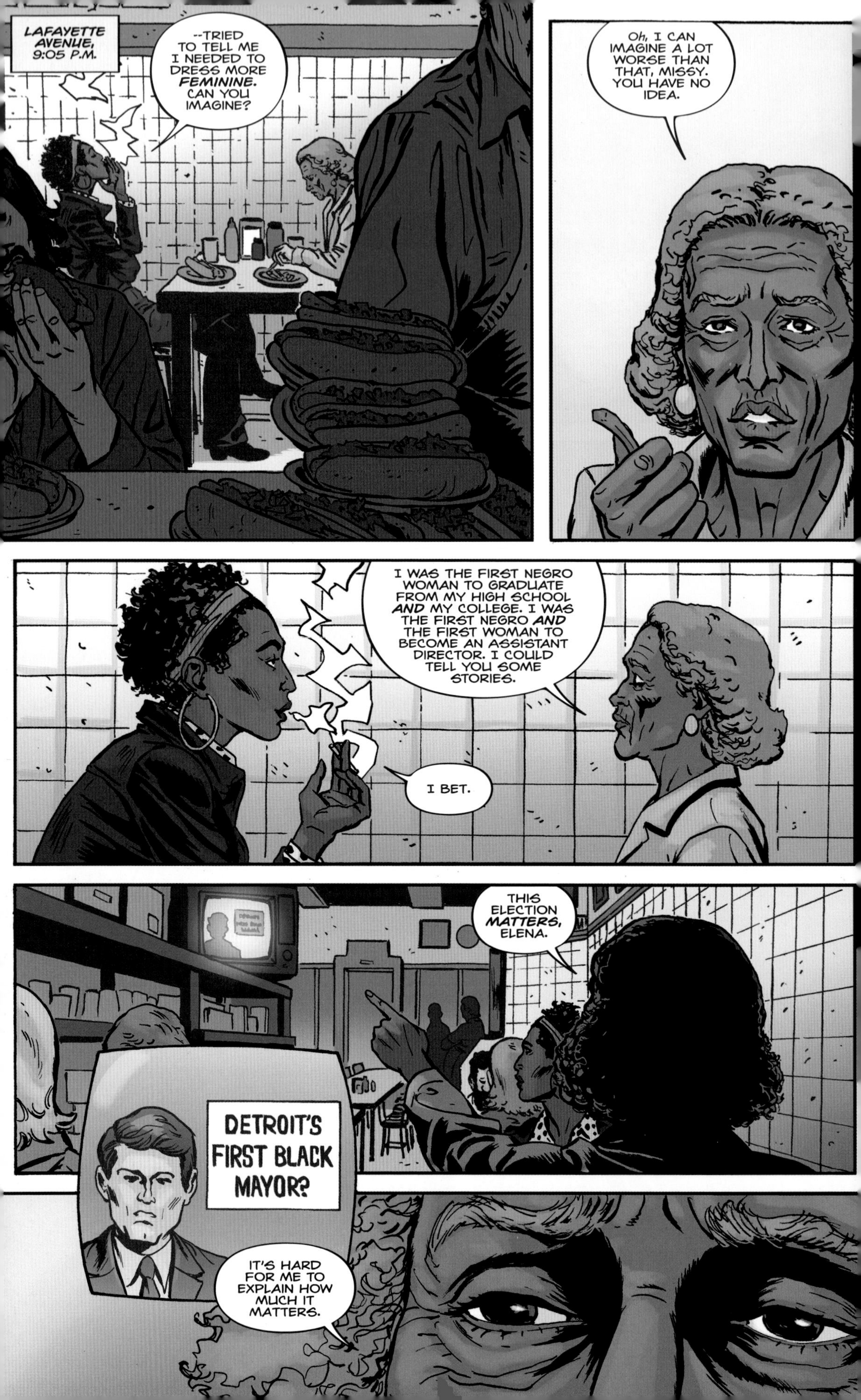
LAFAYETTE AVENUE, 9:05 P.M.
--TRIED TO TELL ME I NEEDED TO DRESS MORE FEMININE. CAN YOU IMAGINE?
Oh, I CAN IMAGINE A LOT WORSE THAN THAT, MISSY. YOU HAVE NO IDEA.
I WAS THE FIRST NEGRO WOMAN TO GRADUATE FROM MY HIGH SCHOOL AND MY COLLEGE. I WAS THE FIRST NEGRO AND THE FIRST WOMAN TO BECOME AN ASSISTANT DIRECTOR. I COULD TELL YOU SOME STORIES.
I BET.
THIS ELECTION MATTERS, ELENA.
DETROIT'S FIRST BLACK MAYOR?
IT'S HARD FOR ME TO EXPLAIN HOW MUCH IT MATTERS.

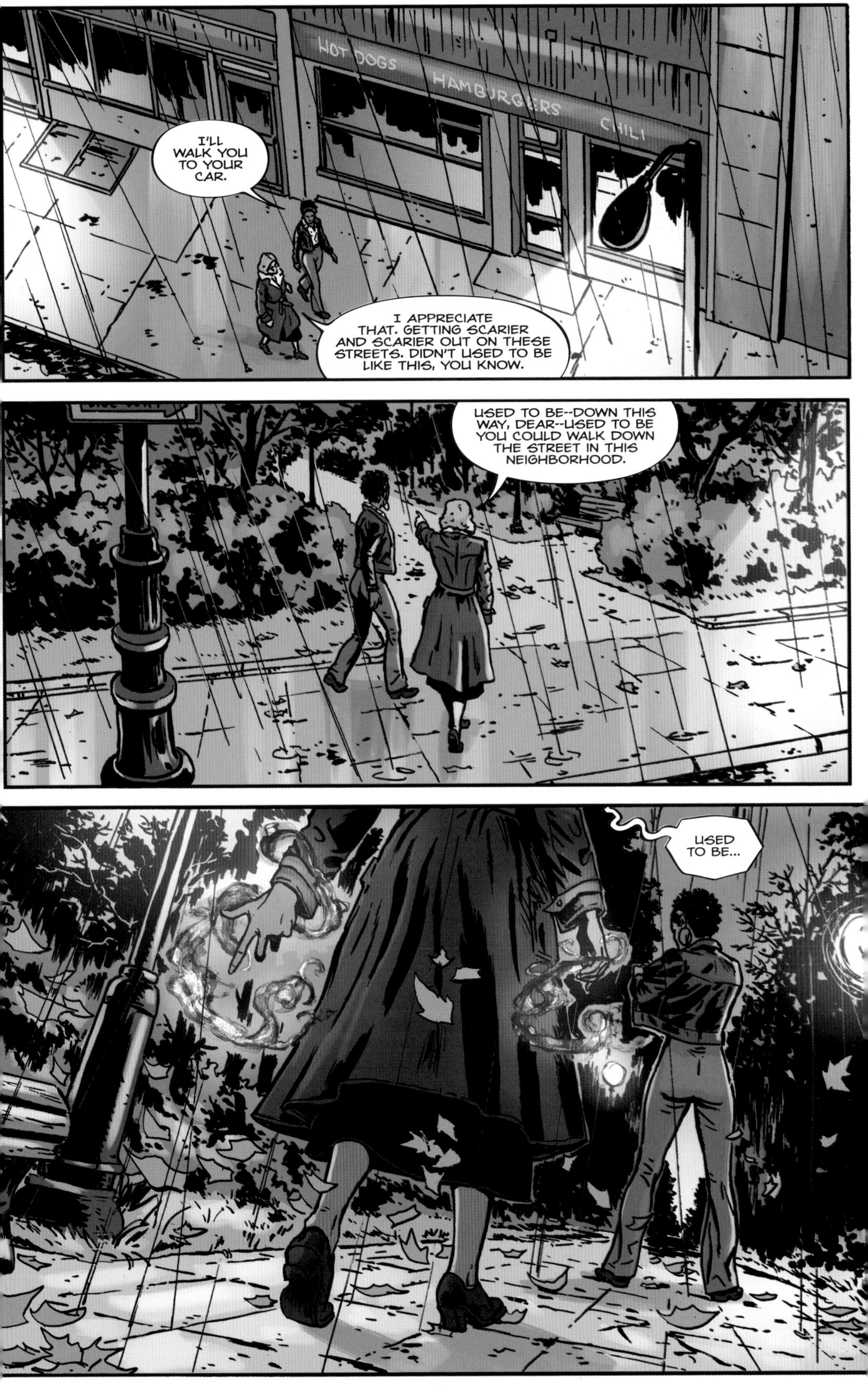
HOT DOGS
HAMBURGERS
CHILI
I'LL WALK YOU TO YOUR CAR.
I APPRECIATE THAT. GETTING SCARIER AND SCARIER OUT ON THESE STREETS. DIDN'T USED TO BE LIKE THIS, YOU KNOW.
USED TO BE--DOWN THIS WAY, DEAR--USED TO BE YOU COULD WALK DOWN THE STREET IN THIS NEIGHBORHOOD.
USED TO BE...

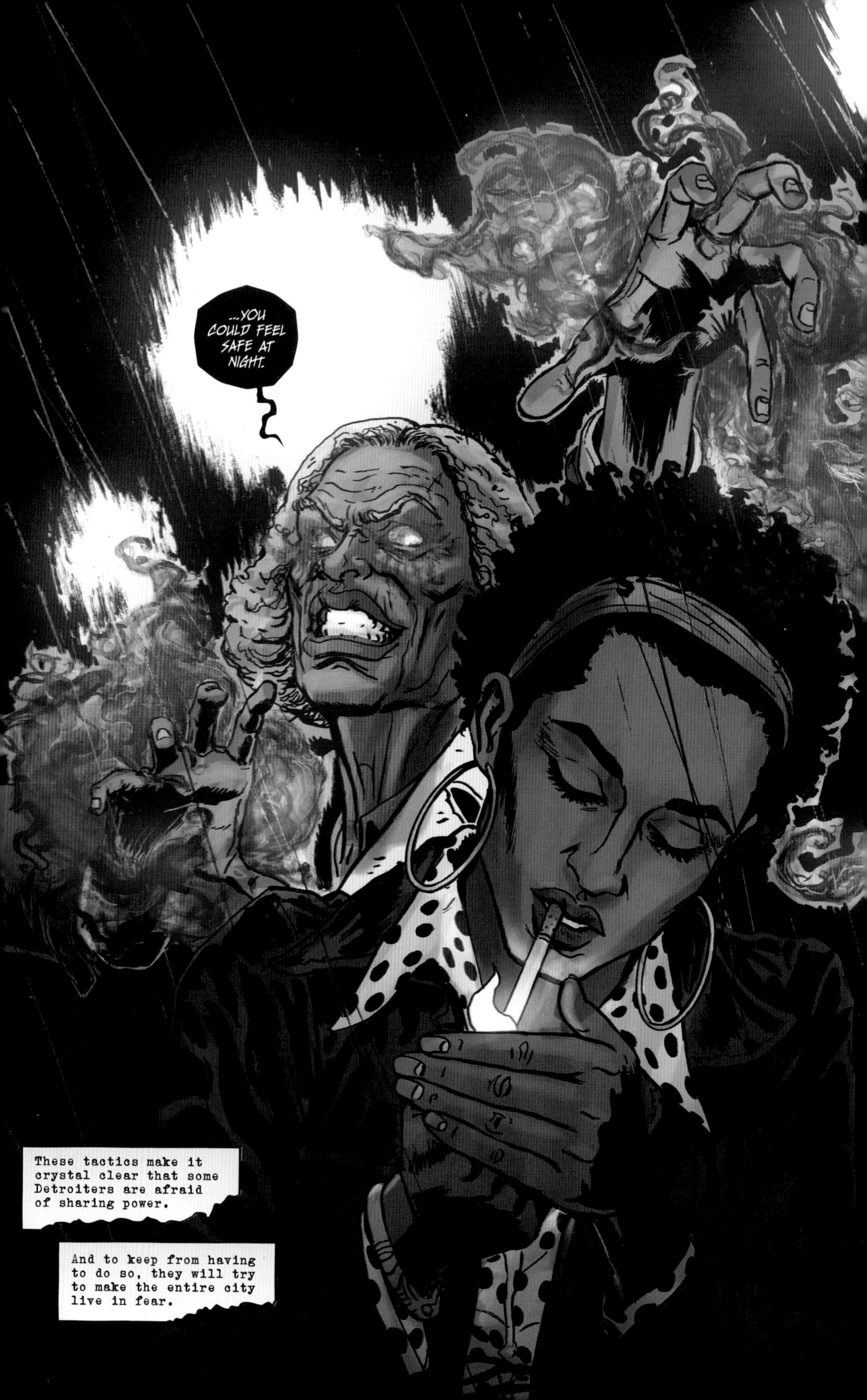
...YOU COULD FEEL SAFE AT NIGHT.
These tactics make it crystal clear that some Detroiters are afraid of sharing power.
And to keep from having to do so, they will try to make the entire city live in fear.

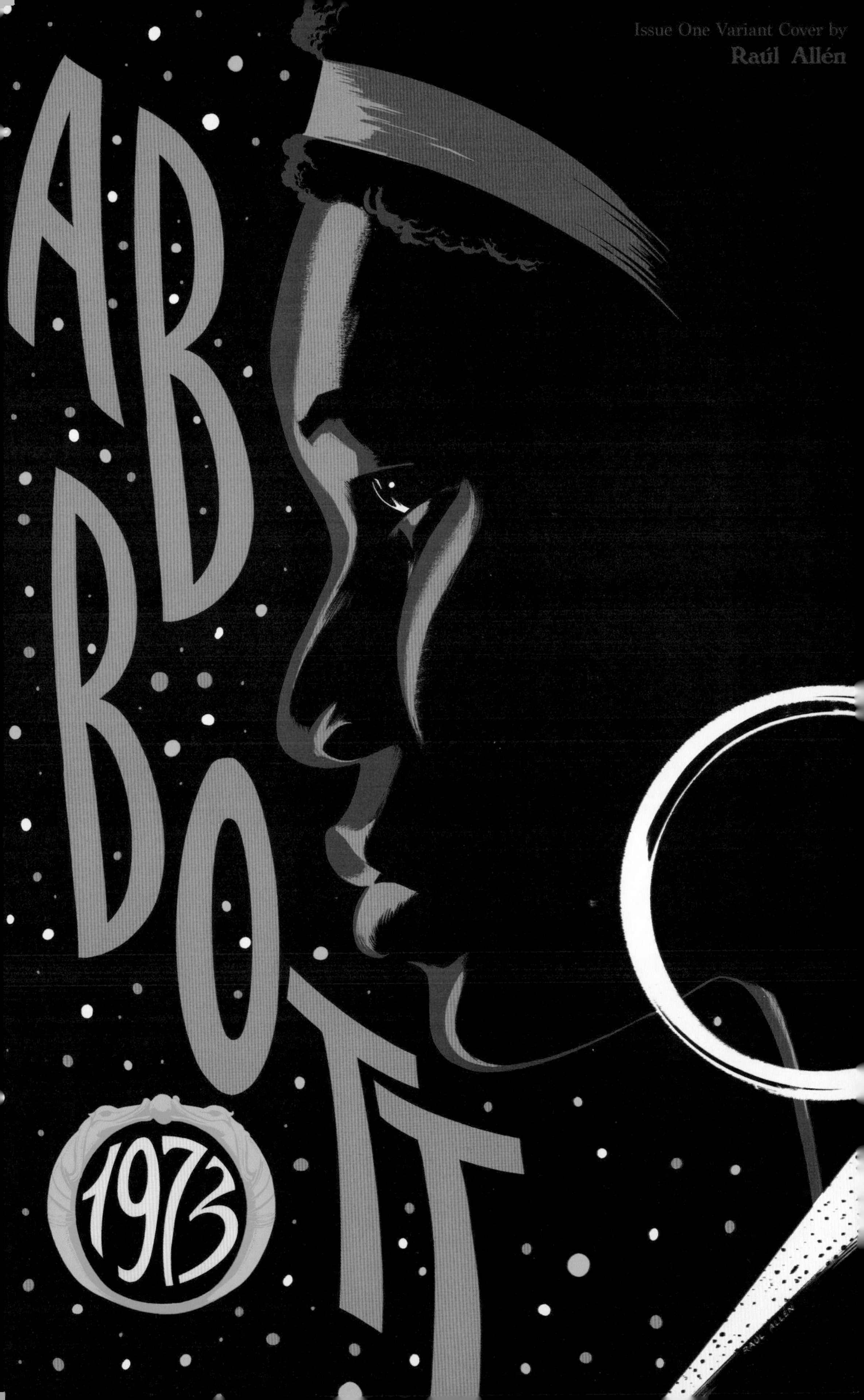
ABBOTT
1973
RAUL ALLEN

Issue One Variant Cover by
Raúl Allén

CHAPTER TWO

Issue Two Cover by Taj Tenfold

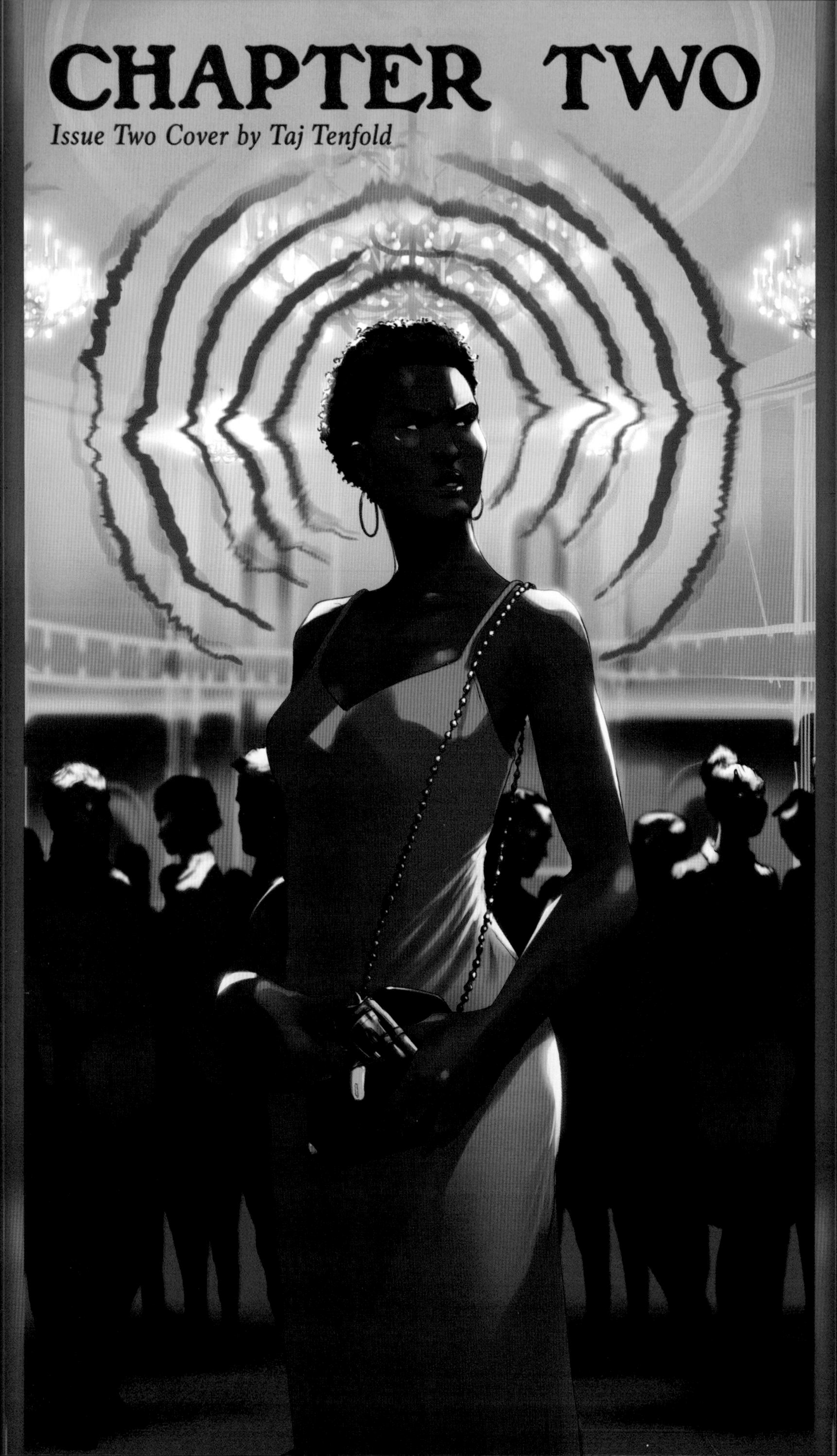

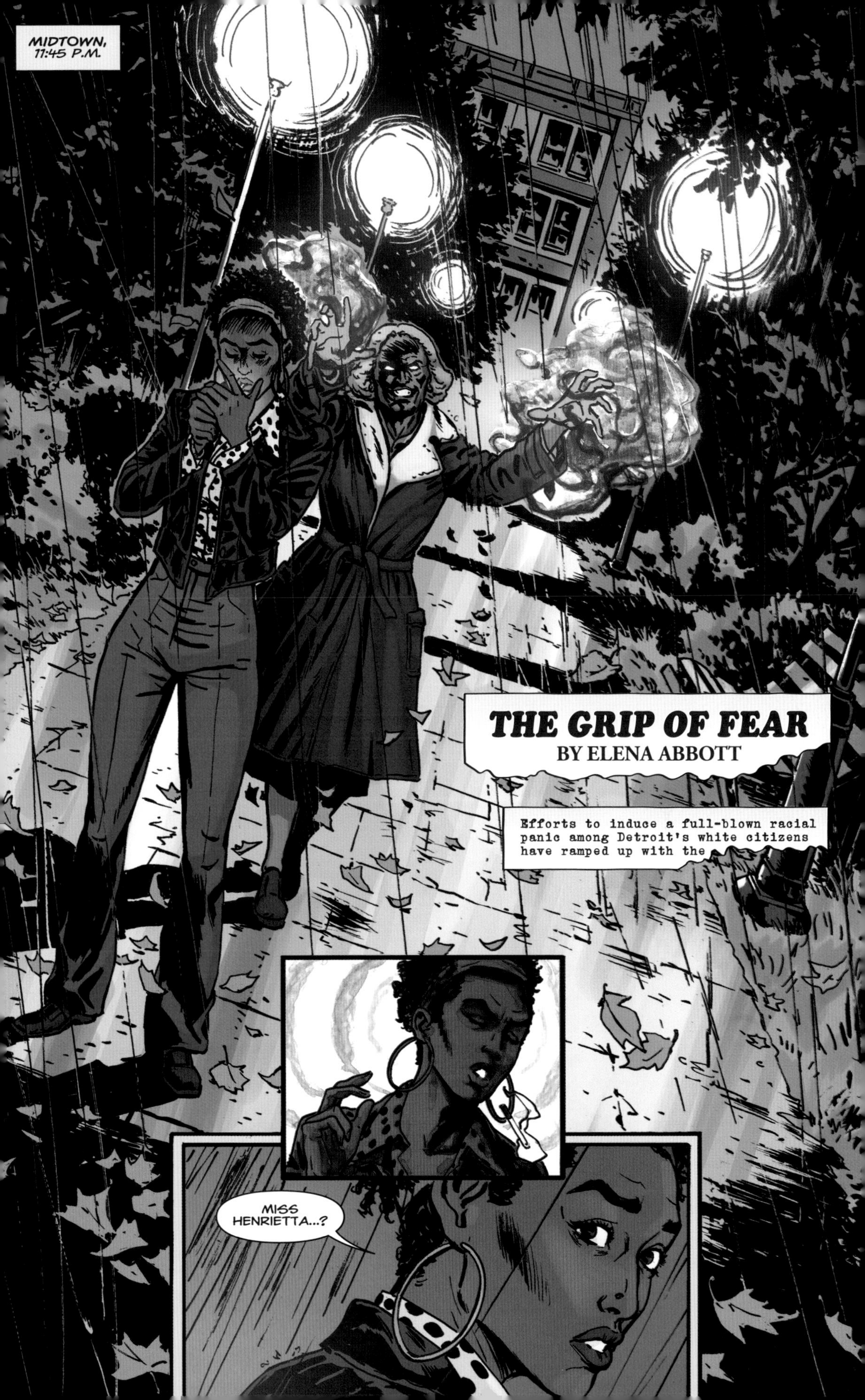
MIDTOWN, 11:45 P.M.
THE GRIP OF FEAR
BY ELENA ABBOTT
Efforts to induce a full-blown racial panic among Detroit's white citizens have ramped up with the
MISS HENRIETTA...?

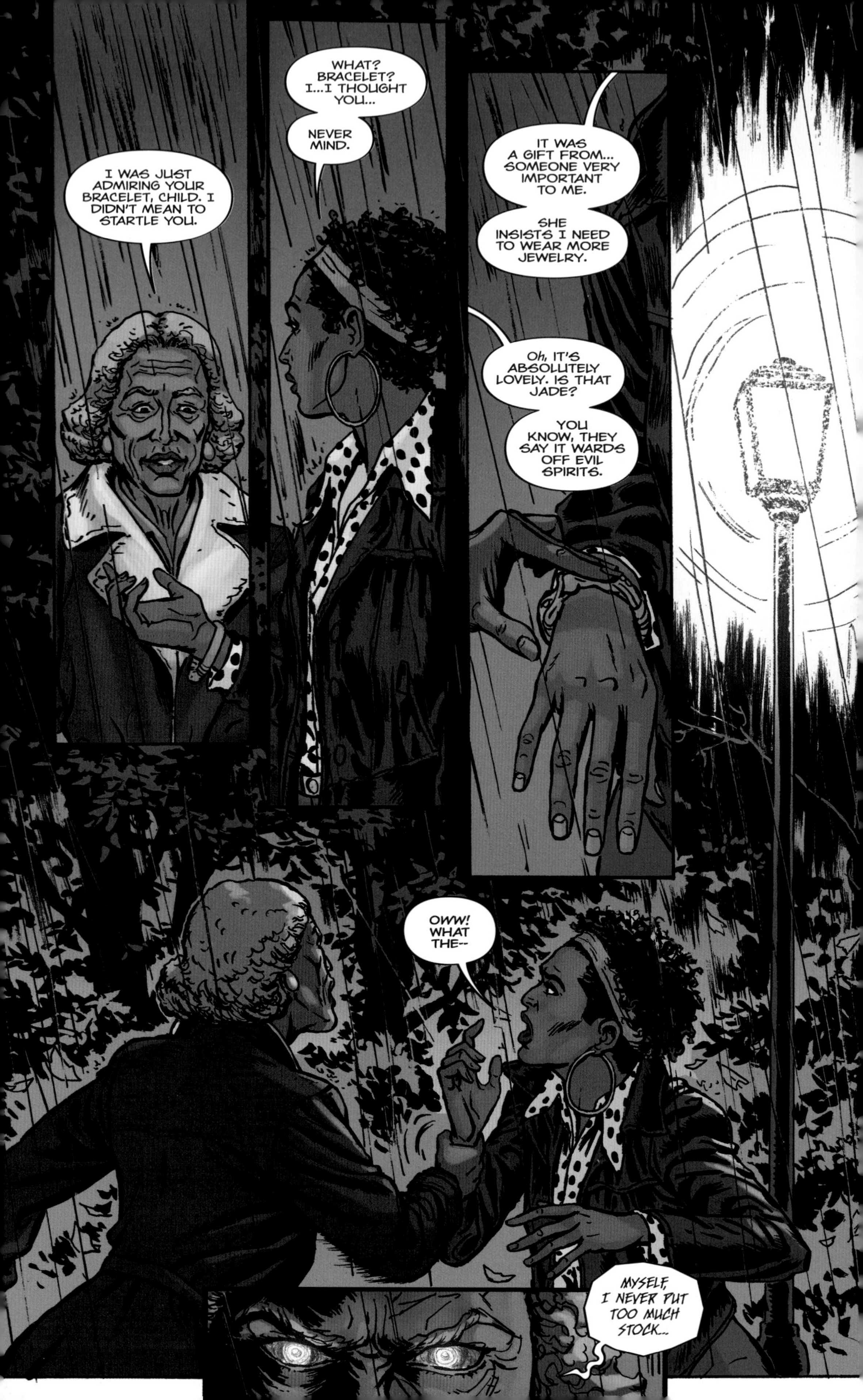
I WAS JUST ADMIRING YOUR BRACELET, CHILD. I DIDN'T MEAN TO STARTLE YOU.
WHAT? BRACELET? I...I THOUGHT YOU...
NEVER MIND.
IT WAS A GIFT FROM... SOMEONE VERY IMPORTANT TO ME.
SHE INSISTS I NEED TO WEAR MORE JEWELRY.
Oh, IT'S ABSOLUTELY LOVELY. IS THAT JADE?
YOU KNOW, THEY SAY IT WARDS OFF EVIL SPIRITS.
OWW! WHAT THE--
MYSELF, I NEVER PUT TOO MUCH STOCK...

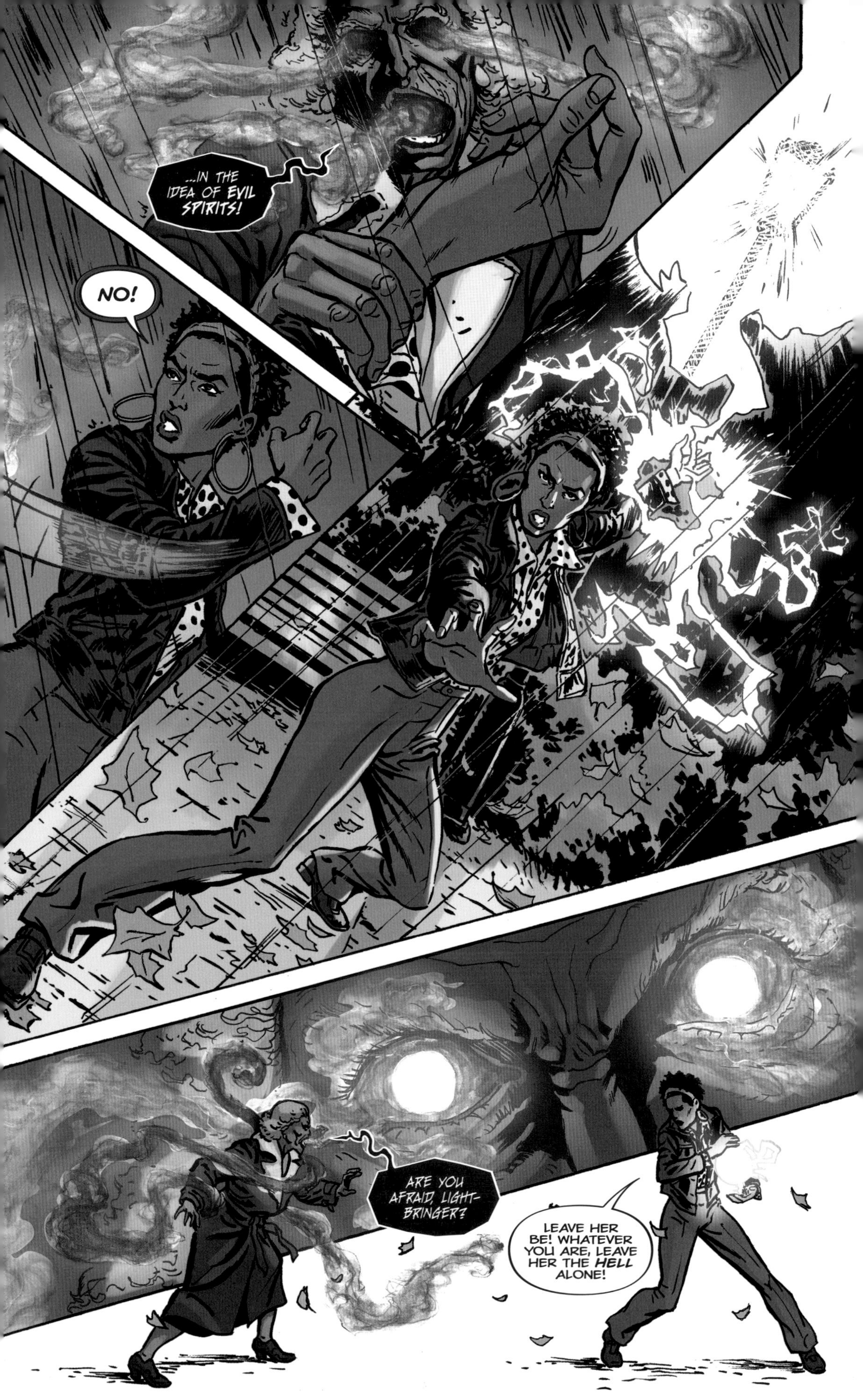
...IN THE IDEA OF EVIL SPIRITS!
NO!
ARE YOU AFRAID, LIGHT-BRINGER?
LEAVE HER BE! WHATEVER YOU ARE, LEAVE HER THE HELL ALONE!

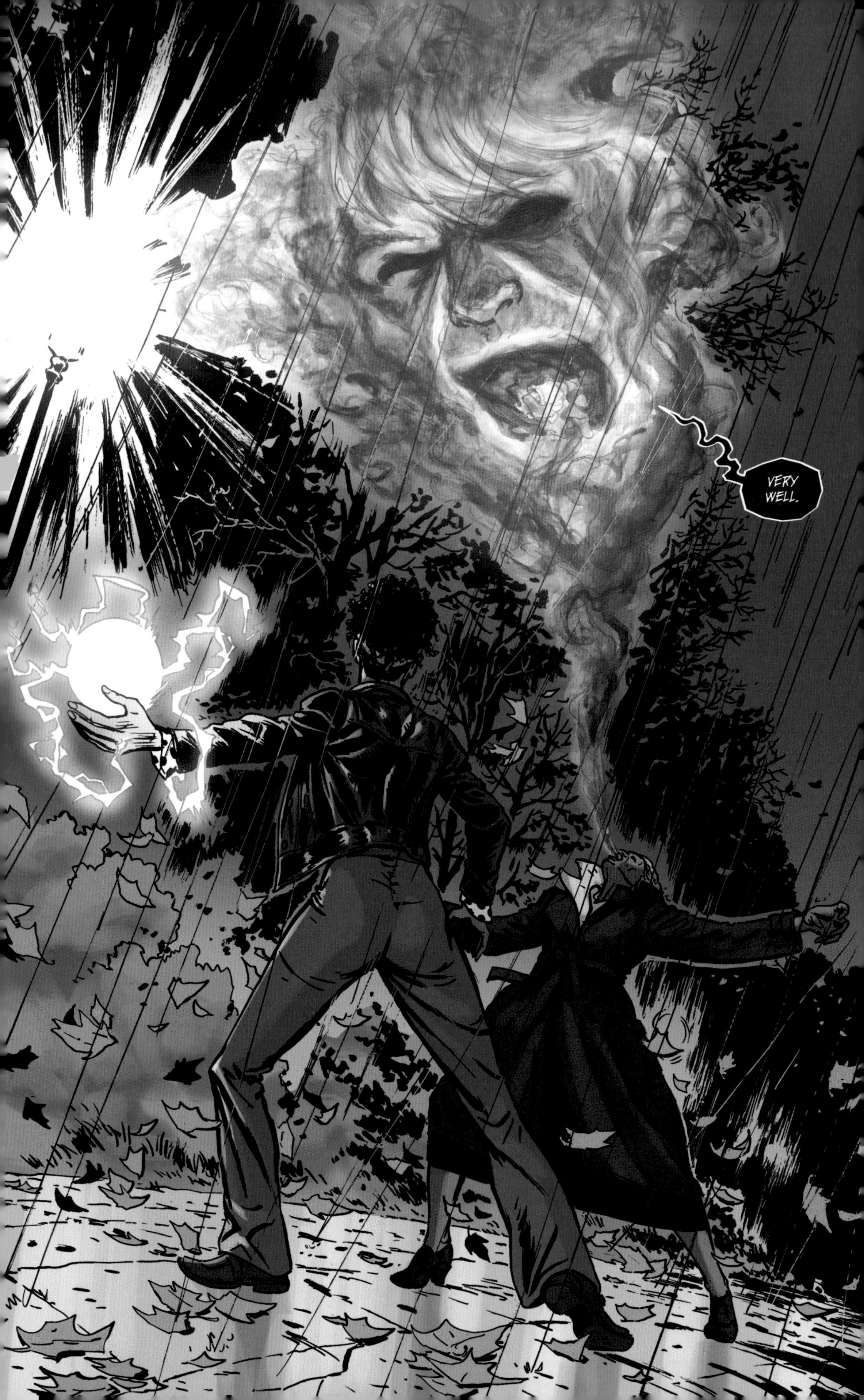
VERY WELL.

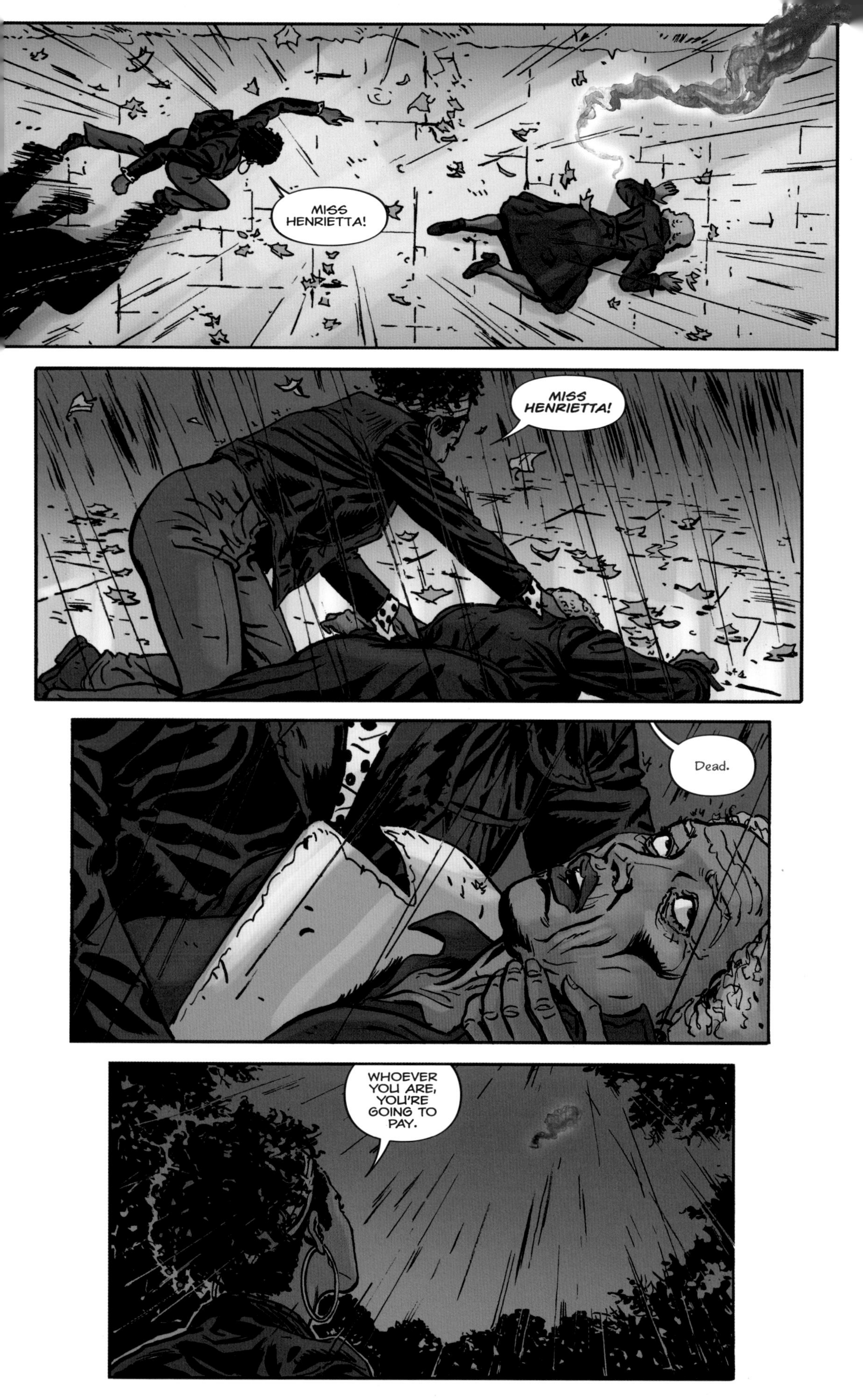
MISS HENRIETTA!
MISS HENRIETTA!
Dead.
WHOEVER YOU ARE, YOU'RE GOING TO PAY.

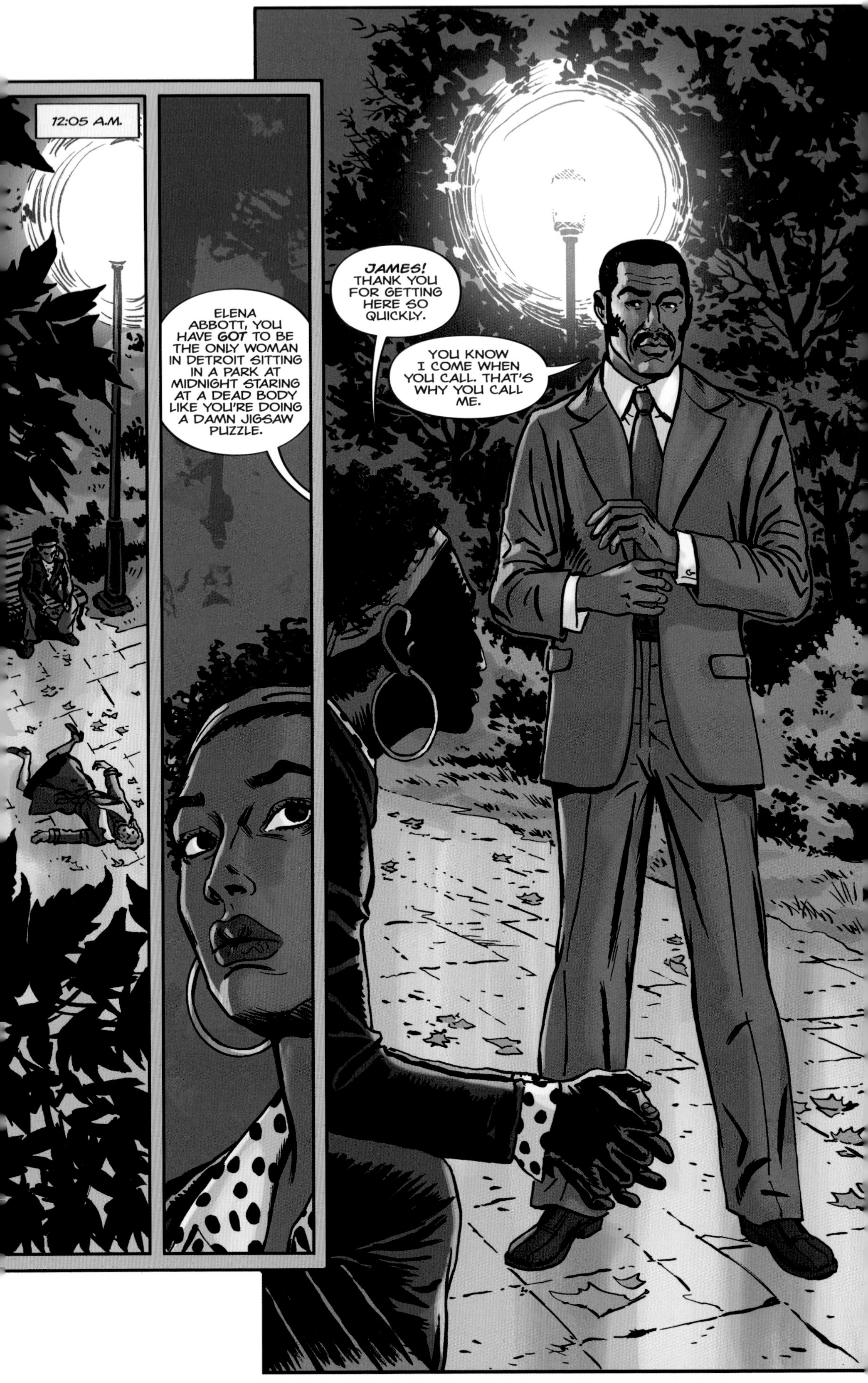
12:05 A.M.
ELENA ABBOTT, YOU HAVE GOT TO BE THE ONLY WOMAN IN DETROIT SITTING IN A PARK AT MIDNIGHT STARING AT A DEAD BODY LIKE YOU'RE DOING A DAMN JIGSAW PUZZLE.
JAMES! THANK YOU FOR GETTING HERE SO QUICKLY.
YOU KNOW I COME WHEN YOU CALL. THAT'S WHY YOU CALL ME.

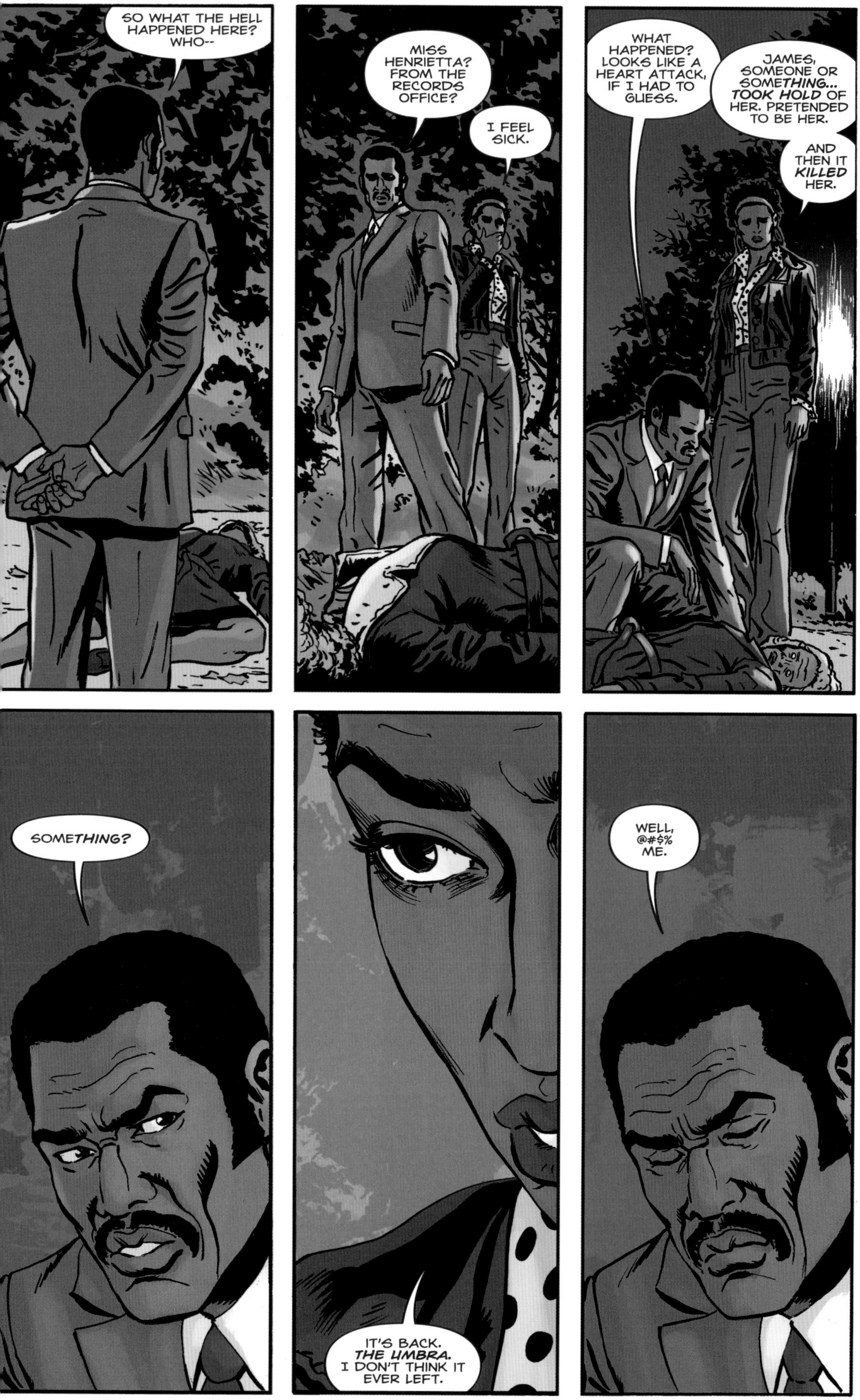
SO WHAT THE HELL HAPPENED HERE? WHO--
MISS HENRIETTA? FROM THE RECORDS OFFICE?
I FEEL SICK.
WHAT HAPPENED? LOOKS LIKE A HEART ATTACK, IF I HAD TO GUESS.
JAMES, SOMEONE OR SOMETHING... TOOK HOLD OF HER. PRETENDED TO BE HER.
AND THEN IT KILLED HER.
SOMETHING?
IT'S BACK. THE UMBRA. I DON'T THINK IT EVER LEFT.
WELL, @#$% ME.

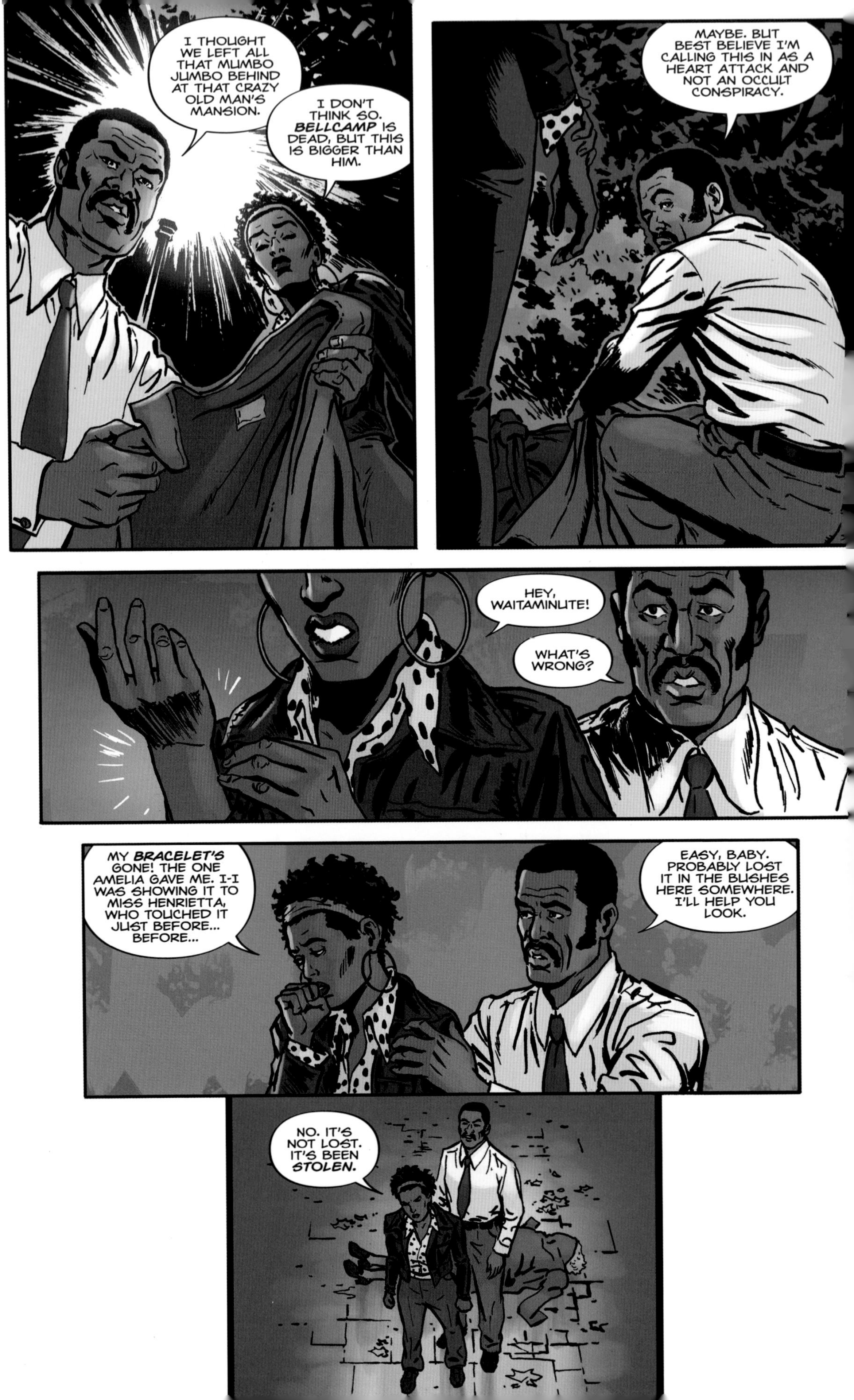
I THOUGHT WE LEFT ALL THAT MUMBO JUMBO BEHIND AT THAT CRAZY OLD MAN'S MANSION.
I DON'T THINK SO. BELLCAMP IS DEAD, BUT THIS IS BIGGER THAN HIM.
MAYBE. BUT BEST BELIEVE I'M CALLING THIS IN AS A HEART ATTACK AND NOT AN OCCULT CONSPIRACY.
HEY, WAITAMINUTE!
WHAT'S WRONG?
MY BRACELET'S GONE! THE ONE AMELIA GAVE ME. I-I WAS SHOWING IT TO MISS HENRIETTA, WHO TOUCHED IT JUST BEFORE... BEFORE...
EASY, BABY. PROBABLY LOST IT IN THE BUSHES HERE SOMEWHERE. I'LL HELP YOU LOOK.
NO. IT'S NOT LOST. IT'S BEEN STOLEN.

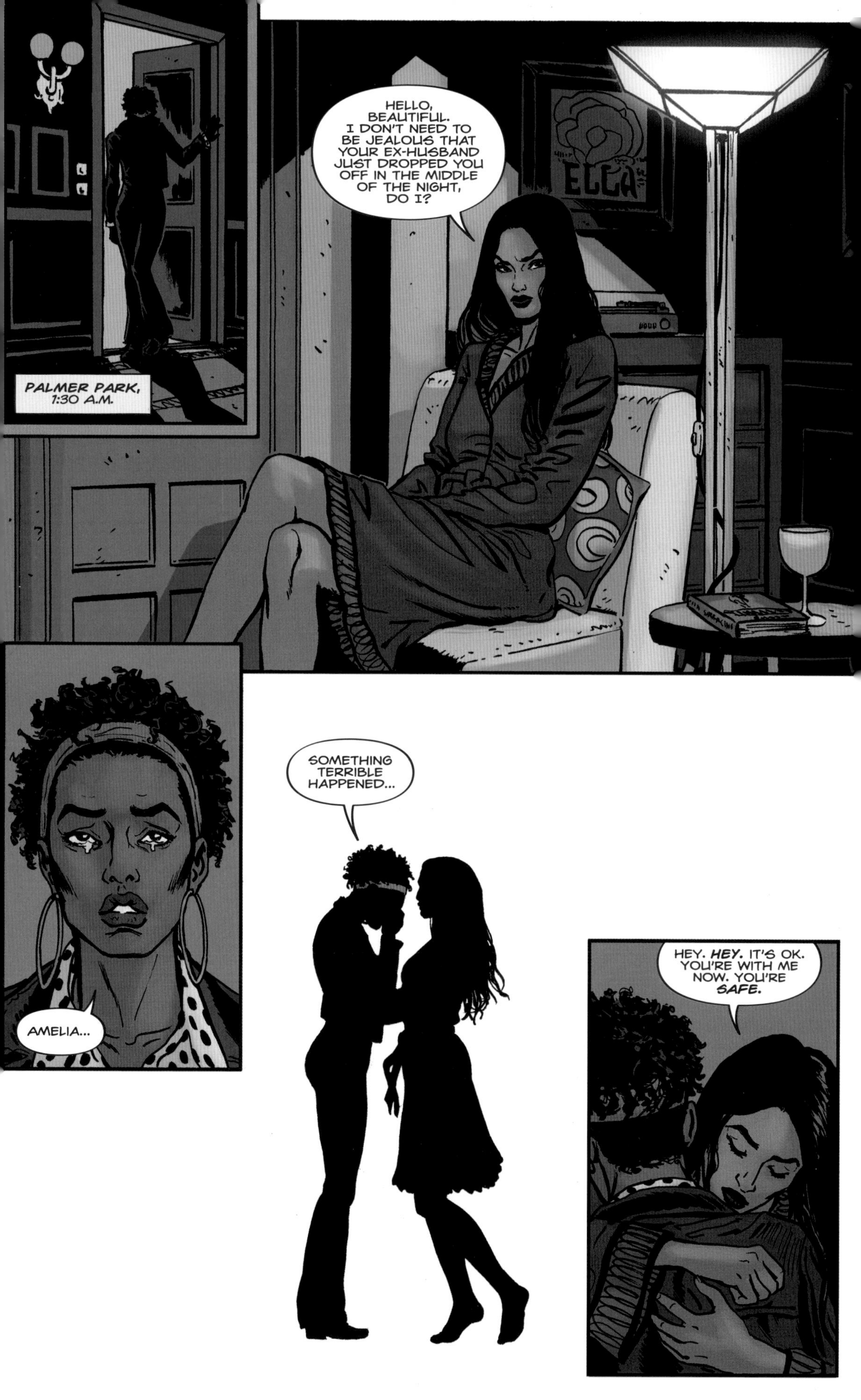
PALMER PARK, 1:30 A.M.
HELLO, BEAUTIFUL. I DON'T NEED TO BE JEALOUS THAT YOUR EX-HUSBAND JUST DROPPED YOU OFF IN THE MIDDLE OF THE NIGHT, DO I?
ELLA
AMELIA...
SOMETHING TERRIBLE HAPPENED...
HEY. HEY. IT'S OK. YOU'RE WITH ME NOW. YOU'RE SAFE.

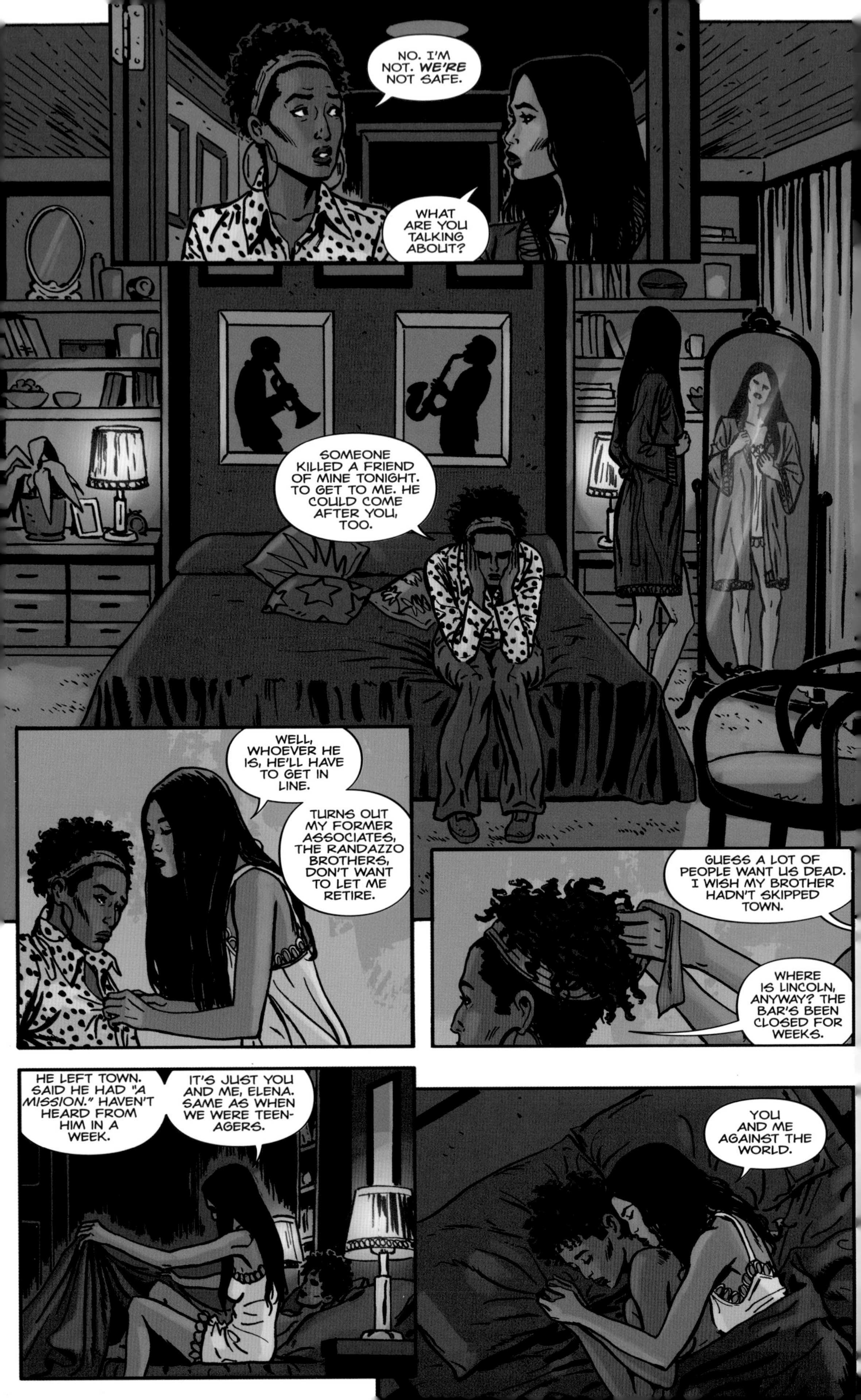
NO. I'M NOT. *WE'RE* NOT SAFE.
WHAT ARE YOU TALKING ABOUT?
SOMEONE KILLED A FRIEND OF MINE TONIGHT. TO GET TO ME. HE COULD COME AFTER YOU, TOO.
WELL, WHOEVER HE IS, HE'LL HAVE TO GET IN LINE.
TURNS OUT MY FORMER ASSOCIATES, THE RANDAZZO BROTHERS, DON'T WANT TO LET ME RETIRE.
GUESS A LOT OF PEOPLE WANT US DEAD. I WISH MY BROTHER HADN'T SKIPPED TOWN.
WHERE IS LINCOLN, ANYWAY? THE BAR'S BEEN CLOSED FOR WEEKS.
HE LEFT TOWN. SAID HE HAD *"A MISSION."* HAVEN'T HEARD FROM HIM IN A WEEK.
IT'S JUST YOU AND ME, ELENA. SAME AS WHEN WE WERE TEEN-AGERS.
YOU AND ME AGAINST THE WORLD.

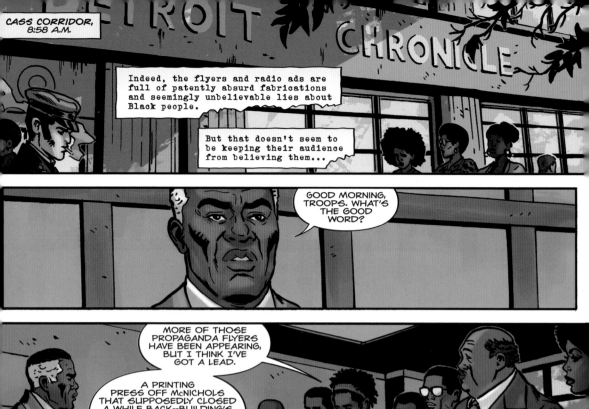

CASS CORRIDOR, 8:58 A.M.
DETROIT CHRONICLE
Indeed, the flyers and radio ads are full of patently absurd fabrications and seemingly unbelievable lies about Black people.
But that doesn't seem to be keeping their audience from believing them...
GOOD MORNING, TROOPS. WHAT'S THE GOOD WORD?
MORE OF THOSE PROPAGANDA FLYERS HAVE BEEN APPEARING, BUT I THINK I'VE GOT A LEAD.
A PRINTING PRESS OFF McNICHOLS THAT SUPPOSEDLY CLOSED A WHILE BACK--BUILDING'S STILL OWNED BY A GUY WHO SHOWED UP IN THE CHRONICLE'S "KNOWN KKK" REGISTRY.
I'VE TOLD YOU BEFORE, THIS FLYERS BUSINESS IS PENNY ANTE.
WITH ALL DUE RESPECT, SIR, I DISAGREE. IF THERE'S EVEN A CHANCE THESE LIES WILL AFFECT THE ELECTION--
FINE, MISS ABBOTT. BUT YOU'LL NEED TO FILE YOUR STORY EARLY TODAY.
WHY?
BECAUSE YOU ARE GOING TO ACCOMPANY ME TONIGHT TO A FUNDRAISING DINNER FOR THE NATIONAL NEGRO COLLEGE FUND WHERE MY DEAR FRIEND, THE FUTURE MAYOR OF THIS CITY, WILL GIVE A KEYNOTE SPEECH.
DINNER? SIR, I--
PLEASE BE SURE TO WEAR SOMETHING ATTRACTIVE AND APPROPRIATE.
NOW, KHALIL, YOU SAID YOU'RE WORKING ON THAT FIRE IN THE HERMAN FIELDS HOUSING PROJECT--

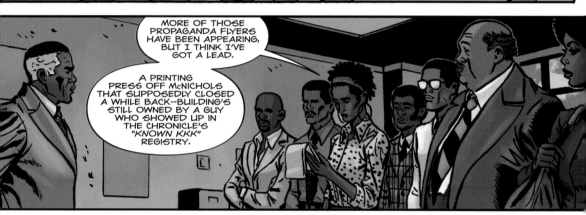

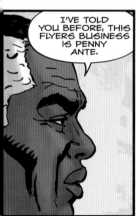

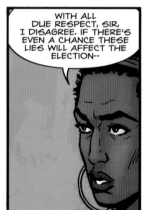

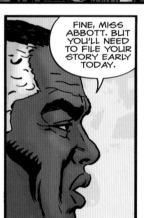

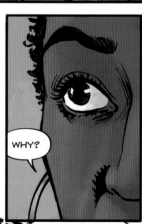

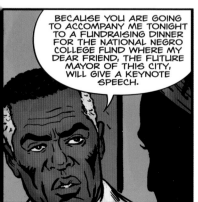

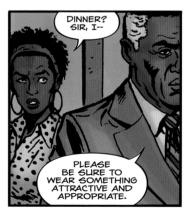

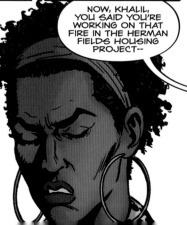

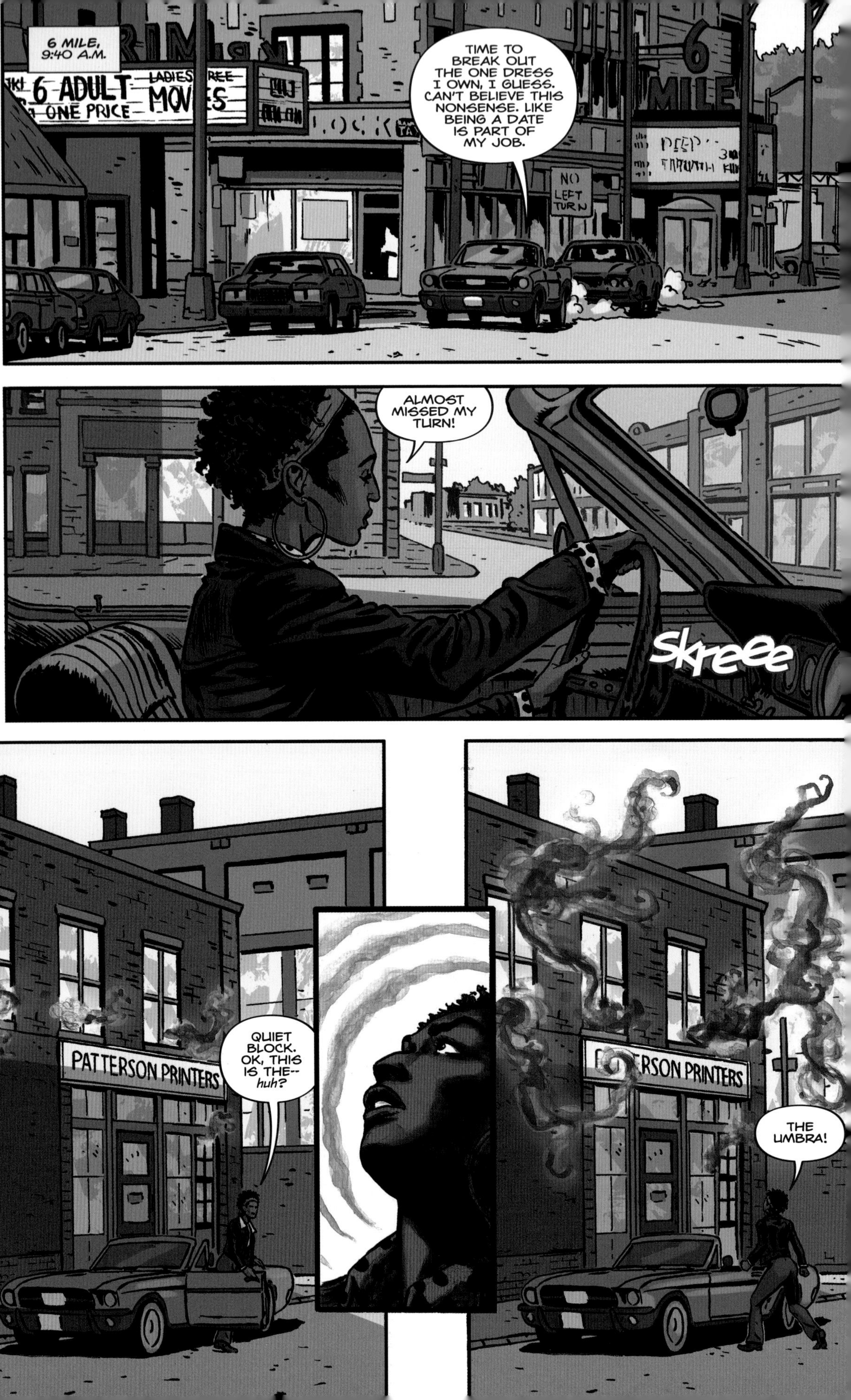
6 MILE, 9:40 A.M.
6 ADULT ONE PRICE
LADIES FREE MOVIES
6 MILE
NO LEFT TURN
TIME TO BREAK OUT THE ONE DRESS I OWN, I GUESS. CAN'T BELIEVE THIS NONSENSE. LIKE BEING A DATE IS PART OF MY JOB.
ALMOST MISSED MY TURN!
Skreeee
PATTERSON PRINTERS
QUIET BLOCK. OK, THIS IS THE-- *huh?*
THE UMBRA!

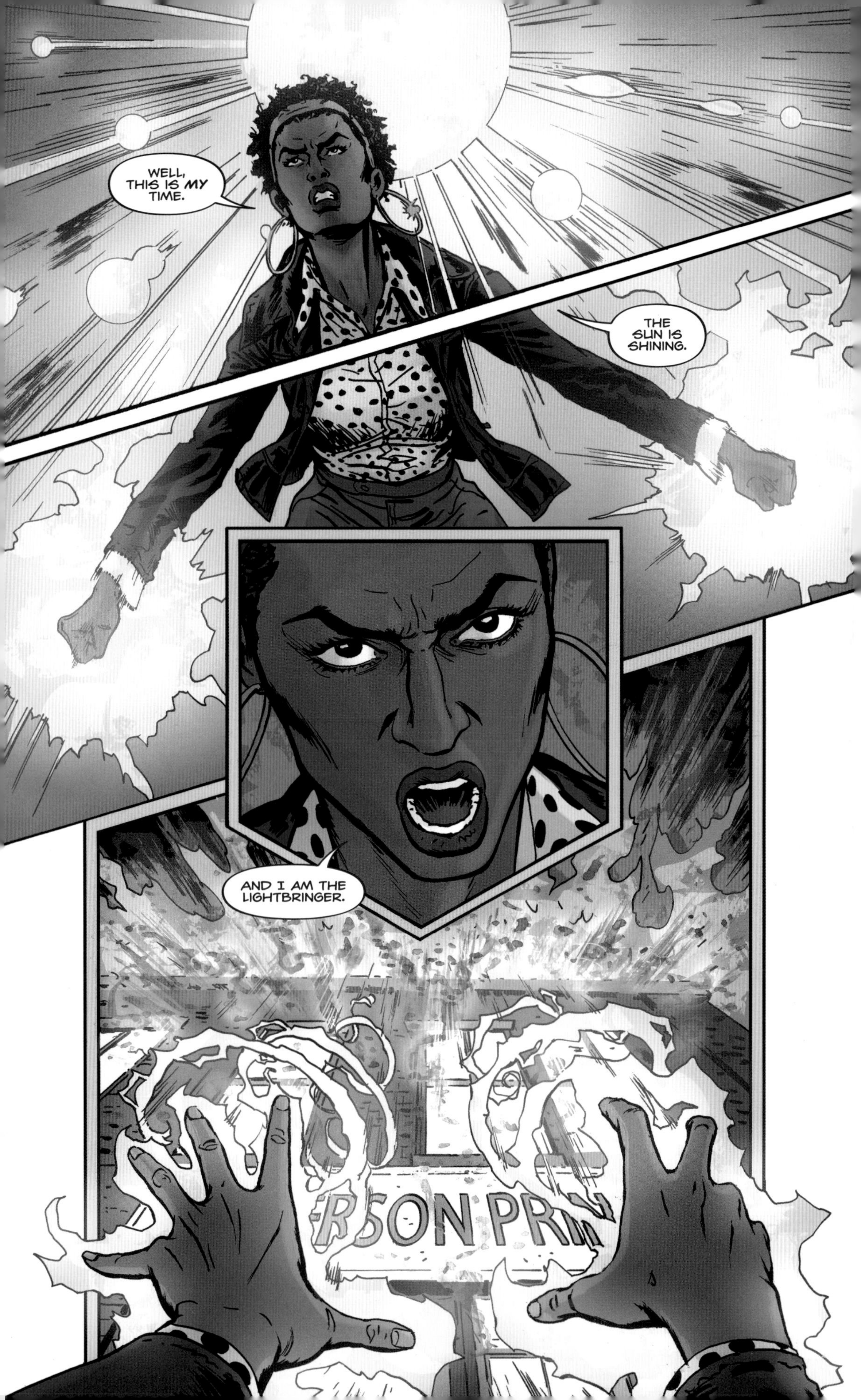
WELL, THIS IS MY TIME.
THE SUN IS SHINING.
AND I AM THE LIGHTBRINGER.
RSON PRI

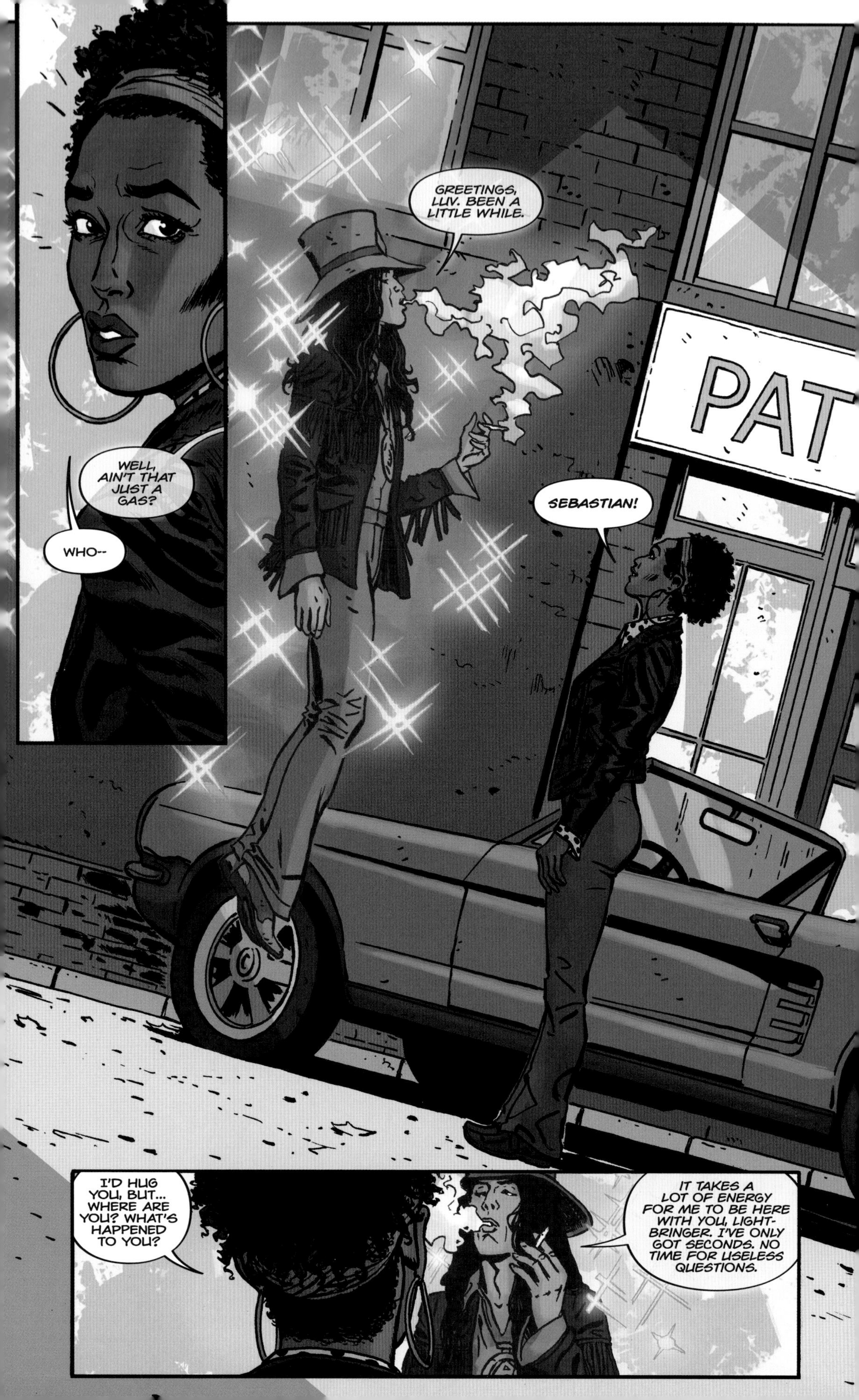
WHO--
WELL, AIN'T THAT JUST A GAS?
GREETINGS, LUV. BEEN A LITTLE WHILE.
PAT
SEBASTIAN!
I'D HUG YOU, BUT... WHERE ARE YOU? WHAT'S HAPPENED TO YOU?
IT TAKES A LOT OF ENERGY FOR ME TO BE HERE WITH YOU, LIGHT-BRINGER. I'VE ONLY GOT SECONDS. NO TIME FOR USELESS QUESTIONS.

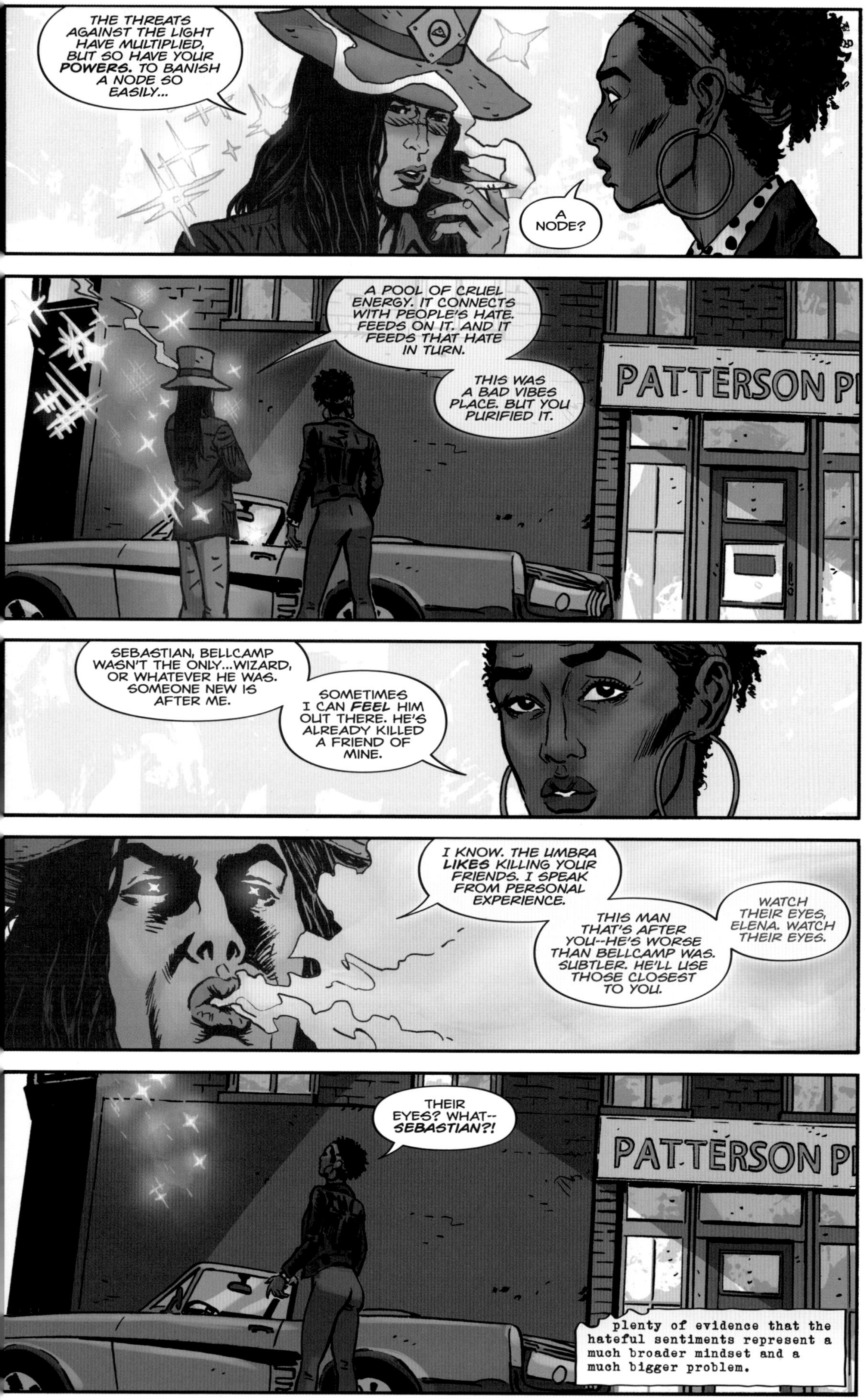
THE THREATS AGAINST THE LIGHT HAVE MULTIPLIED, BUT SO HAVE YOUR **POWERS.** TO BANISH A NODE SO EASILY...
A NODE?
A POOL OF CRUEL ENERGY. IT CONNECTS WITH PEOPLE'S HATE. FEEDS ON IT. AND IT FEEDS THAT HATE IN TURN.
THIS WAS A BAD VIBES PLACE. BUT YOU PURIFIED IT.
PATTERSON P
SEBASTIAN, BELLCAMP WASN'T THE ONLY...WIZARD, OR WHATEVER HE WAS. SOMEONE NEW IS AFTER ME.
SOMETIMES I CAN ***FEEL*** HIM OUT THERE. HE'S ALREADY KILLED A FRIEND OF MINE.
I KNOW. THE UMBRA ***LIKES*** KILLING YOUR FRIENDS. I SPEAK FROM PERSONAL EXPERIENCE.
THIS MAN THAT'S AFTER YOU--HE'S WORSE THAN BELLCAMP WAS. SUBTLER. HE'LL USE THOSE CLOSEST TO YOU.
WATCH THEIR EYES, ELENA. WATCH THEIR EYES.
THEIR EYES? WHAT-- ***SEBASTIAN?!***
PATTERSON P
plenty of evidence that the hateful sentiments represent a much broader mindset and a much bigger problem.

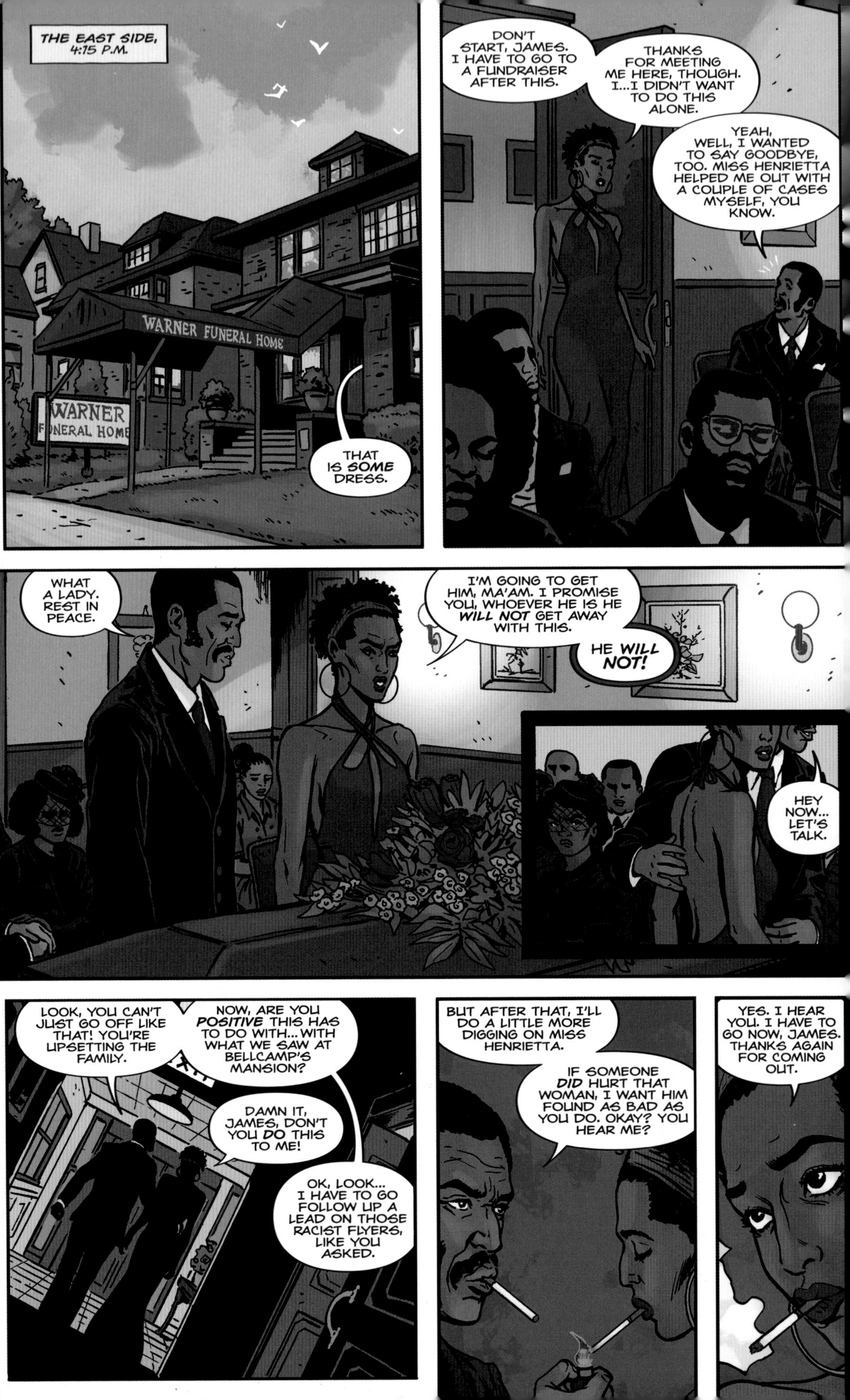
THE EAST SIDE, 4:15 P.M.
WARNER FUNERAL HOME
WARNER FUNERAL HOME
THAT IS SOME DRESS.
DON'T START, JAMES. I HAVE TO GO TO A FUNDRAISER AFTER THIS.
THANKS FOR MEETING ME HERE, THOUGH. I...I DIDN'T WANT TO DO THIS ALONE.
YEAH, WELL, I WANTED TO SAY GOODBYE, TOO. MISS HENRIETTA HELPED ME OUT WITH A COUPLE OF CASES MYSELF, YOU KNOW.
WHAT A LADY. REST IN PEACE.
I'M GOING TO GET HIM, MA'AM. I PROMISE YOU, WHOEVER HE IS HE WILL NOT GET AWAY WITH THIS.
HE WILL NOT!
HEY NOW... LET'S TALK.
LOOK, YOU CAN'T JUST GO OFF LIKE THAT! YOU'RE UPSETTING THE FAMILY.
NOW, ARE YOU POSITIVE THIS HAS TO DO WITH... WITH WHAT WE SAW AT BELLCAMP'S MANSION?
DAMN IT, JAMES, DON'T YOU DO THIS TO ME!
OK, LOOK... I HAVE TO GO FOLLOW UP A LEAD ON THOSE RACIST FLYERS, LIKE YOU ASKED.
BUT AFTER THAT, I'LL DO A LITTLE MORE DIGGING ON MISS HENRIETTA.
IF SOMEONE DID HURT THAT WOMAN, I WANT HIM FOUND AS BAD AS YOU DO. OKAY? YOU HEAR ME?
YES. I HEAR YOU. I HAVE TO GO NOW, JAMES. THANKS AGAIN FOR COMING OUT.

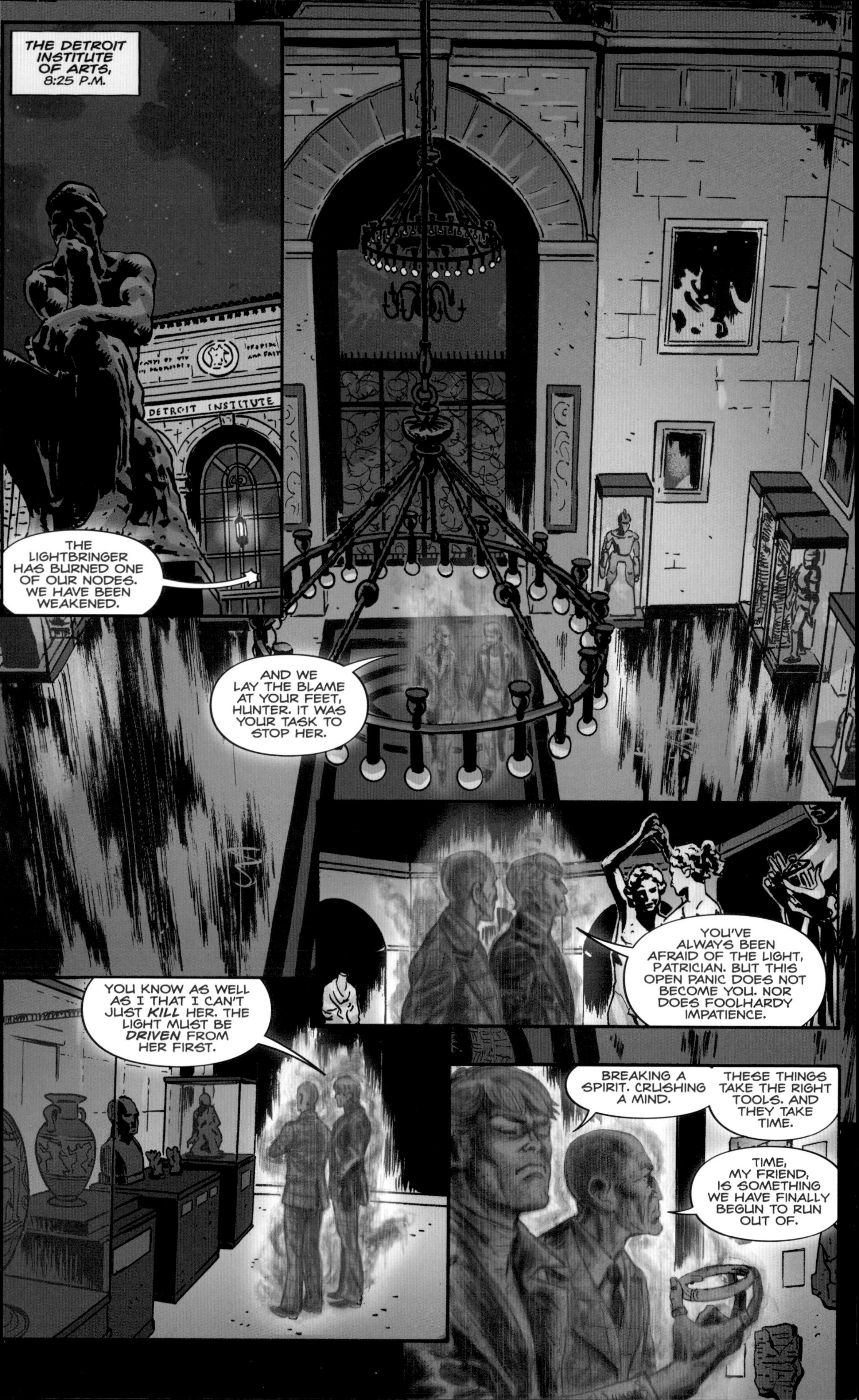
THE DETROIT INSTITUTE OF ARTS, 8:25 P.M.
DETROIT INSTITUTE
THE LIGHTBRINGER HAS BURNED ONE OF OUR NODES. WE HAVE BEEN WEAKENED.
AND WE LAY THE BLAME AT YOUR FEET, HUNTER. IT WAS YOUR TASK TO STOP HER.
YOU'VE ALWAYS BEEN AFRAID OF THE LIGHT, PATRICIAN. BUT THIS OPEN PANIC DOES NOT BECOME YOU. NOR DOES FOOLHARDY IMPATIENCE.
YOU KNOW AS WELL AS I THAT I CAN'T JUST KILL HER. THE LIGHT MUST BE DRIVEN FROM HER FIRST.
BREAKING A SPIRIT. CRUSHING A MIND.
THESE THINGS TAKE THE RIGHT TOOLS. AND THEY TAKE TIME.
TIME, MY FRIEND, IS SOMETHING WE HAVE FINALLY BEGUN TO RUN OUT OF.

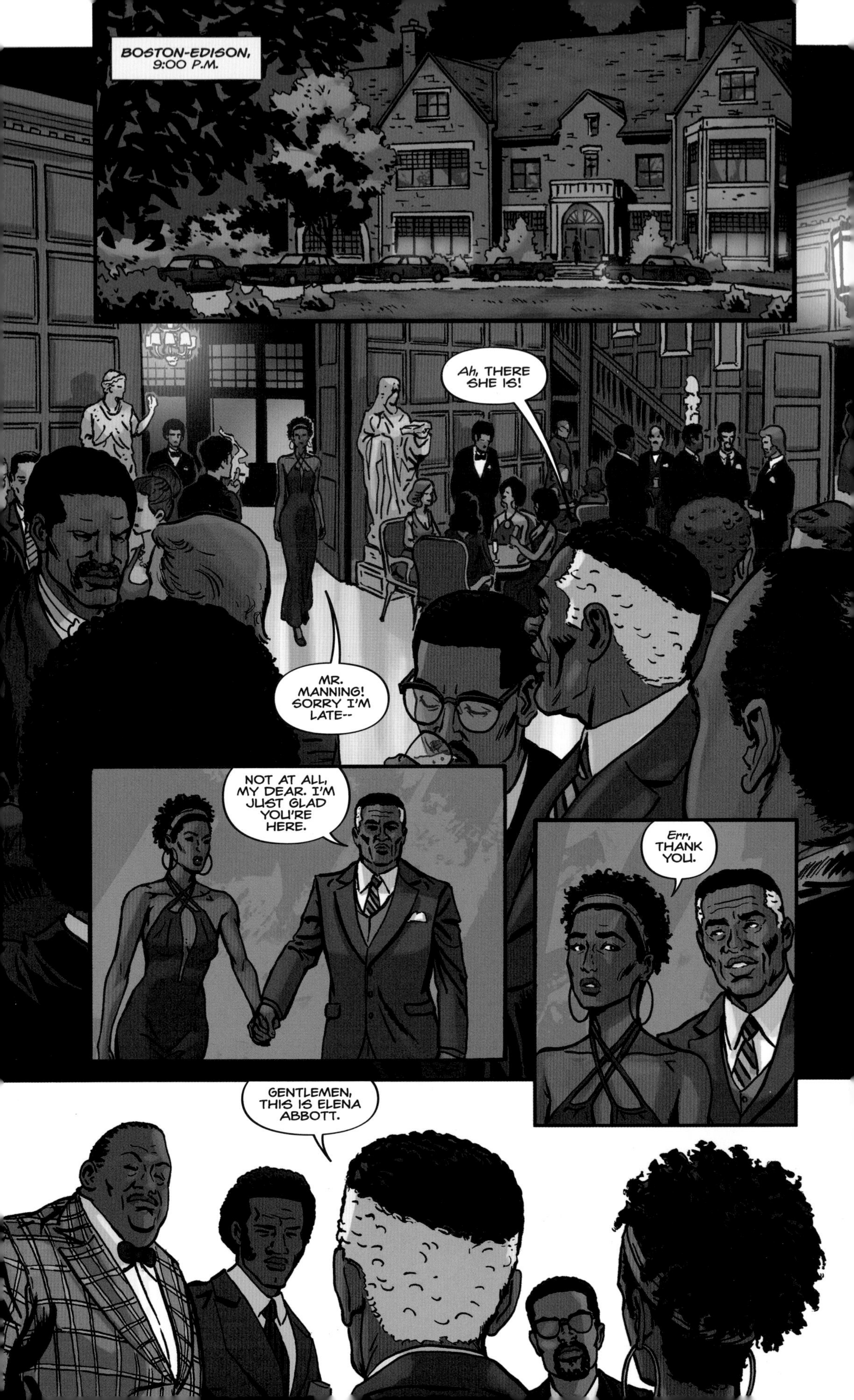
BOSTON-EDISON, 9:00 P.M.
Ah, THERE SHE IS!
MR. MANNING! SORRY I'M LATE--
NOT AT ALL, MY DEAR. I'M JUST GLAD YOU'RE HERE.
Err, THANK YOU.
GENTLEMEN, THIS IS ELENA ABBOTT.

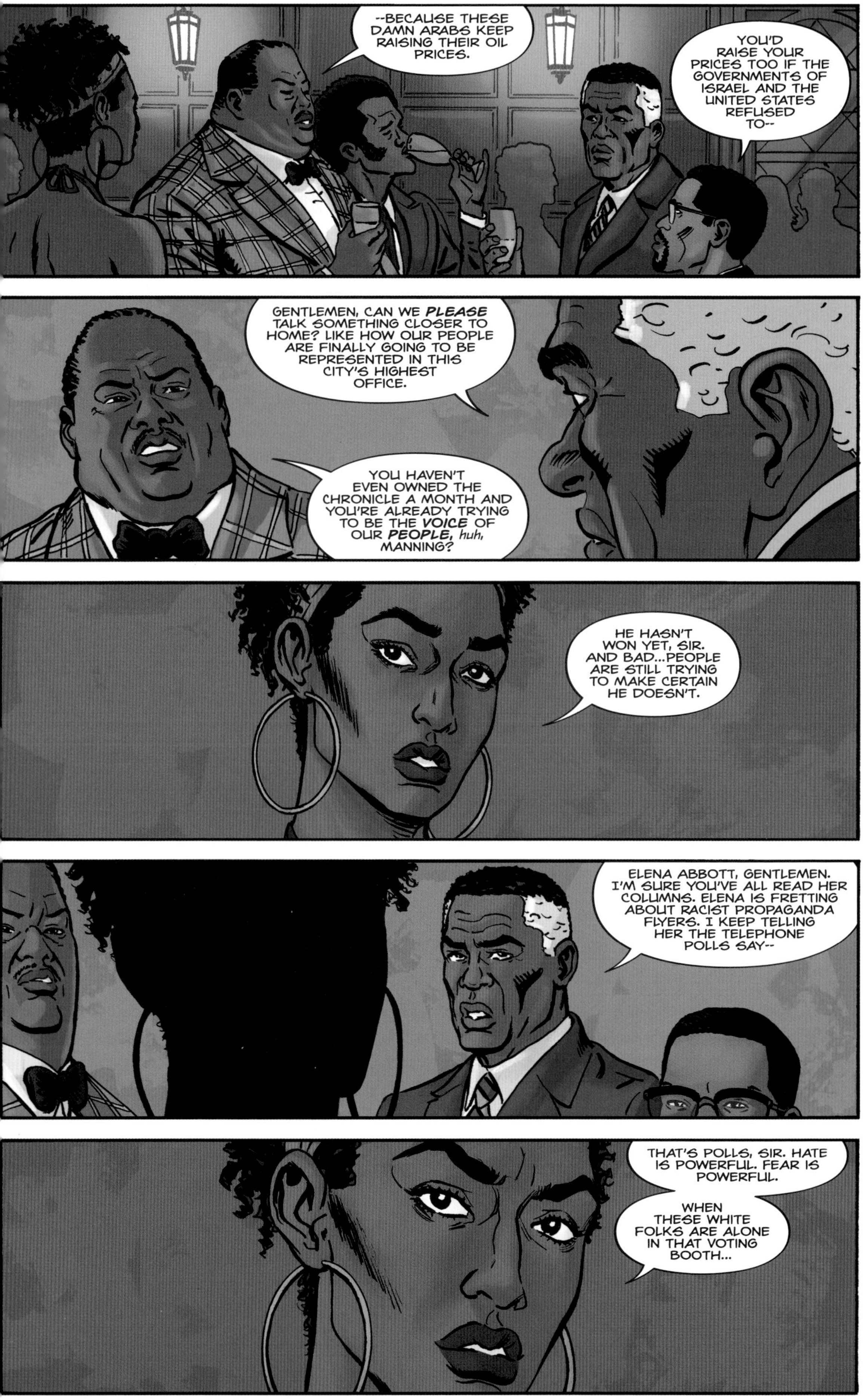
--BECAUSE THESE DAMN ARABS KEEP RAISING THEIR OIL PRICES.
YOU'D RAISE YOUR PRICES TOO IF THE GOVERNMENTS OF ISRAEL AND THE UNITED STATES REFUSED TO--
GENTLEMEN, CAN WE *PLEASE* TALK SOMETHING CLOSER TO HOME? LIKE HOW OUR PEOPLE ARE FINALLY GOING TO BE REPRESENTED IN THIS CITY'S HIGHEST OFFICE.
YOU HAVEN'T EVEN OWNED THE CHRONICLE A MONTH AND YOU'RE ALREADY TRYING TO BE THE *VOICE* OF OUR *PEOPLE, huh,* MANNING?
HE HASN'T WON YET, SIR. AND BAD...PEOPLE ARE STILL TRYING TO MAKE CERTAIN HE DOESN'T.
ELENA ABBOTT, GENTLEMEN. I'M SURE YOU'VE ALL READ HER COLUMNS. ELENA IS FRETTING ABOUT RACIST PROPAGANDA FLYERS. I KEEP TELLING HER THE TELEPHONE POLLS SAY--
THAT'S POLLS, SIR. HATE IS POWERFUL. FEAR IS POWERFUL.
WHEN THESE WHITE FOLKS ARE ALONE IN THAT VOTING BOOTH...

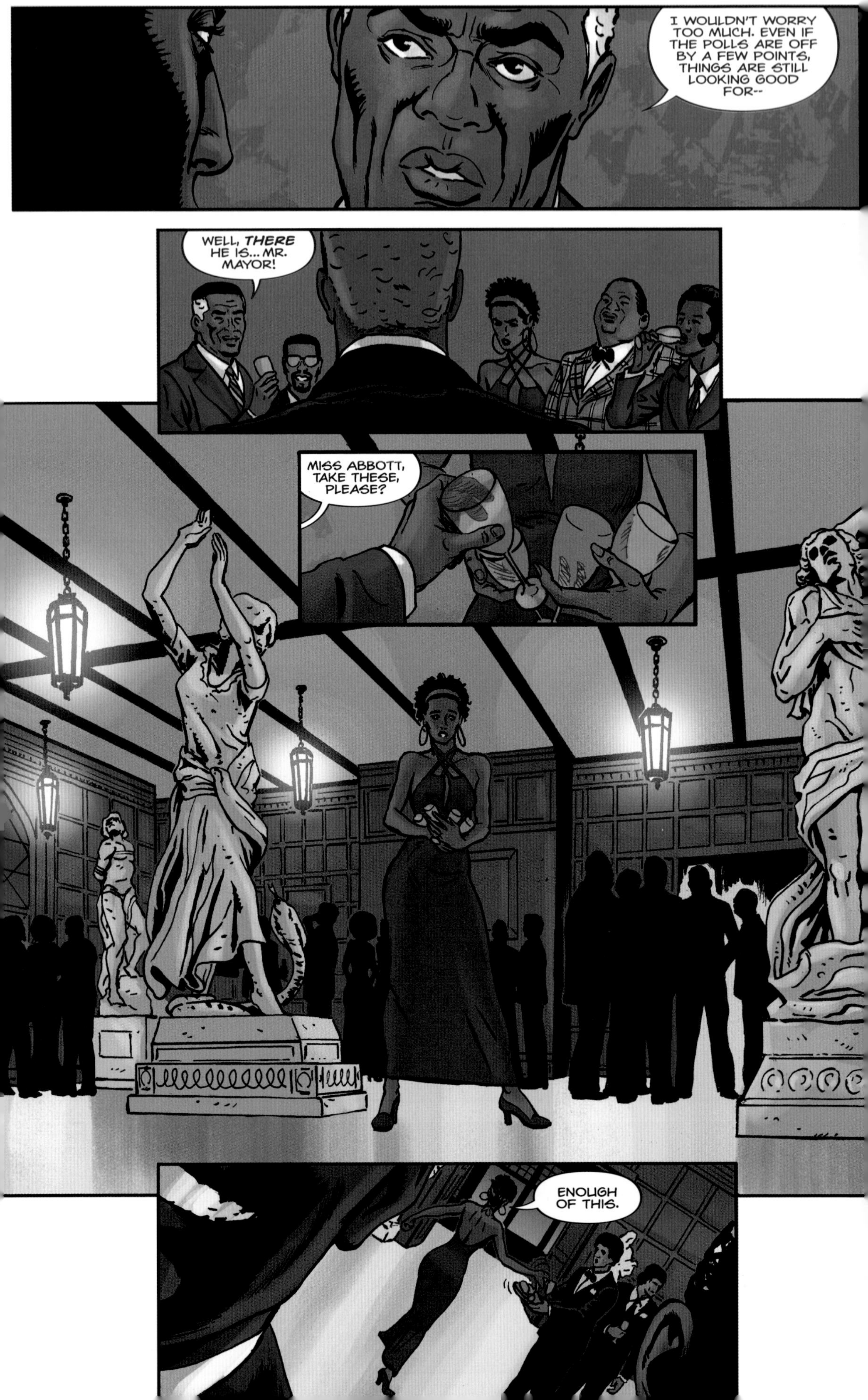
I WOULDN'T WORRY TOO MUCH. EVEN IF THE POLLS ARE OFF BY A FEW POINTS, THINGS ARE STILL LOOKING GOOD FOR--
WELL, *THERE* HE IS... MR. MAYOR!
MISS ABBOTT, TAKE THESE, PLEASE?
ENOUGH OF THIS.

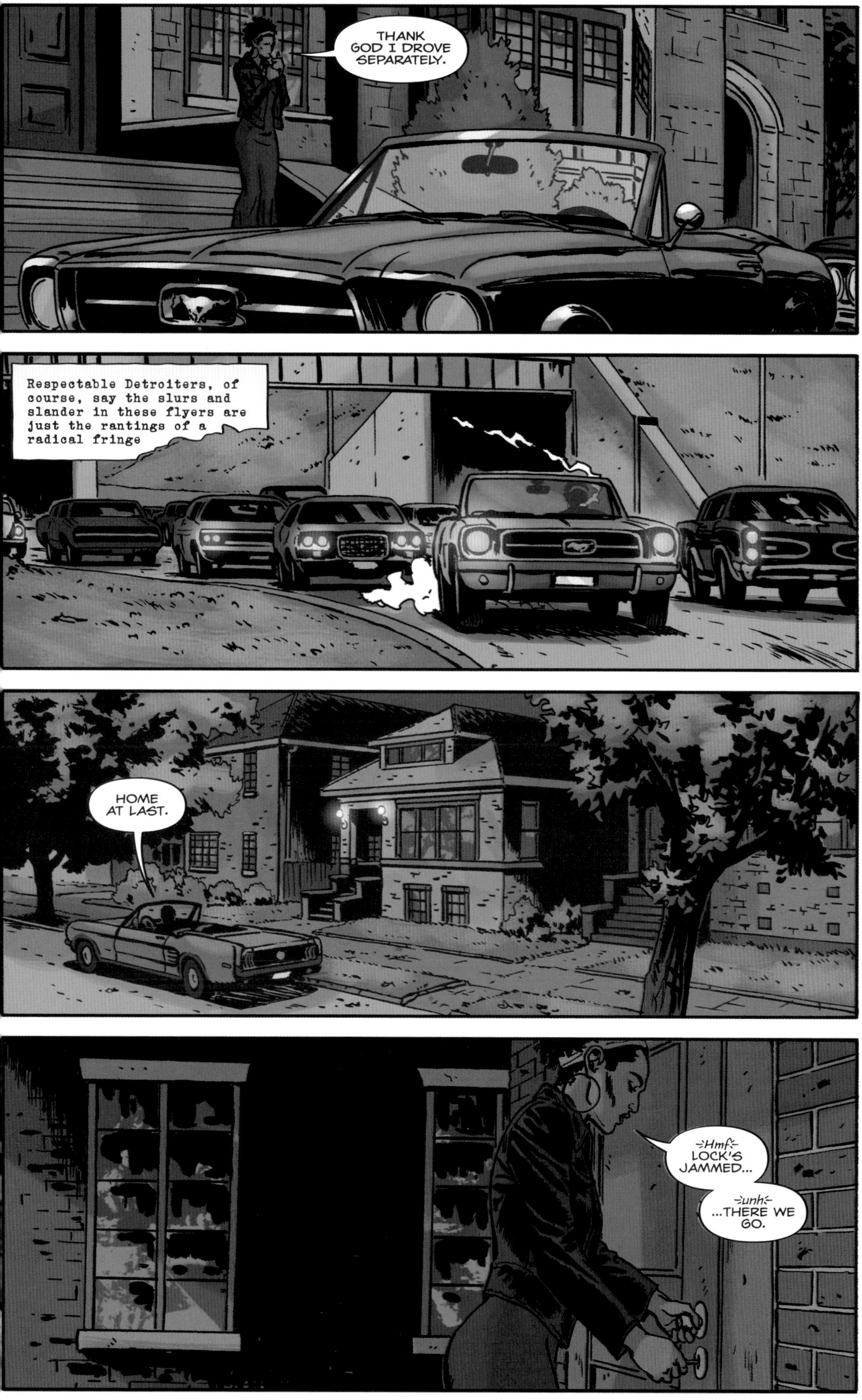
THANK GOD I DROVE SEPARATELY.
Respectable Detroiters, of course, say the slurs and slander in these flyers are just the rantings of a radical fringe
HOME AT LAST.
Hmf LOCK'S JAMMED...
unh ...THERE WE GO.

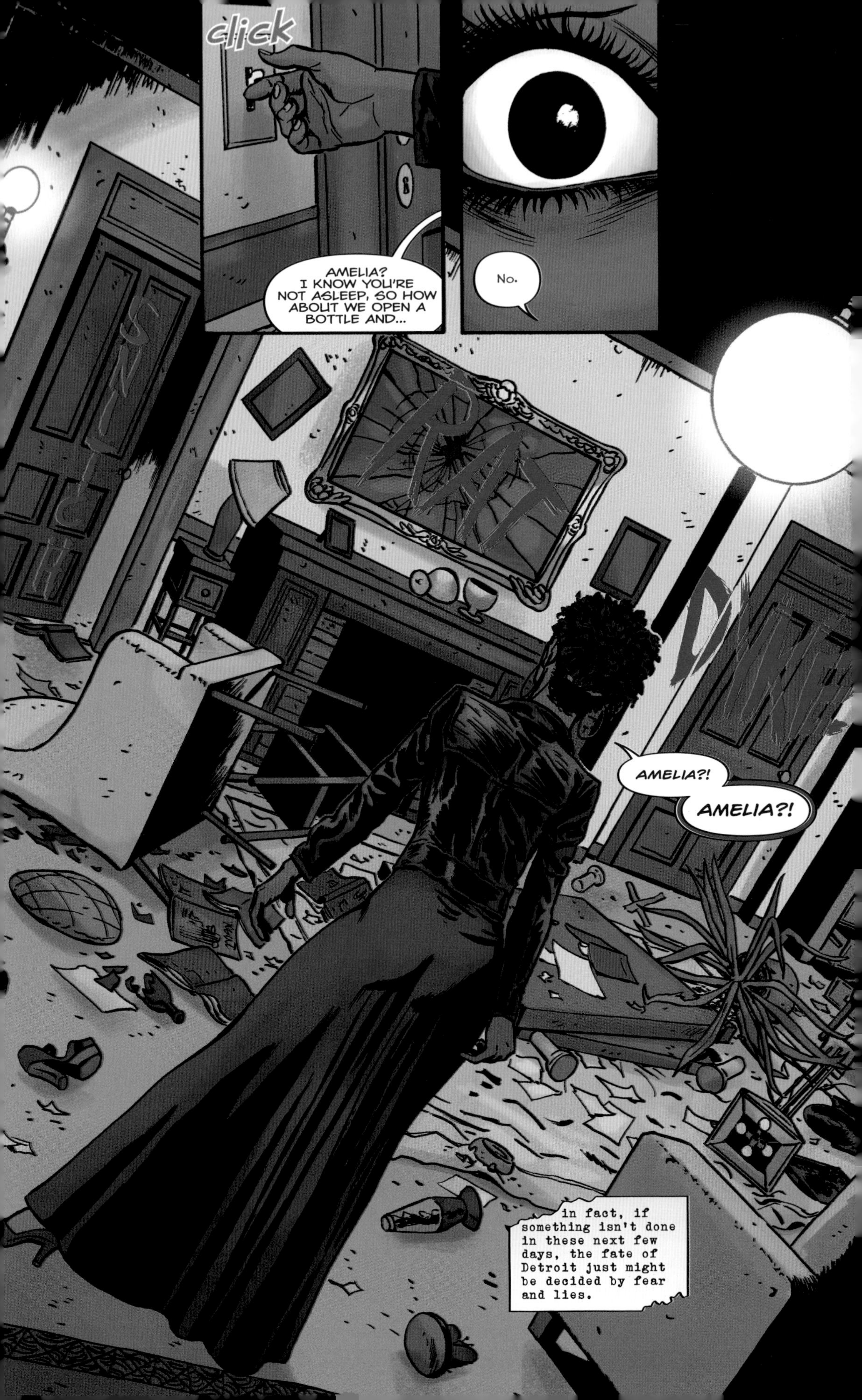
click
AMELIA? I KNOW YOU'RE NOT ASLEEP, SO HOW ABOUT WE OPEN A BOTTLE AND...
No.
SNITCH
RAT
AMELIA?!
AMELIA?!
in fact, if something isn't done in these next few days, the fate of Detroit just might be decided by fear and lies.

Issue Two Variant Cover by

Raúl Allén

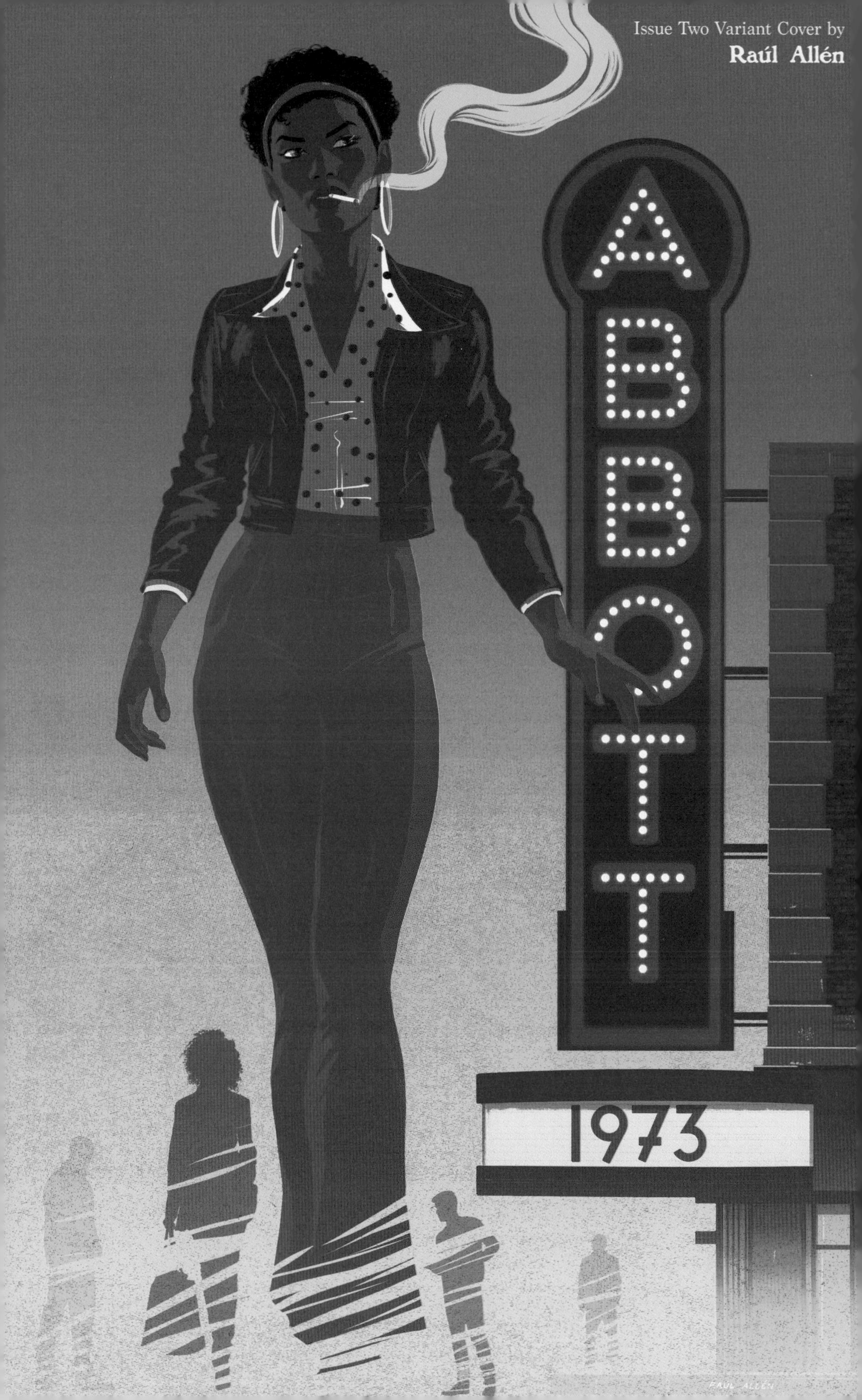
ABBOTT
1973
RAUL ALLEN

CHAPTER THREE

Issue Three Cover by Taj Tenfold

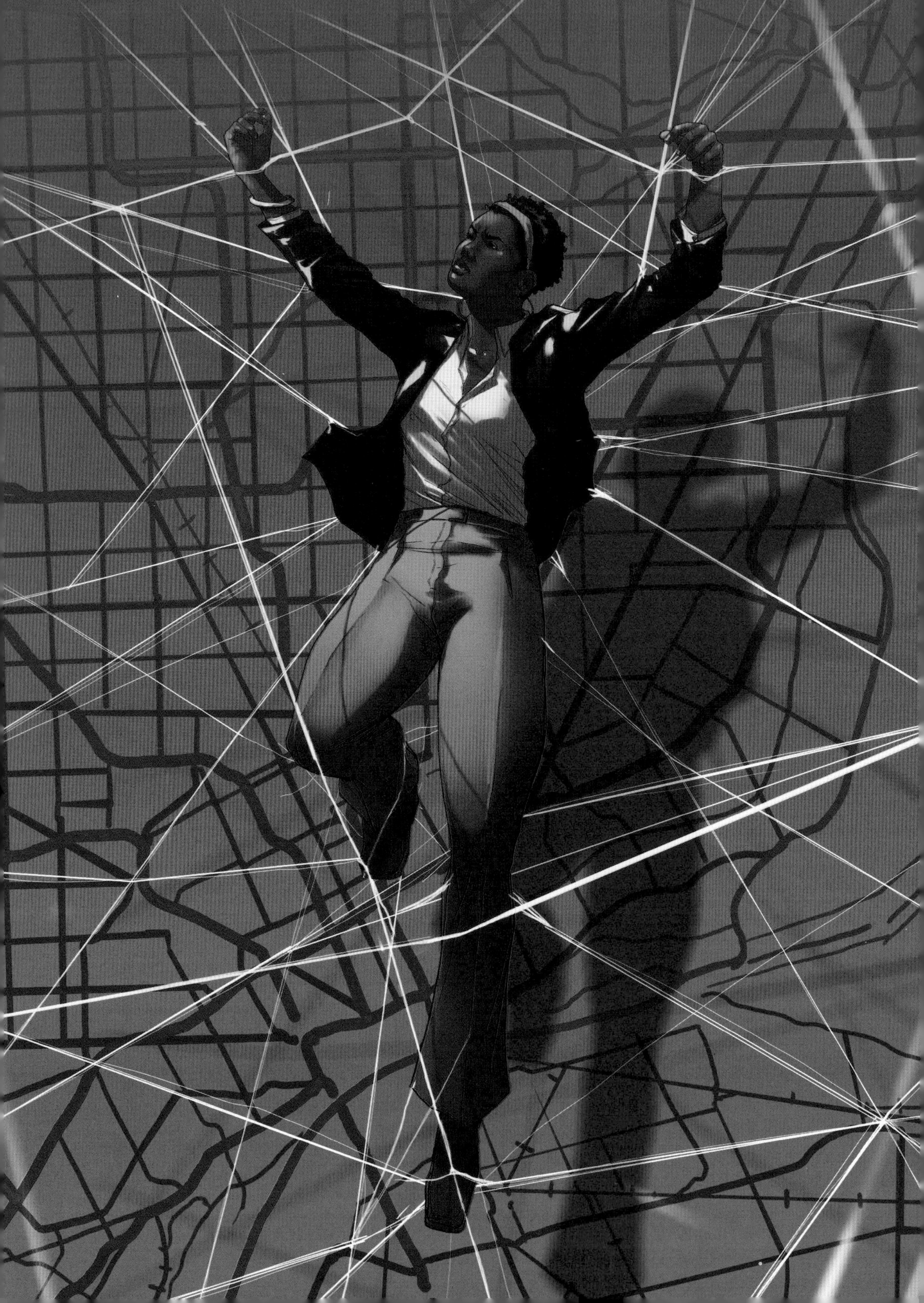

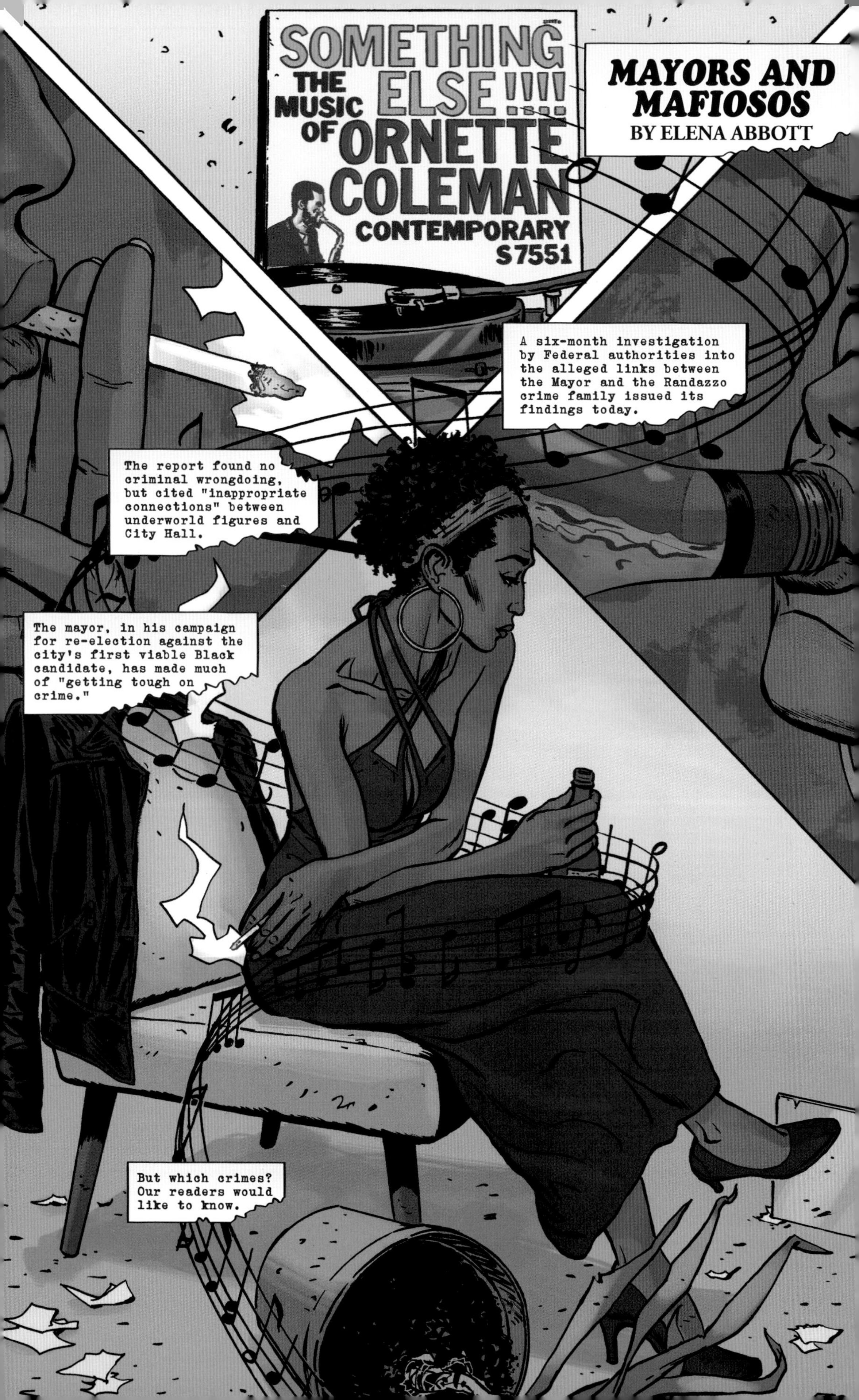
SOMETHING ELSE!!!! THE MUSIC OF ORNETTE COLEMAN
CONTEMPORARY S7551
MAYORS AND MAFIOSOS
BY ELENA ABBOTT
A six-month investigation by Federal authorities into the alleged links between the Mayor and the Randazzo crime family issued its findings today.
The report found no criminal wrongdoing, but cited "inappropriate connections" between underworld figures and City Hall.
The mayor, in his campaign for re-election against the city's first viable Black candidate, has made much of "getting tough on crime."
But which crimes? Our readers would like to know.

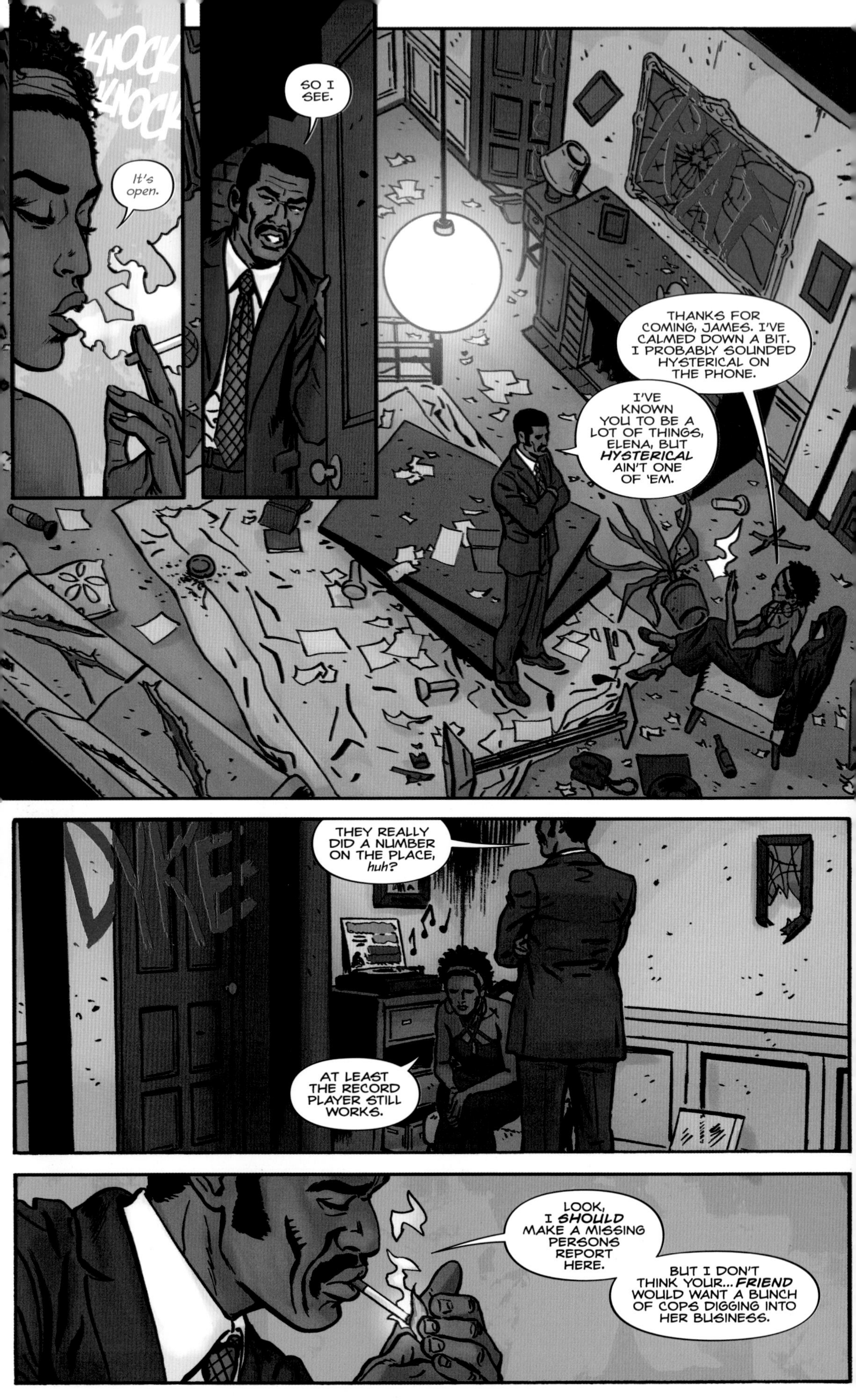
KNOCK
KNOCK
It's open.
SO I SEE.
RAT
THANKS FOR COMING, JAMES. I'VE CALMED DOWN A BIT. I PROBABLY SOUNDED HYSTERICAL ON THE PHONE.
I'VE KNOWN YOU TO BE A LOT OF THINGS, ELENA, BUT ***HYSTERICAL*** AIN'T ONE OF 'EM.
DYKE
THEY REALLY DID A NUMBER ON THE PLACE, *huh?*
AT LEAST THE RECORD PLAYER STILL WORKS.
LOOK, I ***SHOULD*** MAKE A MISSING PERSONS REPORT HERE.
BUT I DON'T THINK YOUR... ***FRIEND*** WOULD WANT A BUNCH OF COPS DIGGING INTO HER BUSINESS.

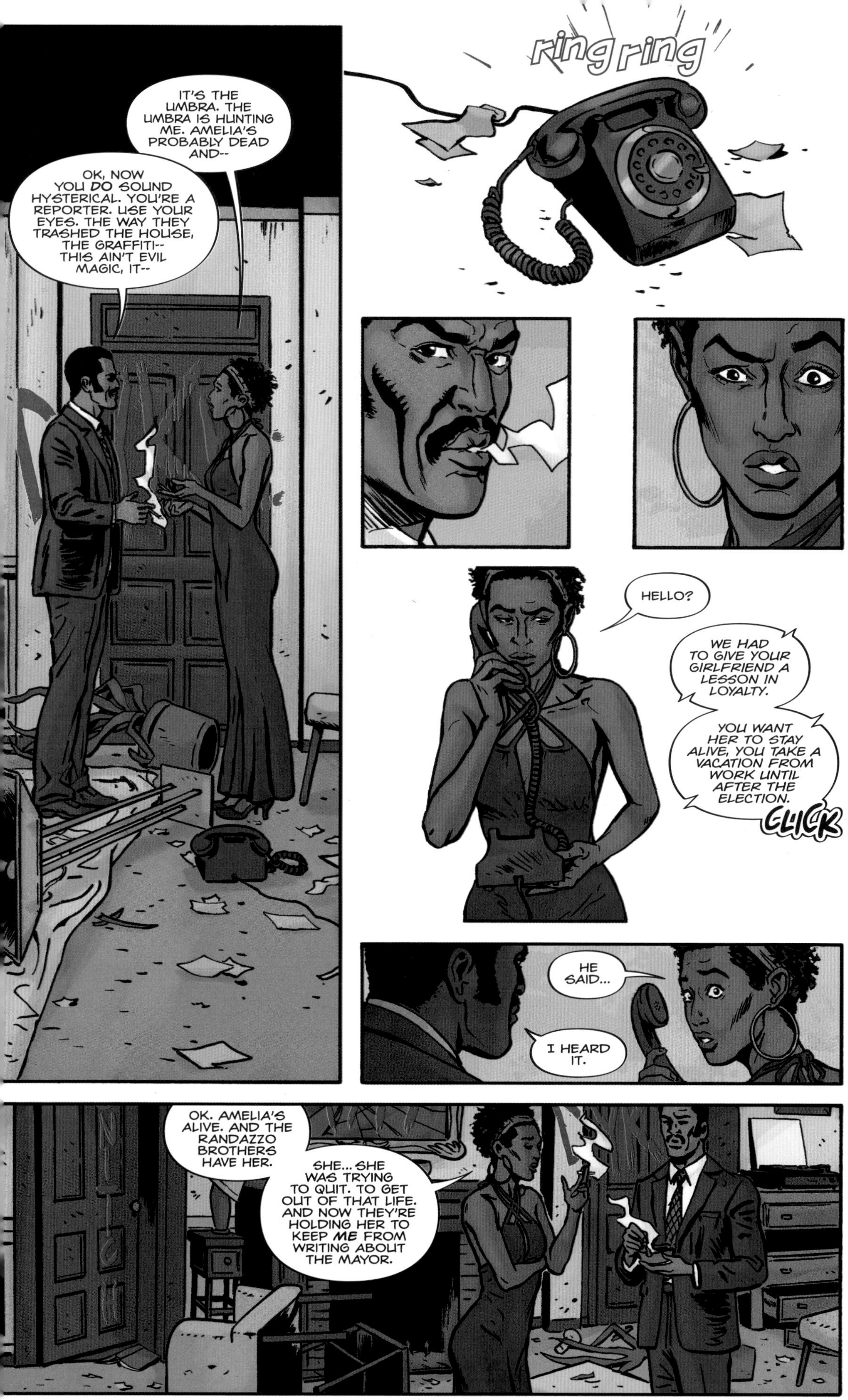
IT'S THE UMBRA. THE UMBRA IS HUNTING ME. AMELIA'S PROBABLY DEAD AND--
OK, NOW YOU *DO* SOUND HYSTERICAL. YOU'RE A REPORTER. USE YOUR EYES. THE WAY THEY TRASHED THE HOUSE, THE GRAFFITI-- THIS AIN'T EVIL MAGIC, IT--
ring ring
HELLO?
WE HAD TO GIVE YOUR GIRLFRIEND A LESSON IN LOYALTY.
YOU WANT HER TO STAY ALIVE, YOU TAKE A VACATION FROM WORK UNTIL AFTER THE ELECTION.
CLICK
HE SAID...
I HEARD IT.
OK. AMELIA'S ALIVE. AND THE RANDAZZO BROTHERS HAVE HER.
SHE... SHE WAS TRYING TO QUIT. TO GET OUT OF THAT LIFE. AND NOW THEY'RE HOLDING HER TO KEEP *ME* FROM WRITING ABOUT THE MAYOR.

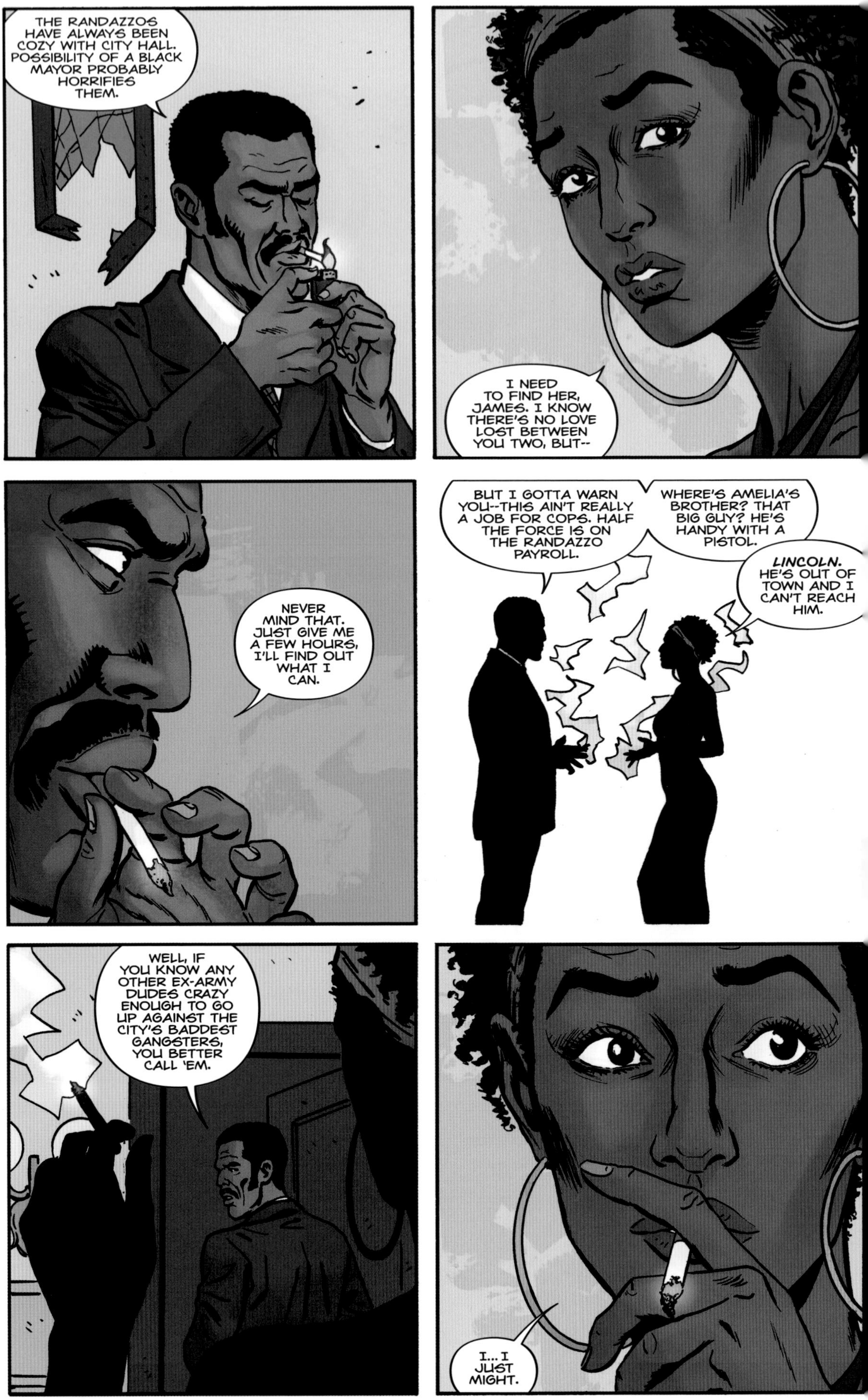
THE RANDAZZOS HAVE ALWAYS BEEN COZY WITH CITY HALL. POSSIBILITY OF A BLACK MAYOR PROBABLY HORRIFIES THEM.
I NEED TO FIND HER, JAMES. I KNOW THERE'S NO LOVE LOST BETWEEN YOU TWO, BUT--
NEVER MIND THAT. JUST GIVE ME A FEW HOURS, I'LL FIND OUT WHAT I CAN.
BUT I GOTTA WARN YOU--THIS AIN'T REALLY A JOB FOR COPS. HALF THE FORCE IS ON THE RANDAZZO PAYROLL.
WHERE'S AMELIA'S BROTHER? THAT BIG GUY? HE'S HANDY WITH A PISTOL.
LINCOLN. HE'S OUT OF TOWN AND I CAN'T REACH HIM.
WELL, IF YOU KNOW ANY OTHER EX-ARMY DUDES CRAZY ENOUGH TO GO UP AGAINST THE CITY'S BADDEST GANGSTERS, YOU BETTER CALL 'EM.
I... I JUST MIGHT.

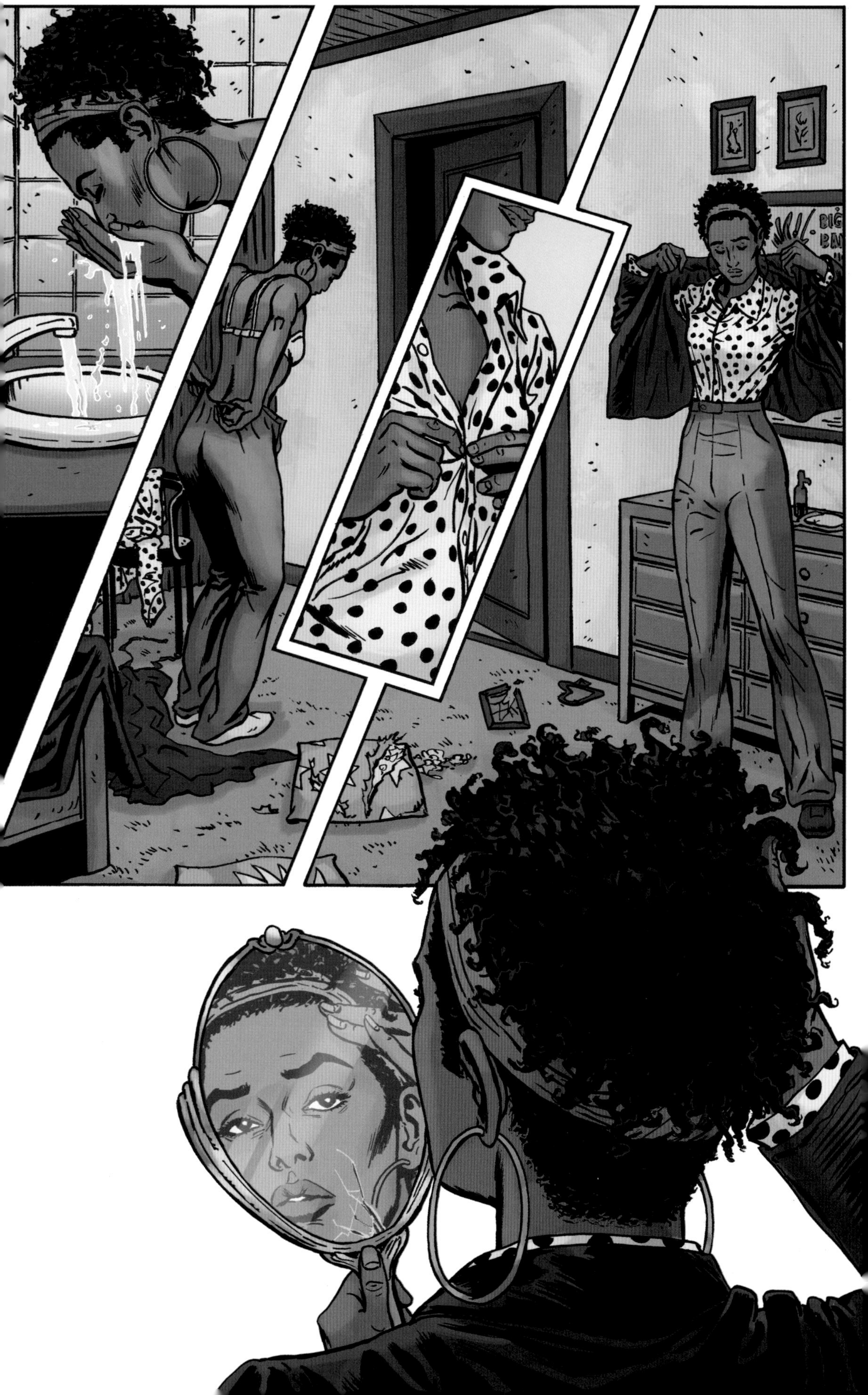

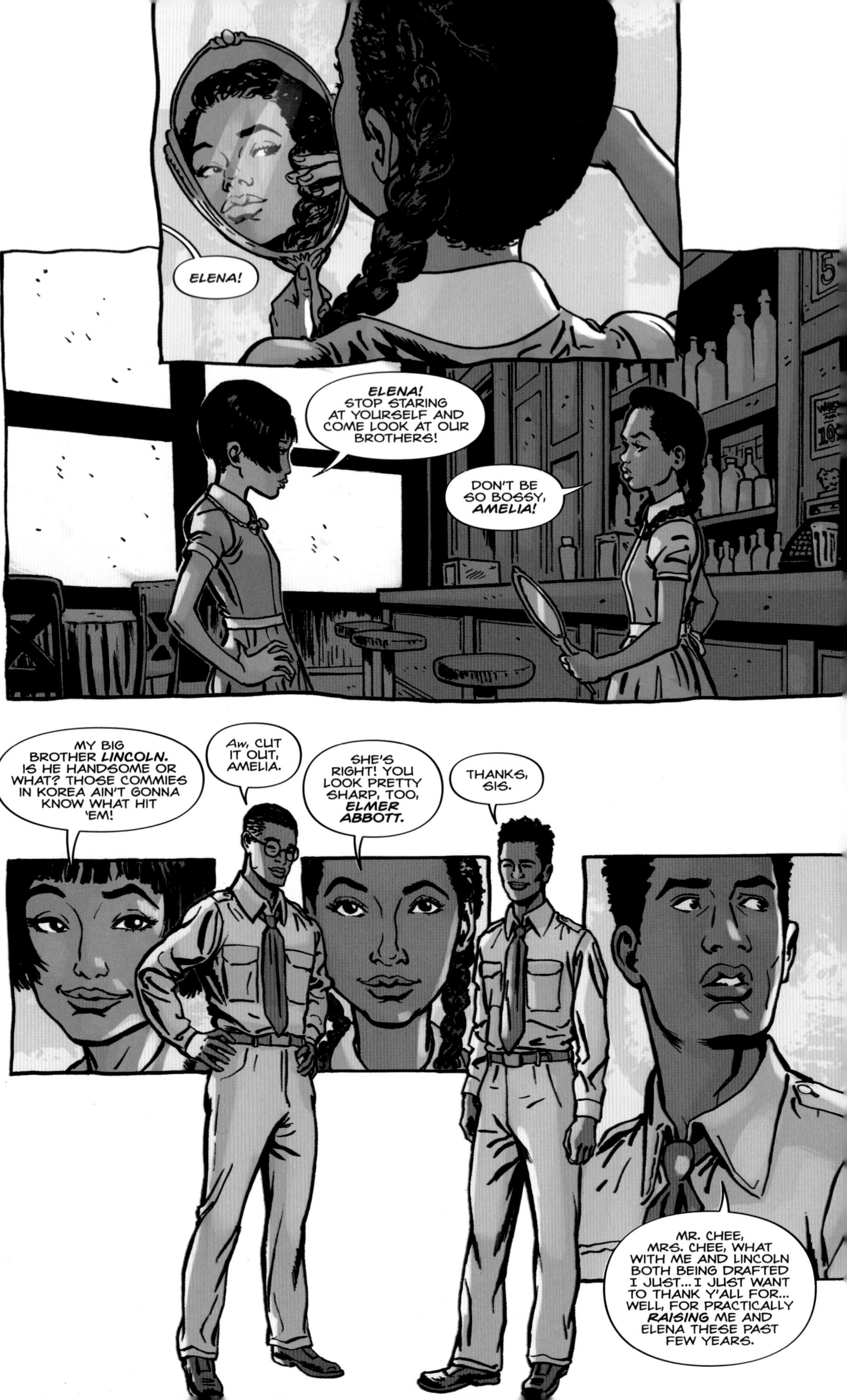
ELENA!
ELENA! STOP STARING AT YOURSELF AND COME LOOK AT OUR BROTHERS!
DON'T BE SO BOSSY, AMELIA!
MY BIG BROTHER LINCOLN. IS HE HANDSOME OR WHAT? THOSE COMMIES IN KOREA AIN'T GONNA KNOW WHAT HIT 'EM!
Aw, CUT IT OUT, AMELIA.
SHE'S RIGHT! YOU LOOK PRETTY SHARP, TOO, ELMER ABBOTT.
THANKS, SIS.
MR. CHEE, MRS. CHEE, WHAT WITH ME AND LINCOLN BOTH BEING DRAFTED I JUST... I JUST WANT TO THANK Y'ALL FOR... WELL, FOR PRACTICALLY RAISING ME AND ELENA THESE PAST FEW YEARS.

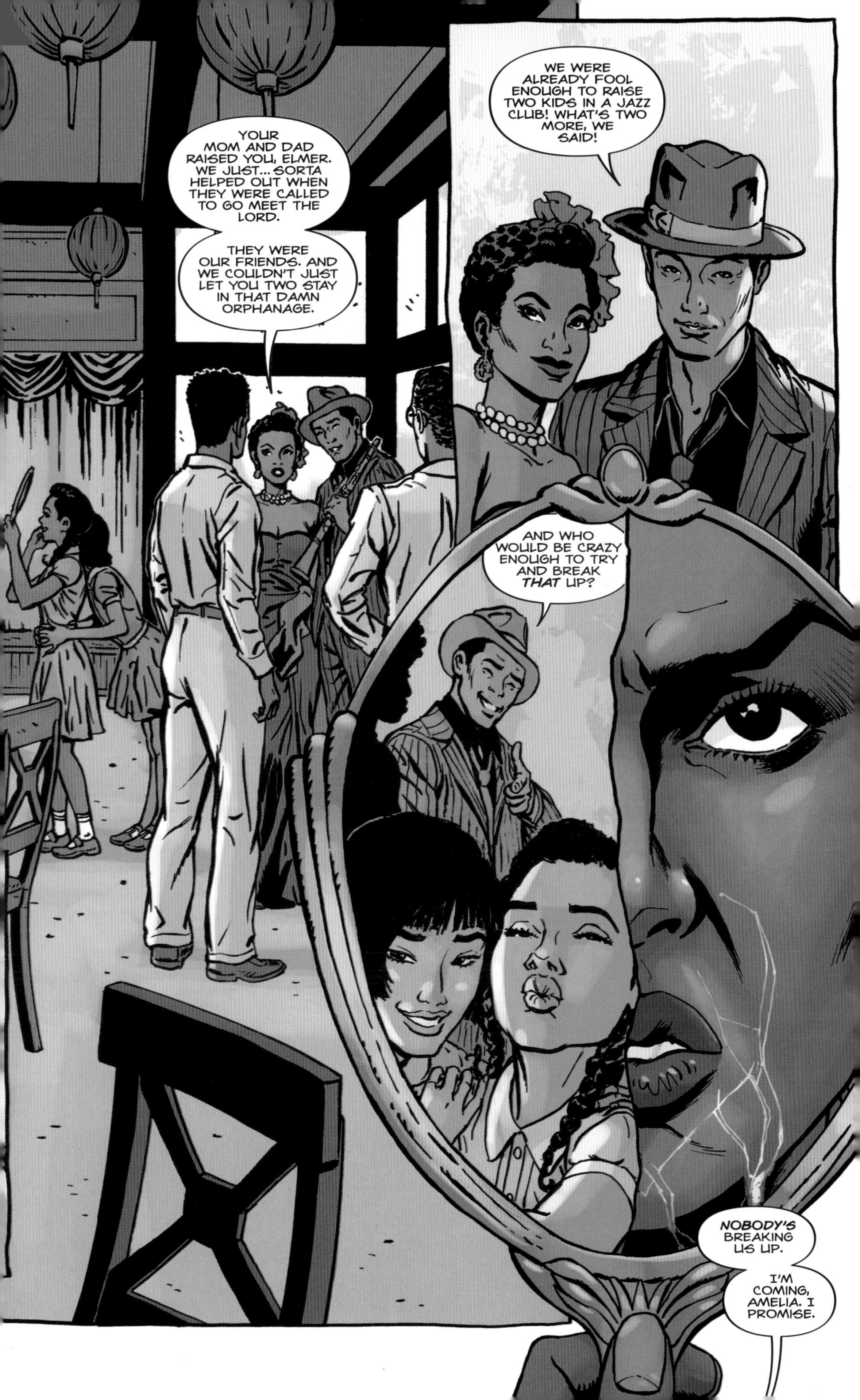
YOUR MOM AND DAD RAISED YOU, ELMER. WE JUST... SORTA HELPED OUT WHEN THEY WERE CALLED TO GO MEET THE LORD.
THEY WERE OUR FRIENDS. AND WE COULDN'T JUST LET YOU TWO STAY IN THAT DAMN ORPHANAGE.
WE WERE ALREADY FOOL ENOUGH TO RAISE TWO KIDS IN A JAZZ CLUB! WHAT'S TWO MORE, WE SAID!
AND WHO WOULD BE CRAZY ENOUGH TO TRY AND BREAK *THAT* UP?
NOBODY'S BREAKING US UP.
I'M COMING, AMELIA. I PROMISE.

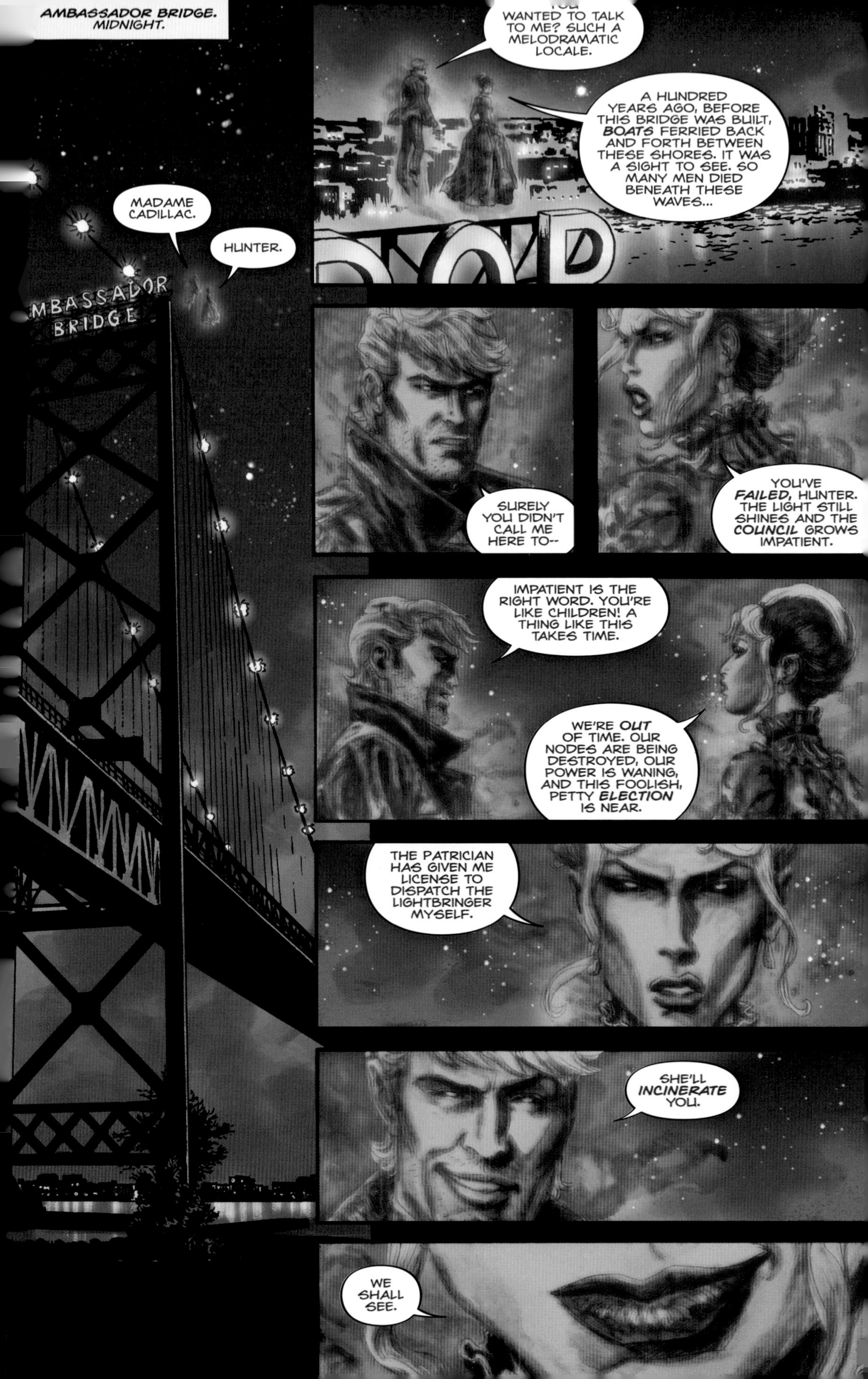
AMBASSADOR BRIDGE. MIDNIGHT.
MADAME CADILLAC.
HUNTER.
AMBASSADOR BRIDGE
YOU WANTED TO TALK TO ME? SUCH A MELODRAMATIC LOCALE.
A HUNDRED YEARS AGO, BEFORE THIS BRIDGE WAS BUILT, BOATS FERRIED BACK AND FORTH BETWEEN THESE SHORES. IT WAS A SIGHT TO SEE. SO MANY MEN DIED BENEATH THESE WAVES...
SURELY YOU DIDN'T CALL ME HERE TO--
YOU'VE FAILED, HUNTER. THE LIGHT STILL SHINES AND THE COUNCIL GROWS IMPATIENT.
IMPATIENT IS THE RIGHT WORD. YOU'RE LIKE CHILDREN! A THING LIKE THIS TAKES TIME.
WE'RE OUT OF TIME. OUR NODES ARE BEING DESTROYED, OUR POWER IS WANING, AND THIS FOOLISH, PETTY ELECTION IS NEAR.
THE PATRICIAN HAS GIVEN ME LICENSE TO DISPATCH THE LIGHTBRINGER MYSELF.
SHE'LL INCINERATE YOU.
WE SHALL SEE.

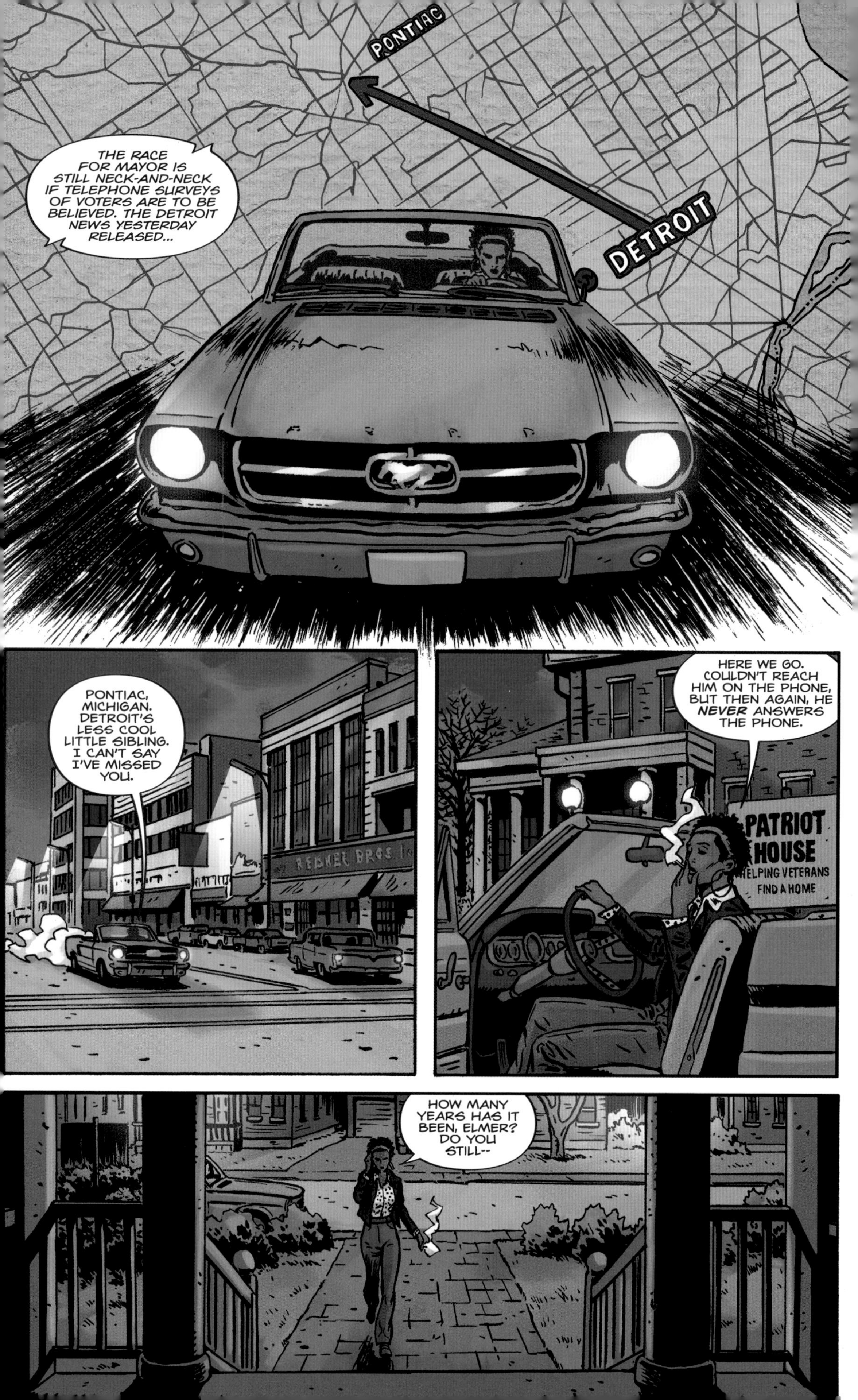
PONTIAC
DETROIT
THE RACE FOR MAYOR IS STILL NECK-AND-NECK IF TELEPHONE SURVEYS OF VOTERS ARE TO BE BELIEVED. THE DETROIT NEWS YESTERDAY RELEASED...
PONTIAC, MICHIGAN. DETROIT'S LESS COOL LITTLE SIBLING. I CAN'T SAY I'VE MISSED YOU.
HERE WE GO. COULDN'T REACH HIM ON THE PHONE, BUT THEN AGAIN, HE ***NEVER*** ANSWERS THE PHONE.
PATRIOT HOUSE
HELPING VETERANS FIND A HOME
HOW MANY YEARS HAS IT BEEN, ELMER? DO YOU STILL--

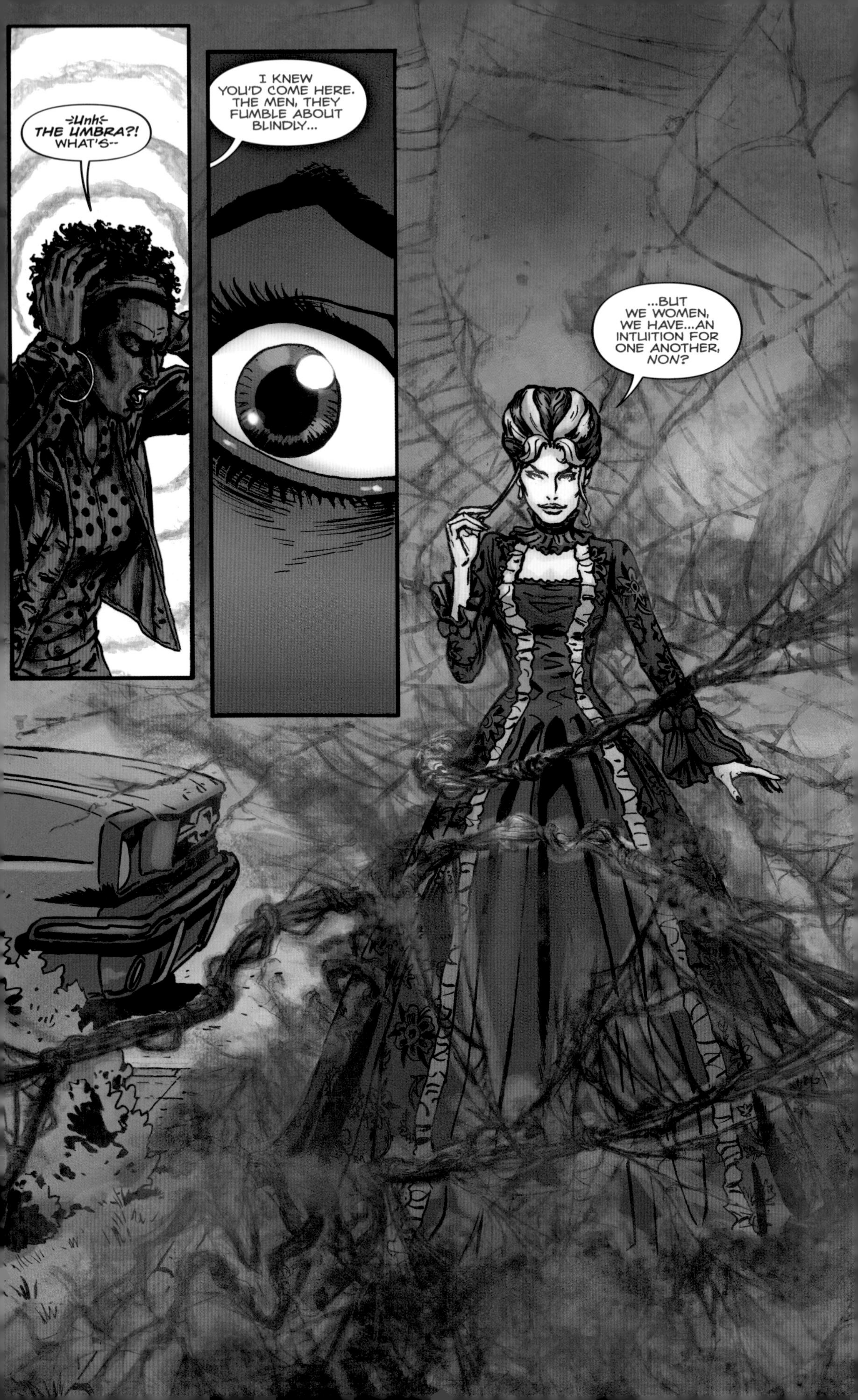

Unh THE UMBRA?! WHAT'S--
I KNEW YOU'D COME HERE. THE MEN, THEY FUMBLE ABOUT BLINDLY...
...BUT WE WOMEN, WE HAVE...AN INTUITION FOR ONE ANOTHER, NON?

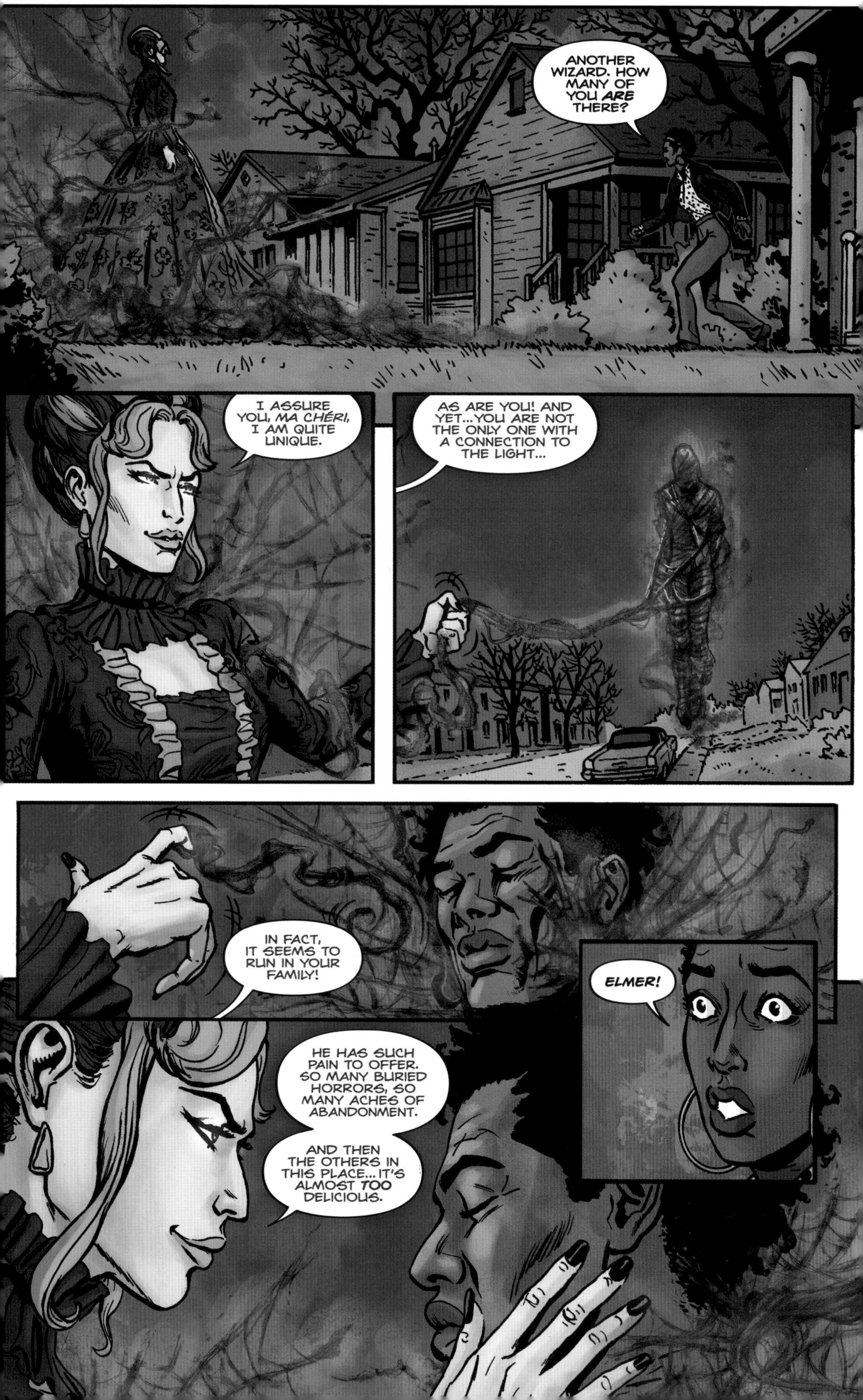
ANOTHER WIZARD. HOW MANY OF YOU *ARE* THERE?
I ASSURE YOU, *MA CHÉRI*, I AM QUITE UNIQUE.
AS ARE YOU! AND YET...YOU ARE NOT THE ONLY ONE WITH A CONNECTION TO THE LIGHT...
IN FACT, IT SEEMS TO RUN IN YOUR FAMILY!
ELMER!
HE HAS SUCH PAIN TO OFFER. SO MANY BURIED HORRORS, SO MANY ACHES OF ABANDONMENT.
AND THEN THE OTHERS IN THIS PLACE... IT'S ALMOST *TOO* DELICIOUS.

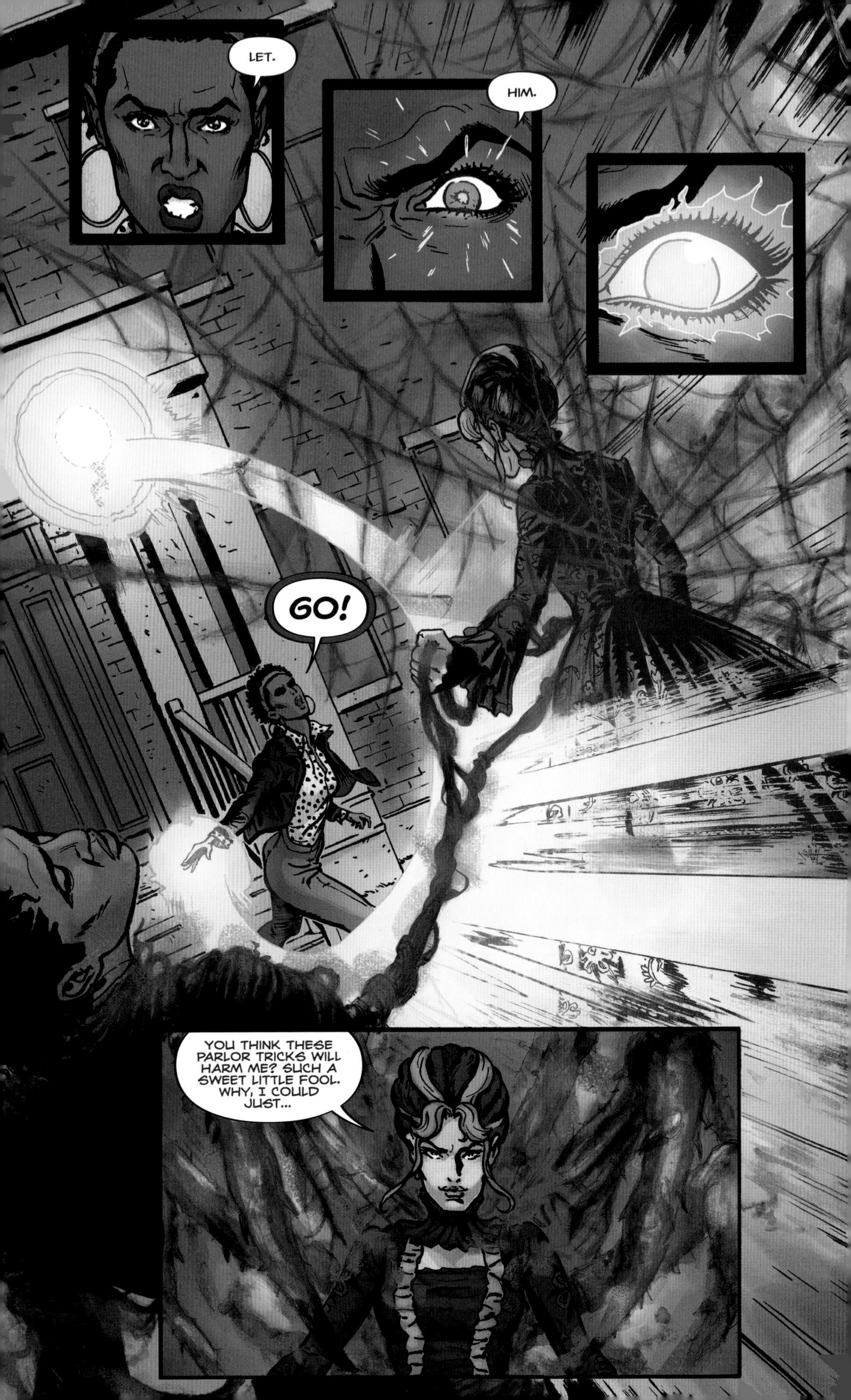
LET.
HIM.
GO!
YOU THINK THESE PARLOR TRICKS WILL HARM ME? SUCH A SWEET LITTLE FOOL. WHY, I COULD JUST...

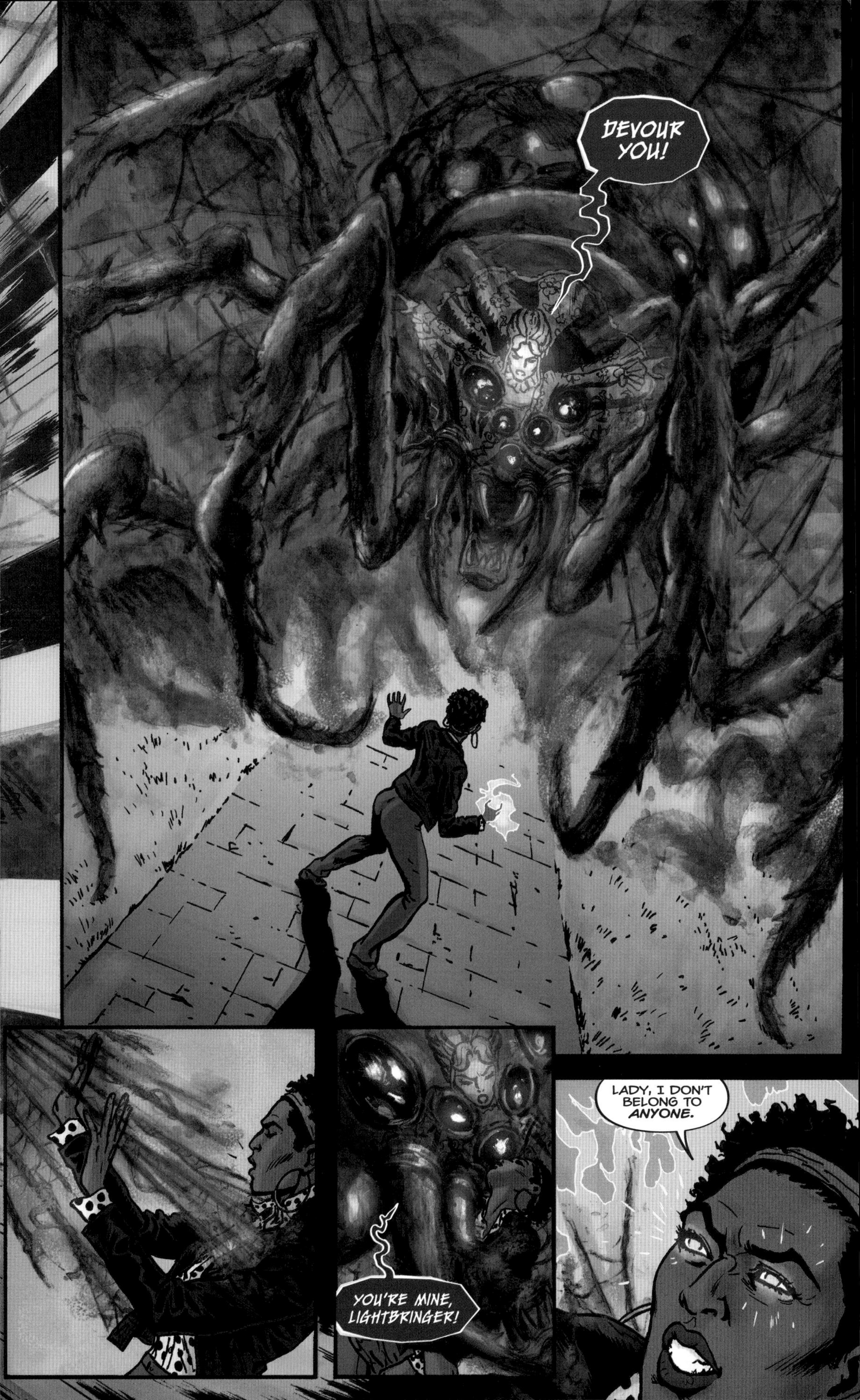
DEVOUR YOU!
YOU'RE MINE, LIGHTBRINGER!
LADY, I DON'T BELONG TO ANYONE.

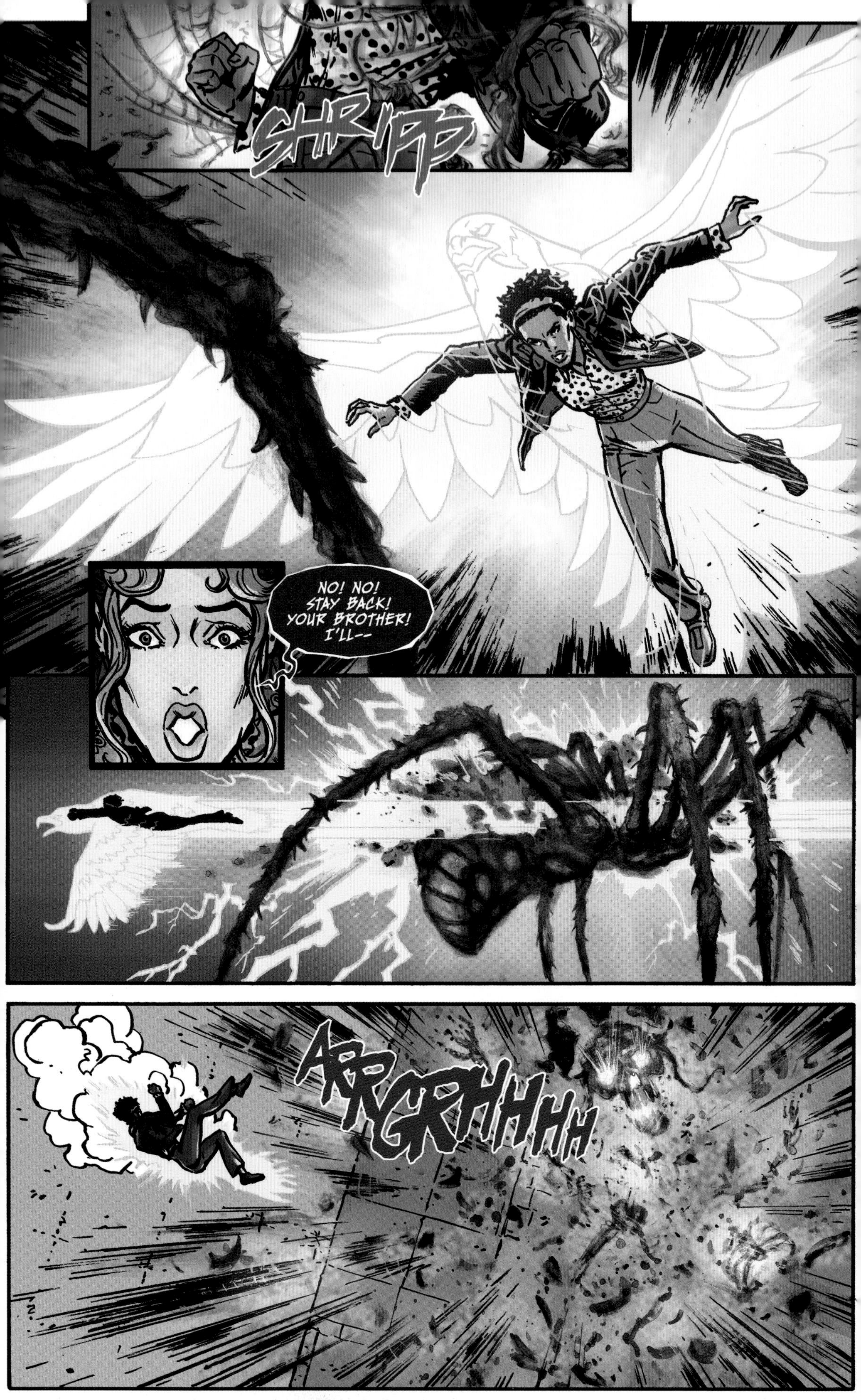
SHRIPP
NO! NO! STAY BACK! YOUR BROTHER! I'LL--
ARRGRHHHHH

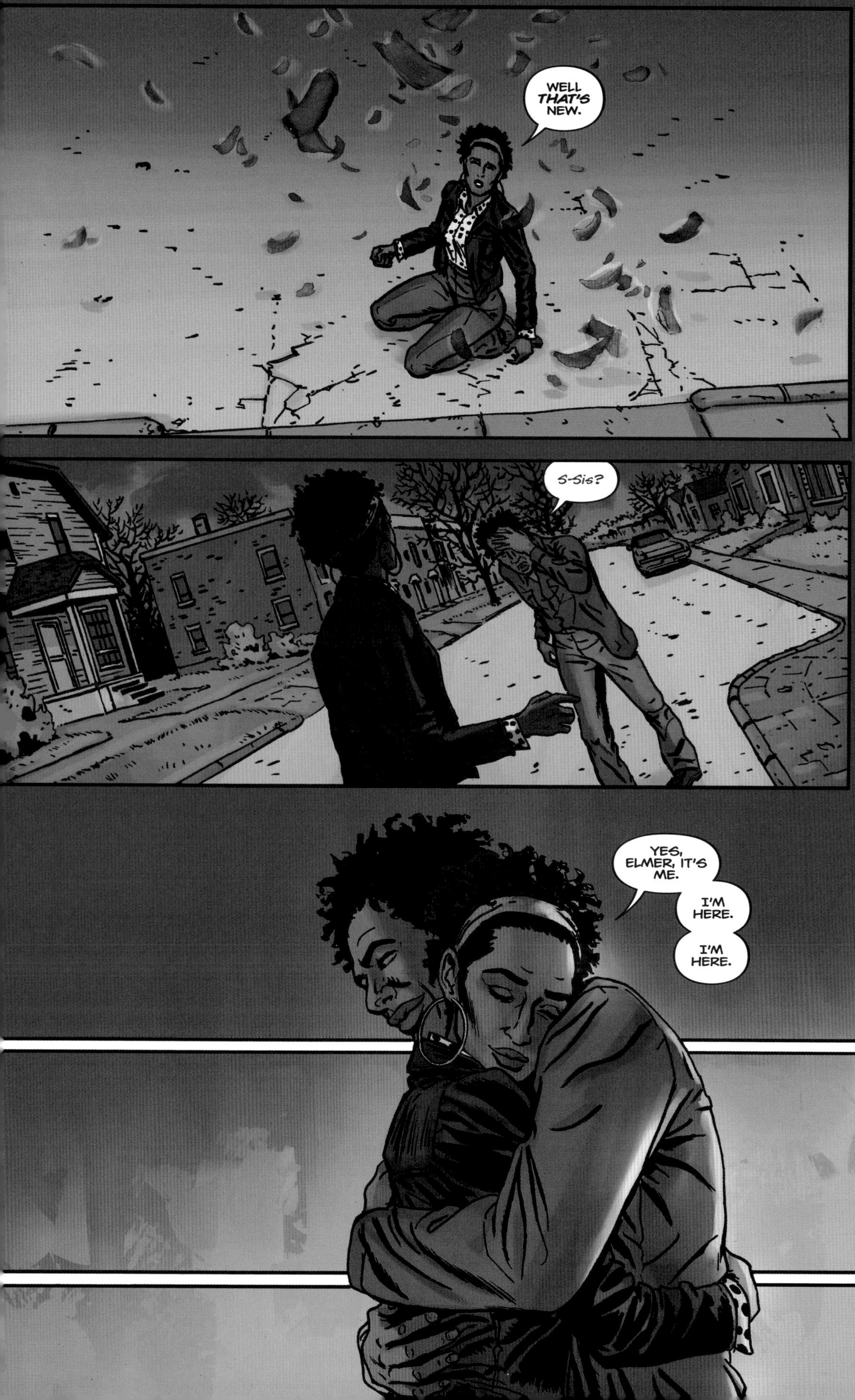
WELL THAT'S NEW.
S-SIS?
YES, ELMER, IT'S ME.
I'M HERE.
I'M HERE.

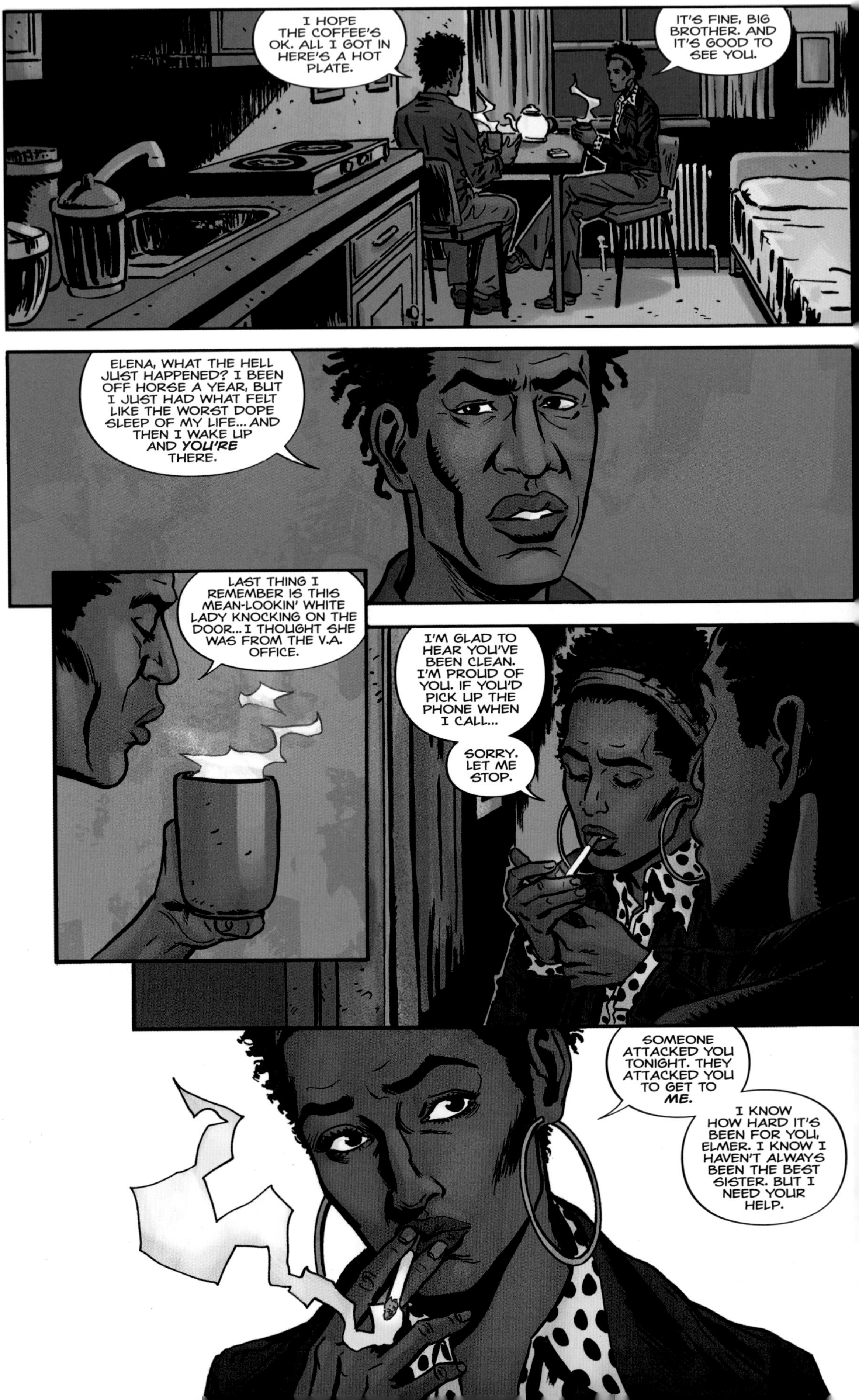
I HOPE THE COFFEE'S OK. ALL I GOT IN HERE'S A HOT PLATE.
IT'S FINE, BIG BROTHER. AND IT'S GOOD TO SEE YOU.
ELENA, WHAT THE HELL JUST HAPPENED? I BEEN OFF HORSE A YEAR, BUT I JUST HAD WHAT FELT LIKE THE WORST DOPE SLEEP OF MY LIFE... AND THEN I WAKE UP AND *YOU'RE* THERE.
LAST THING I REMEMBER IS THIS MEAN-LOOKIN' WHITE LADY KNOCKING ON THE DOOR... I THOUGHT SHE WAS FROM THE V.A. OFFICE.
I'M GLAD TO HEAR YOU'VE BEEN CLEAN. I'M PROUD OF YOU. IF YOU'D PICK UP THE PHONE WHEN I CALL...
SORRY. LET ME STOP.
SOMEONE ATTACKED YOU TONIGHT. THEY ATTACKED YOU TO GET TO *ME*.
I KNOW HOW HARD IT'S BEEN FOR YOU, ELMER. I KNOW I HAVEN'T ALWAYS BEEN THE BEST SISTER. BUT I NEED YOUR HELP.

COME ON, NOW. YOU HAVEN'T BEEN A BAD SISTER. I JUST... YOU KNOW I DON'T LIKE COMING OUT OF THE HOUSE.

OR HAVING VISITORS.

THE NOISE. THE PEOPLE.

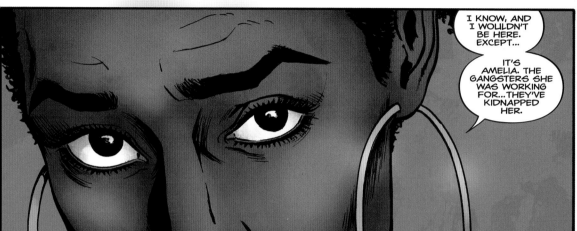

I KNOW, AND I WOULDN'T BE HERE. EXCEPT...

IT'S AMELIA. THE GANGSTERS SHE WAS WORKING FOR...THEY'VE KIDNAPPED HER.

OK. OK, LET'S GO HELP HER.

BUT FIRST WE GOTTA MAKE A STOP.

KNOCK KNOCK

NUTCASE! OPEN UP, IT'S ELMER!

SARGE!

NUTCASE, THIS IS MY SISTER ELENA.

PLEASED TO MEET YOU, MA'AM.

ELENA, THIS IS MY FRIEND NUTCASE. THIS YOUNG MAN SERVED IN THE SAME UNIT AS ME, JUST TWENTY YEARS LATER AND A DIFFERENT WAR.

H-HELLO.

I'LL KEEP IT SHORT: WE'RE IN TROUBLE AND WE NEED HARDWARE PRONTO.

I GOT YOU, SARGE.

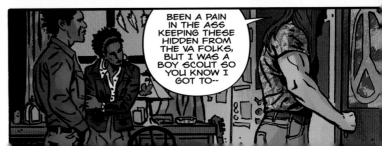

BEEN A PAIN IN THE ASS KEEPING THESE HIDDEN FROM THE VA FOLKS, BUT I WAS A BOY SCOUT SO YOU KNOW I GOT TO--

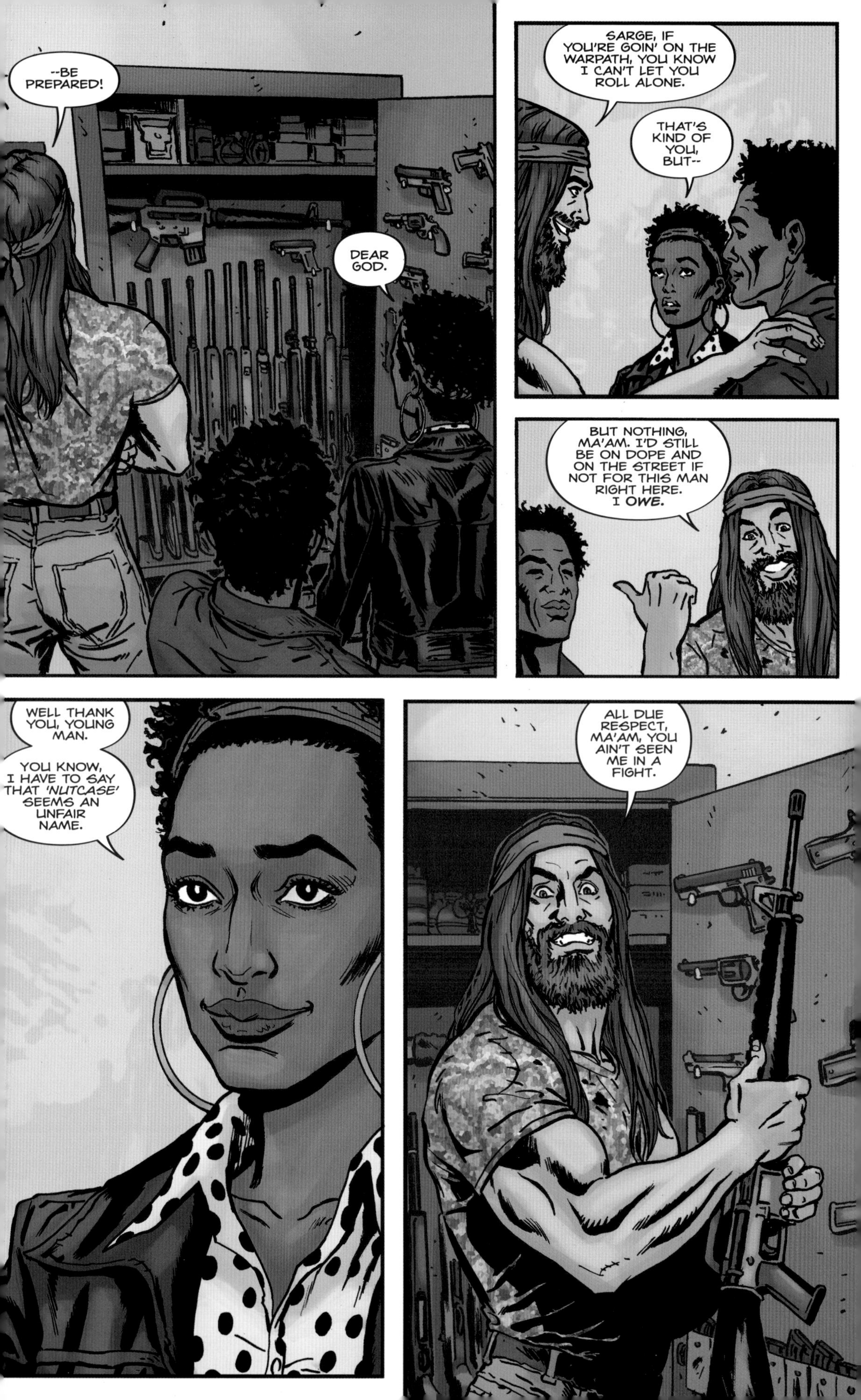
--BE PREPARED!
DEAR GOD.
SARGE, IF YOU'RE GOIN' ON THE WARPATH, YOU KNOW I CAN'T LET YOU ROLL ALONE.
THAT'S KIND OF YOU, BUT--
BUT NOTHING, MA'AM. I'D STILL BE ON DOPE AND ON THE STREET IF NOT FOR THIS MAN RIGHT HERE. I OWE.
WELL THANK YOU, YOUNG MAN.
YOU KNOW, I HAVE TO SAY THAT 'NUTCASE' SEEMS AN UNFAIR NAME.
ALL DUE RESPECT, MA'AM, YOU AIN'T SEEN ME IN A FIGHT.

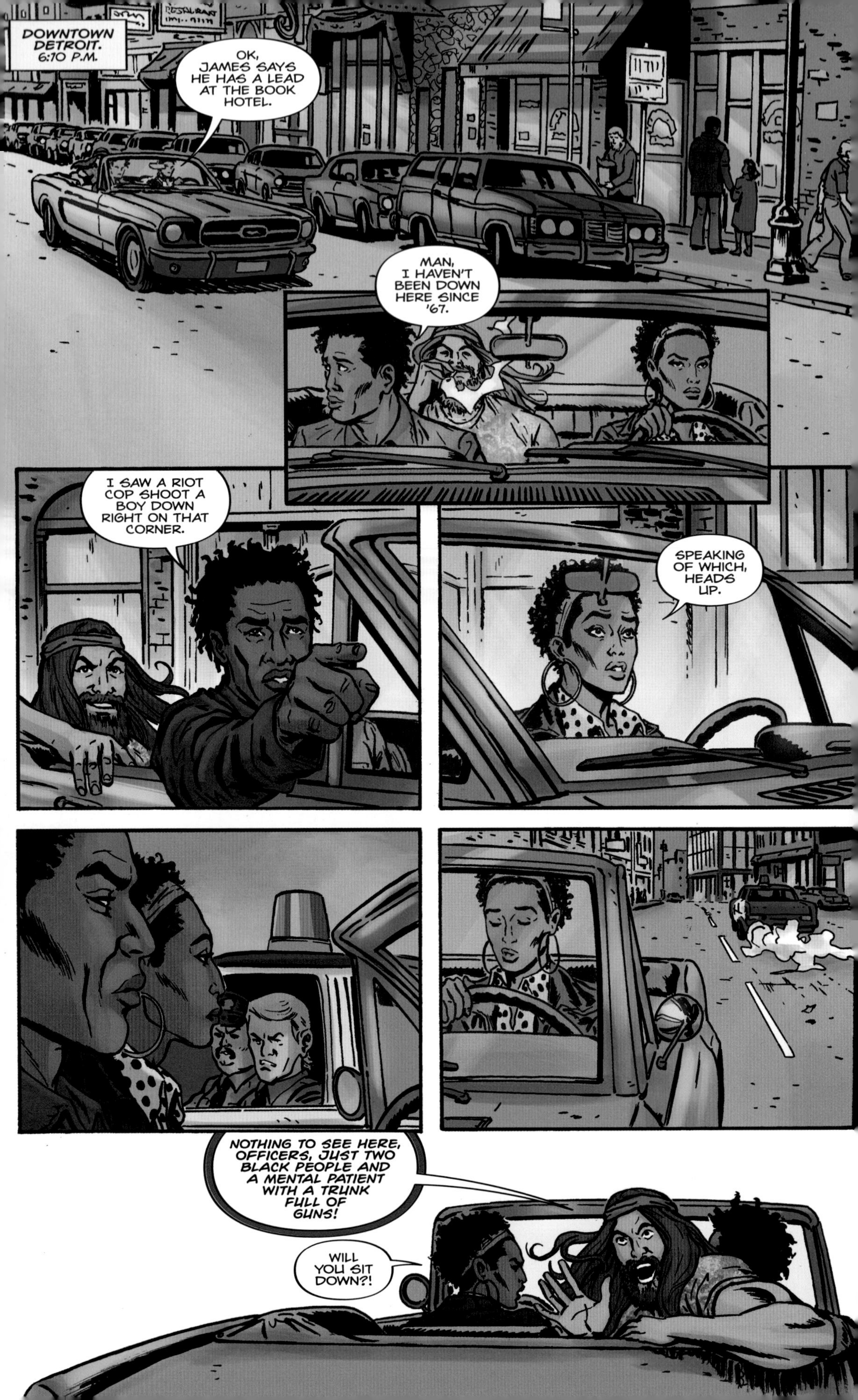
DOWNTOWN DETROIT. 6:10 P.M.
OK, JAMES SAYS HE HAS A LEAD AT THE BOOK HOTEL.
MAN, I HAVEN'T BEEN DOWN HERE SINCE '67.
I SAW A RIOT COP SHOOT A BOY DOWN RIGHT ON THAT CORNER.
SPEAKING OF WHICH, HEADS UP.
NOTHING TO SEE HERE, OFFICERS, JUST TWO BLACK PEOPLE AND A MENTAL PATIENT WITH A TRUNK FULL OF GUNS!
WILL YOU SIT DOWN?!

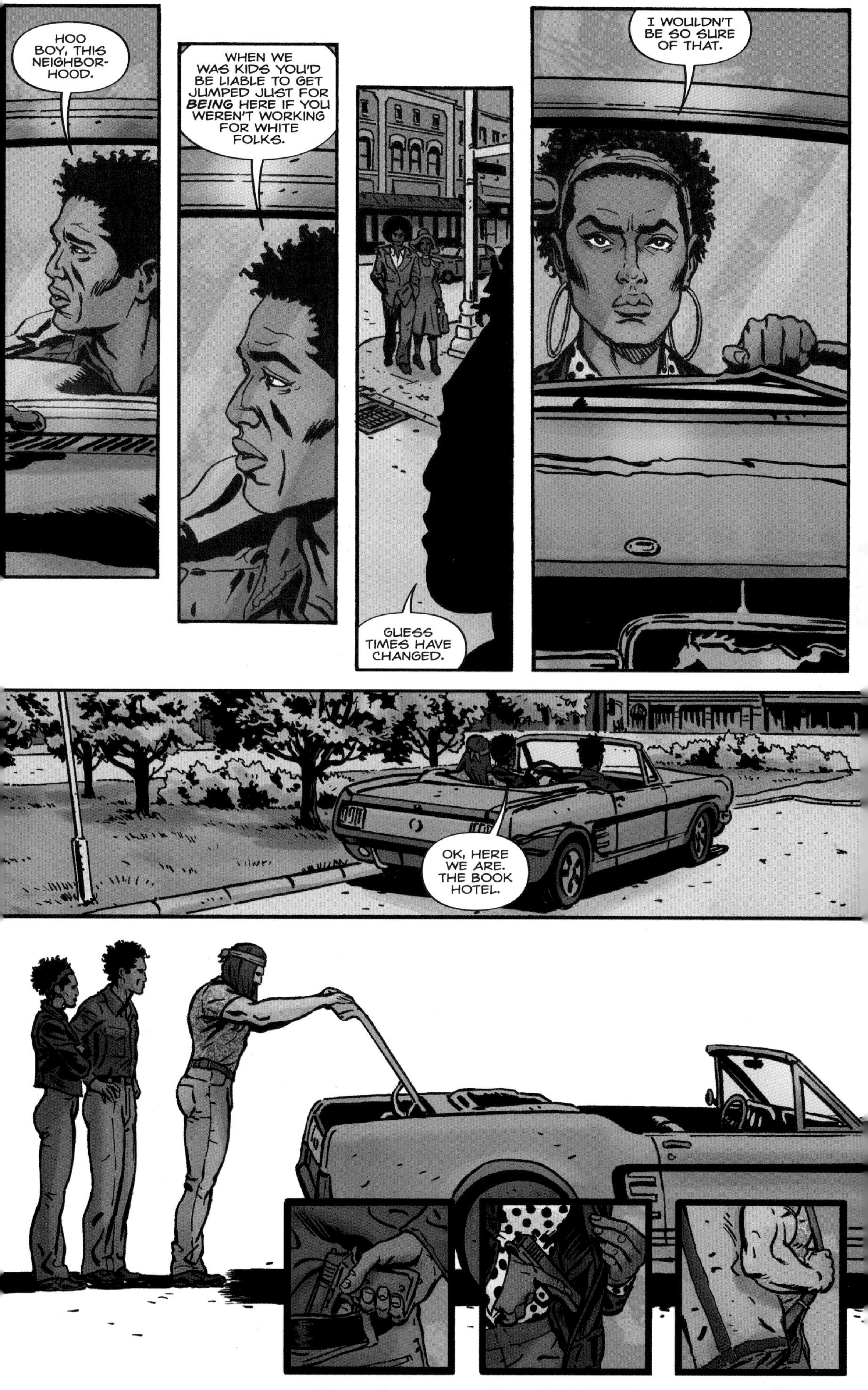
HOO BOY, THIS NEIGHBOR-HOOD.
WHEN WE WAS KIDS YOU'D BE LIABLE TO GET JUMPED JUST FOR *BEING* HERE IF YOU WEREN'T WORKING FOR WHITE FOLKS.
GUESS TIMES HAVE CHANGED.
I WOULDN'T BE SO SURE OF THAT.
OK, HERE WE ARE. THE BOOK HOTEL.

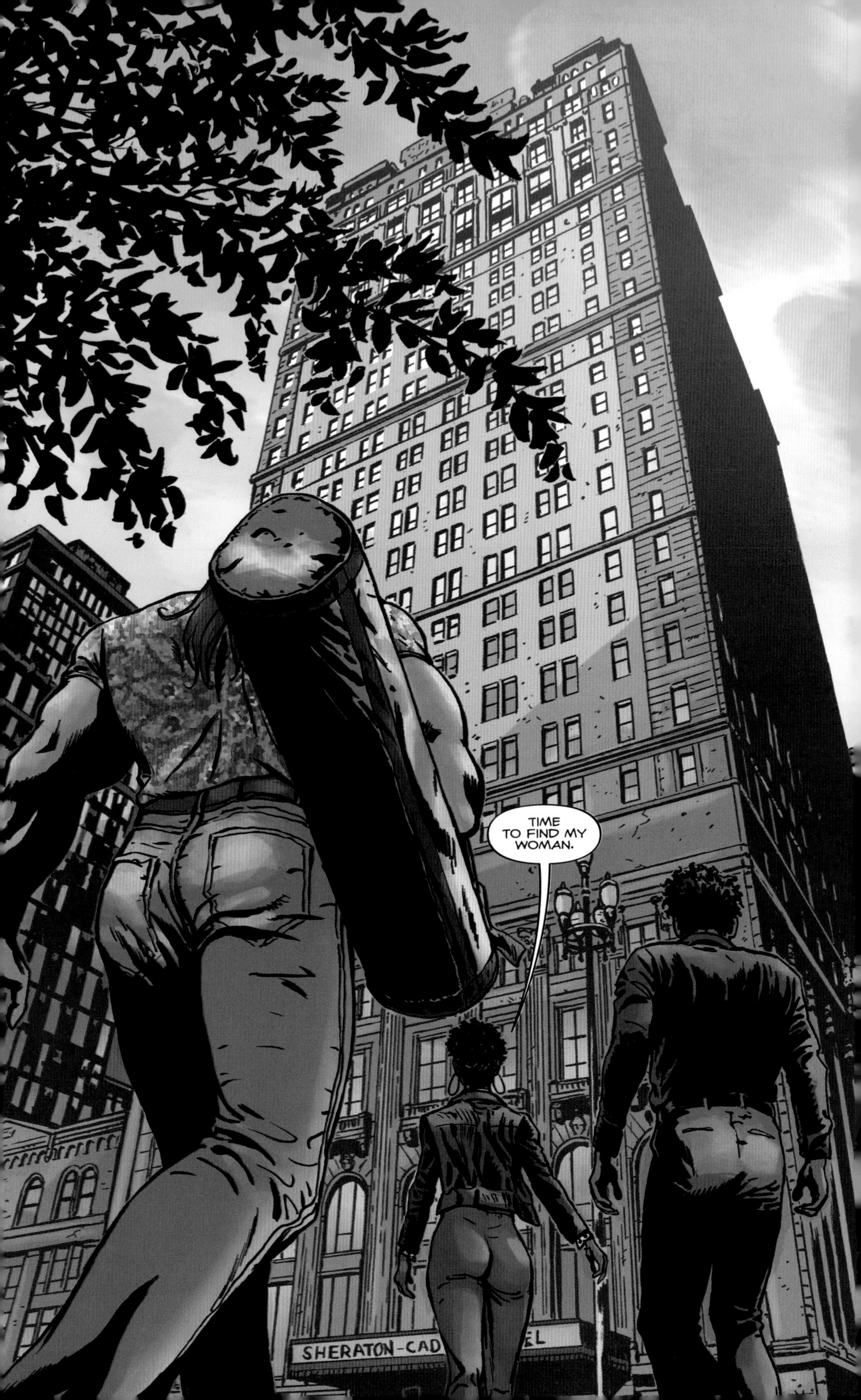
TIME TO FIND MY WOMAN.
SHERATON-CAD
EL

Issue Three Variant Cover by
Raúl Allén

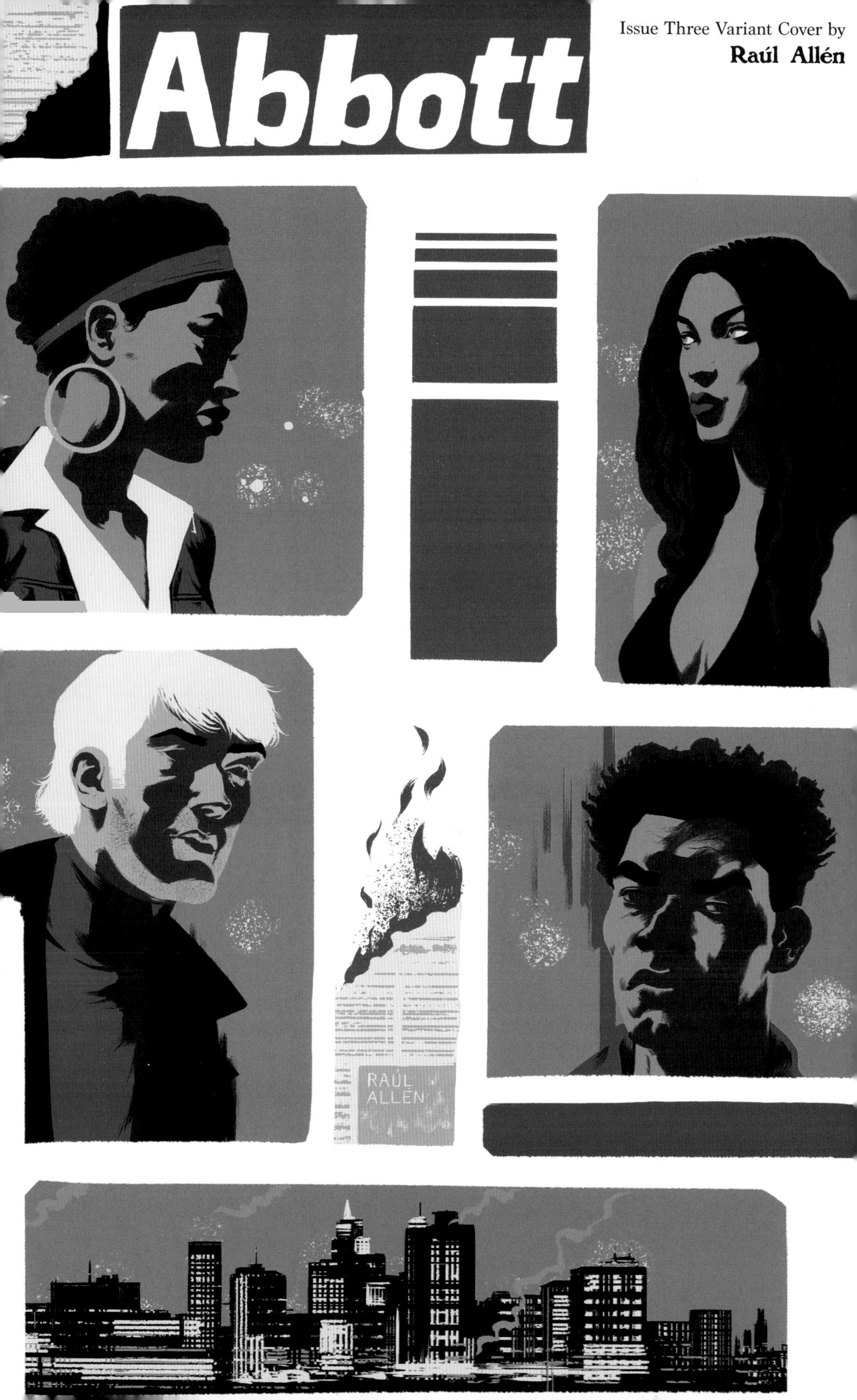

Abbott
RAÚL
ALLÉN

CHAPTER FOUR

Issue Four Cover by Taj Tenfold

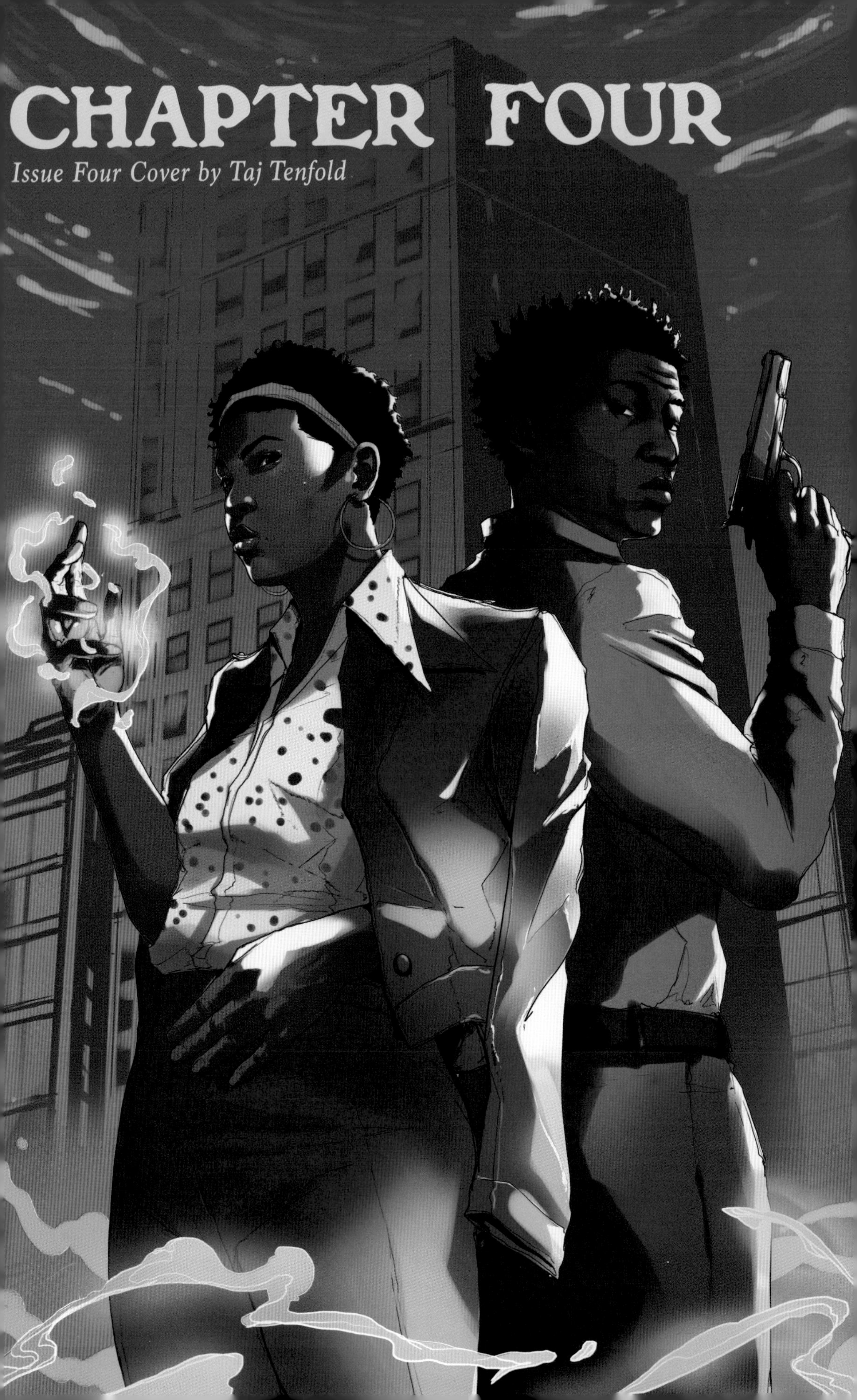

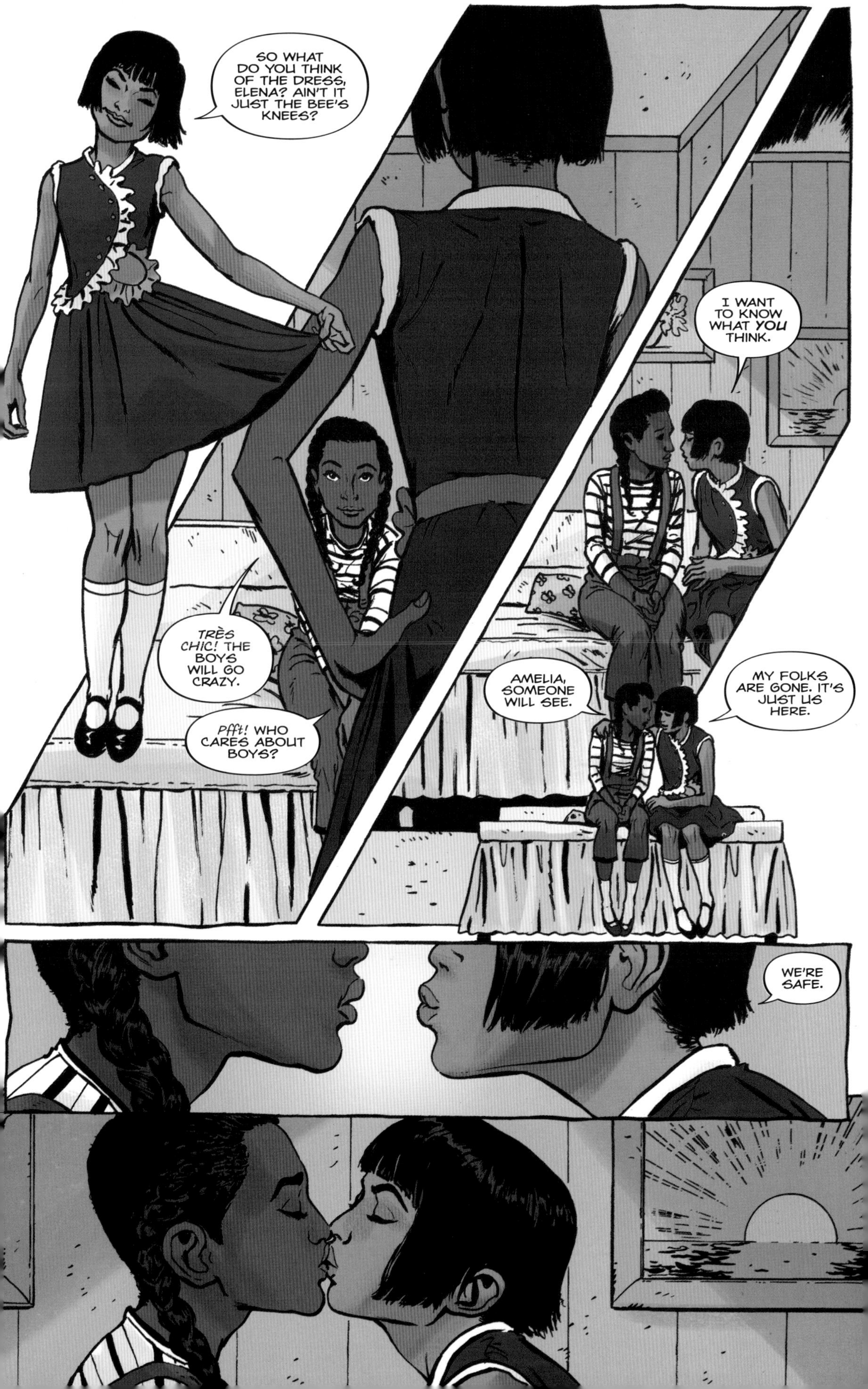
SO WHAT DO YOU THINK OF THE DRESS, ELENA? AIN'T IT JUST THE BEE'S KNEES?
TRÈS CHIC! THE BOYS WILL GO CRAZY.
Pfft! WHO CARES ABOUT BOYS?
I WANT TO KNOW WHAT **YOU** THINK.
AMELIA, SOMEONE WILL SEE.
MY FOLKS ARE GONE. IT'S JUST US HERE.
WE'RE SAFE.

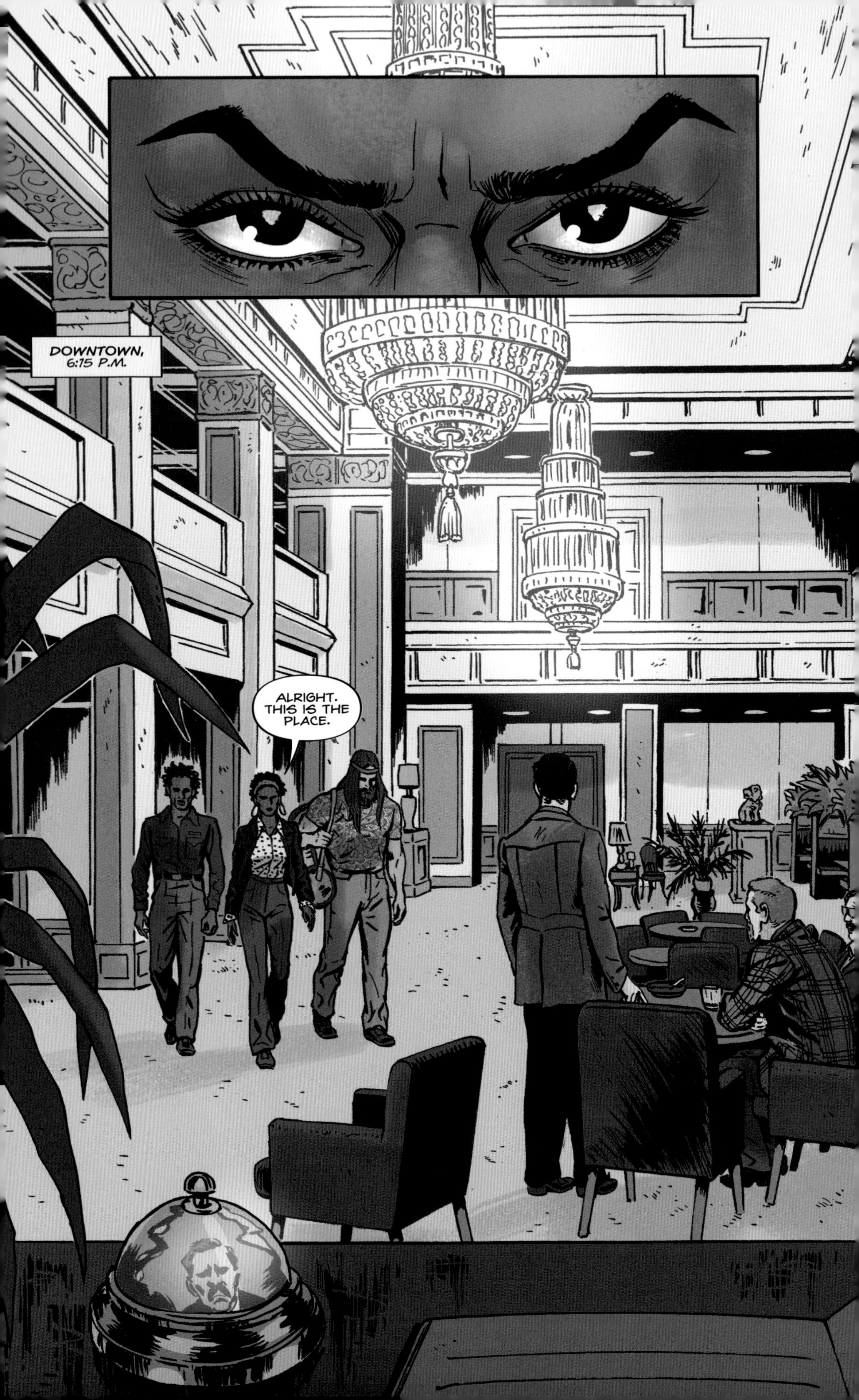
DOWNTOWN, 6:15 P.M.
ALRIGHT. THIS IS THE PLACE.

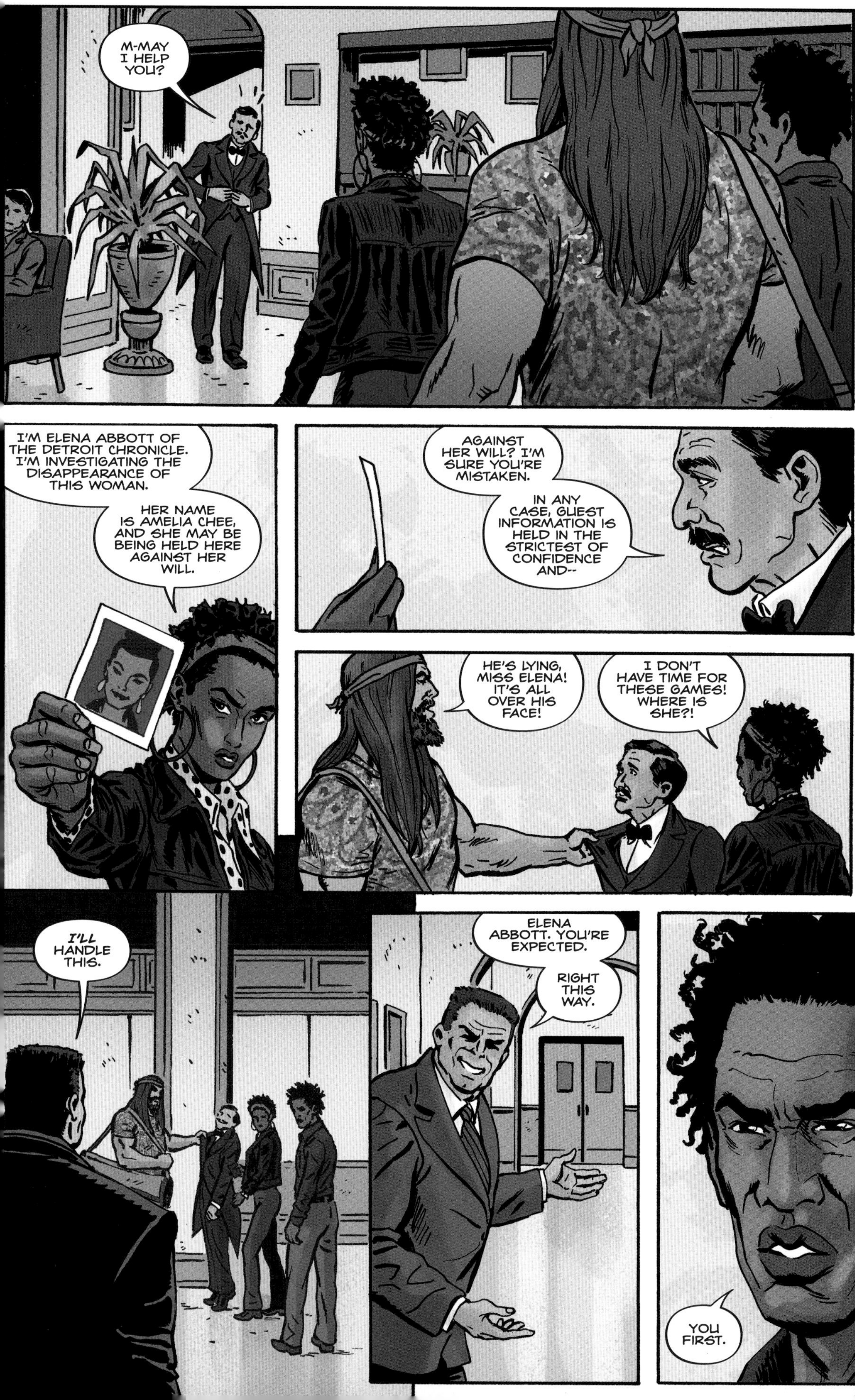
M-MAY I HELP YOU?
I'M ELENA ABBOTT OF THE DETROIT CHRONICLE. I'M INVESTIGATING THE DISAPPEARANCE OF THIS WOMAN.
HER NAME IS AMELIA CHEE, AND SHE MAY BE BEING HELD HERE AGAINST HER WILL.
AGAINST HER WILL? I'M SURE YOU'RE MISTAKEN.
IN ANY CASE, GUEST INFORMATION IS HELD IN THE STRICTEST OF CONFIDENCE AND--
HE'S LYING, MISS ELENA! IT'S ALL OVER HIS FACE!
I DON'T HAVE TIME FOR THESE GAMES! WHERE IS SHE?!
I'LL HANDLE THIS.
ELENA ABBOTT. YOU'RE EXPECTED.
RIGHT THIS WAY.
YOU FIRST.

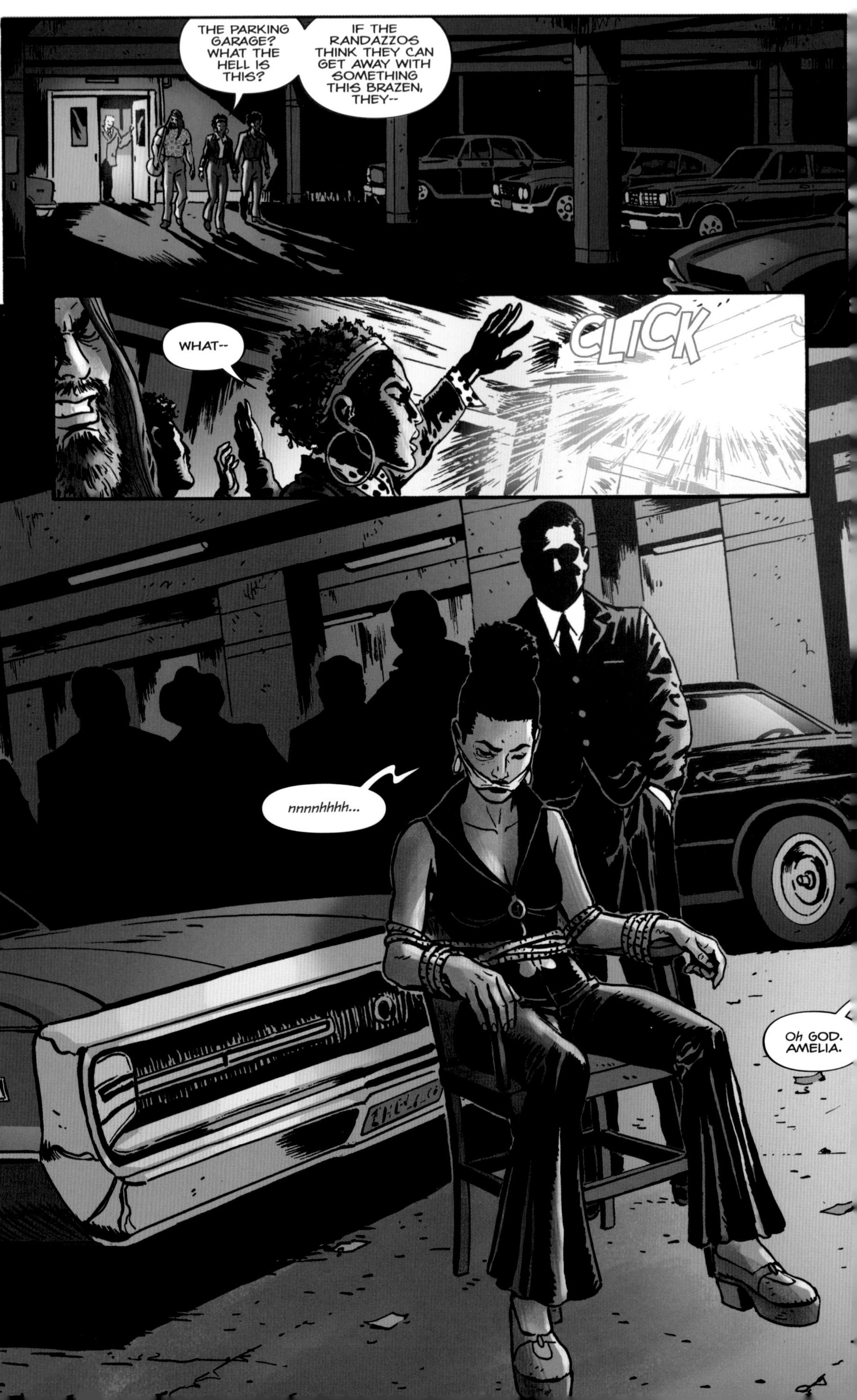
THE PARKING GARAGE? WHAT THE HELL IS THIS?
IF THE RANDAZZOS THINK THEY CAN GET AWAY WITH SOMETHING THIS BRAZEN, THEY--
WHAT--
CLICK
nnnnhhhh...
Oh GOD. AMELIA.

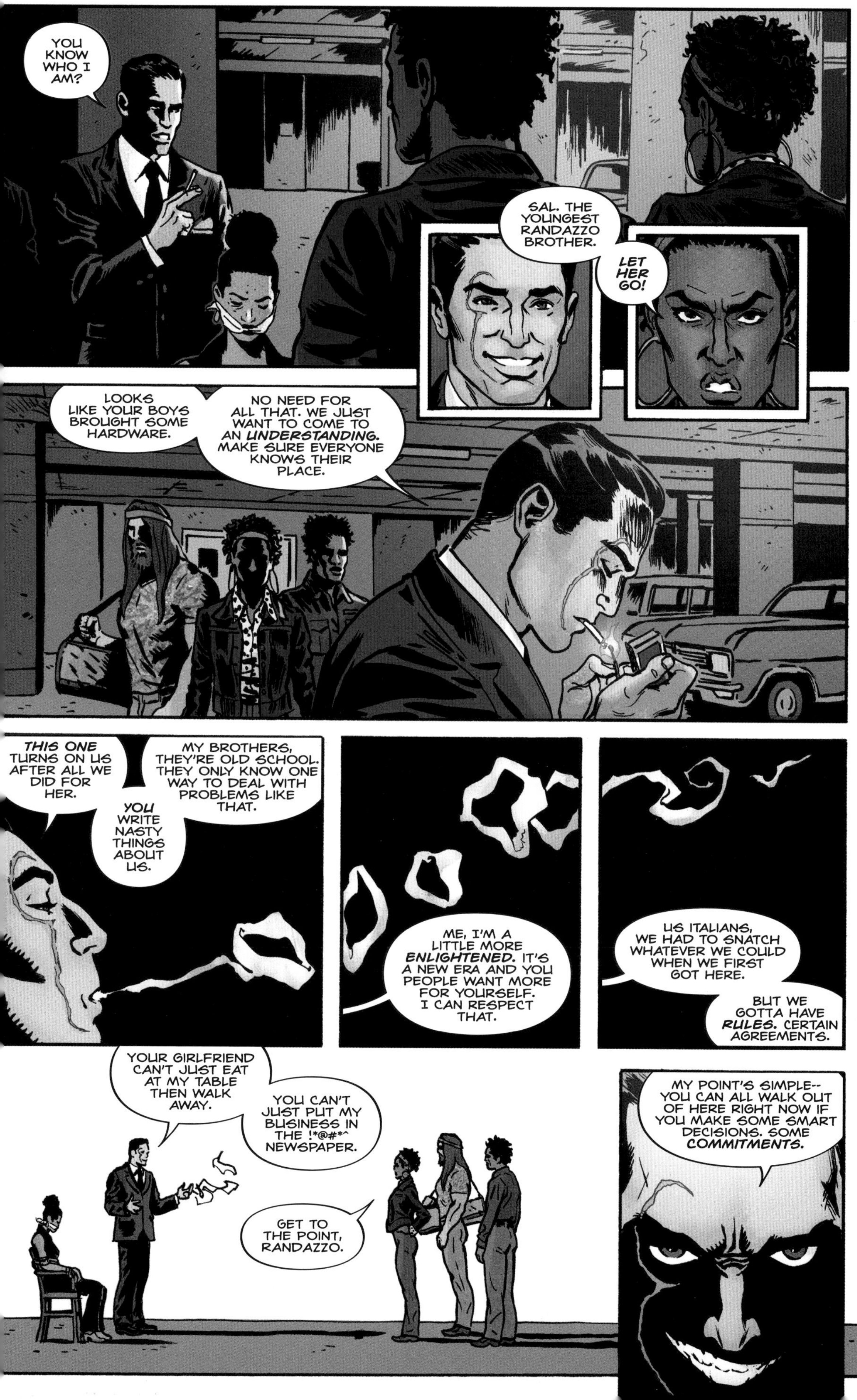
YOU KNOW WHO I AM?
SAL. THE YOUNGEST RANDAZZO BROTHER.
LET HER GO!
LOOKS LIKE YOUR BOYS BROUGHT SOME HARDWARE.
NO NEED FOR ALL THAT. WE JUST WANT TO COME TO AN UNDERSTANDING. MAKE SURE EVERYONE KNOWS THEIR PLACE.
THIS ONE TURNS ON US AFTER ALL WE DID FOR HER.
YOU WRITE NASTY THINGS ABOUT US.
MY BROTHERS, THEY'RE OLD SCHOOL. THEY ONLY KNOW ONE WAY TO DEAL WITH PROBLEMS LIKE THAT.
ME, I'M A LITTLE MORE ENLIGHTENED. IT'S A NEW ERA AND YOU PEOPLE WANT MORE FOR YOURSELF. I CAN RESPECT THAT.
US ITALIANS, WE HAD TO SNATCH WHATEVER WE COULD WHEN WE FIRST GOT HERE.
BUT WE GOTTA HAVE RULES. CERTAIN AGREEMENTS.
YOUR GIRLFRIEND CAN'T JUST EAT AT MY TABLE THEN WALK AWAY.
YOU CAN'T JUST PUT MY BUSINESS IN THE !*@#*^ NEWSPAPER.
GET TO THE POINT, RANDAZZO.
MY POINT'S SIMPLE-- YOU CAN ALL WALK OUT OF HERE RIGHT NOW IF YOU MAKE SOME SMART DECISIONS. SOME COMMITMENTS.

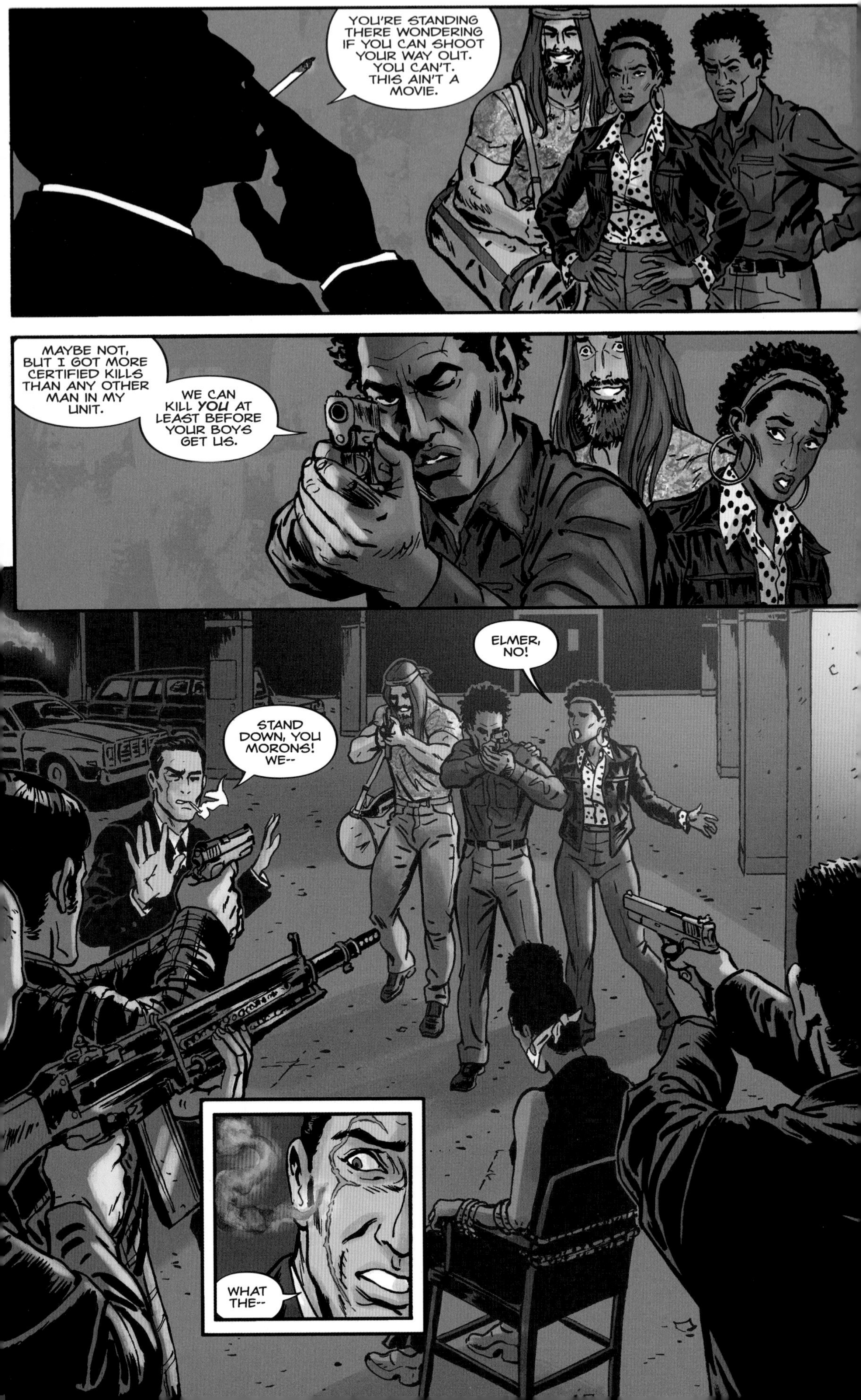
YOU'RE STANDING THERE WONDERING IF YOU CAN SHOOT YOUR WAY OUT. YOU CAN'T. THIS AIN'T A MOVIE.
MAYBE NOT, BUT I GOT MORE CERTIFIED KILLS THAN ANY OTHER MAN IN MY UNIT.
WE CAN KILL YOU AT LEAST BEFORE YOUR BOYS GET US.
ELMER, NO!
STAND DOWN, YOU MORONS! WE--
WHAT THE--

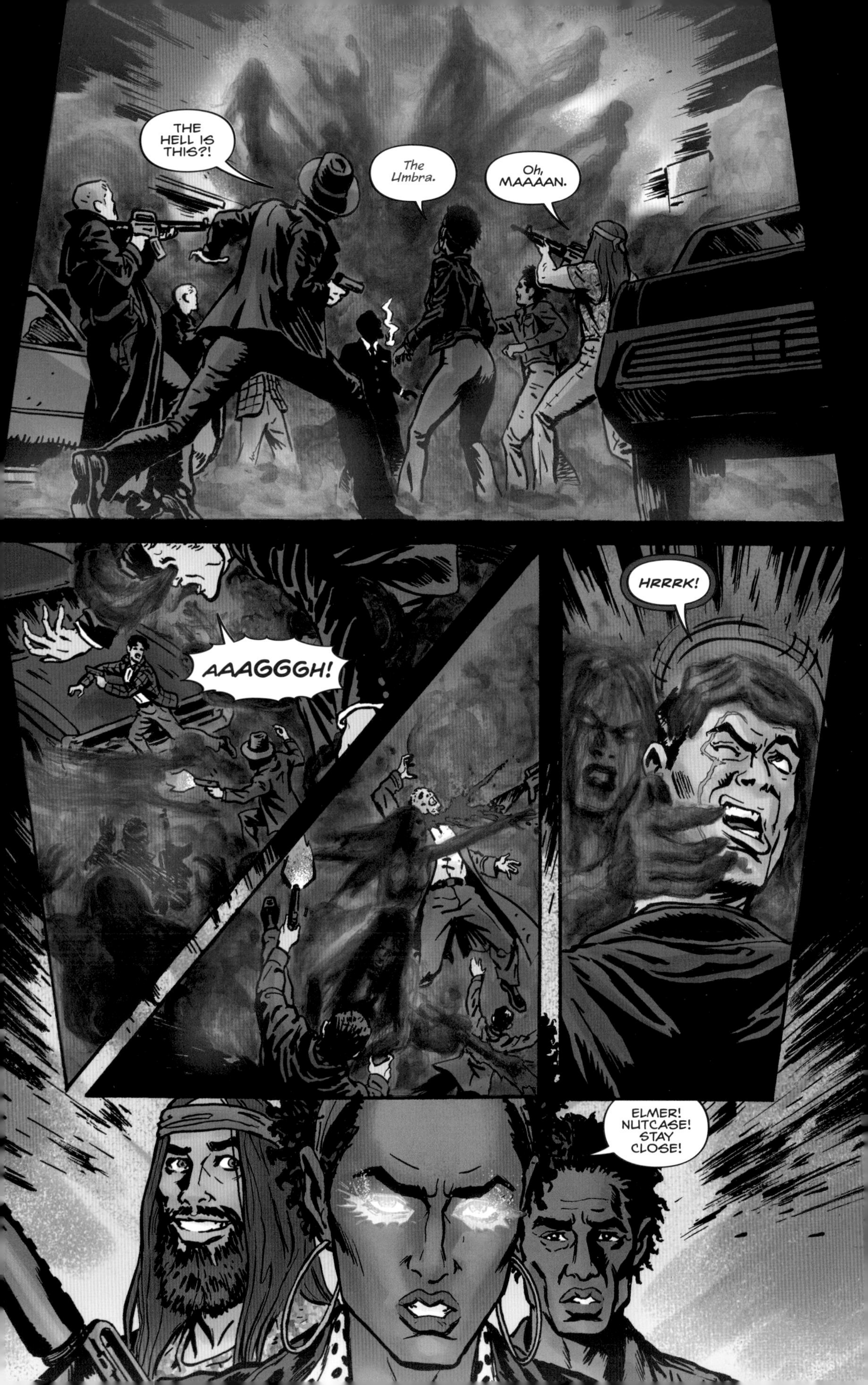
THE HELL IS THIS?!
The Umbra.
Oh, MAAAAN.
AAAGGGH!
HRRRK!
ELMER! NUTCASE! STAY CLOSE!

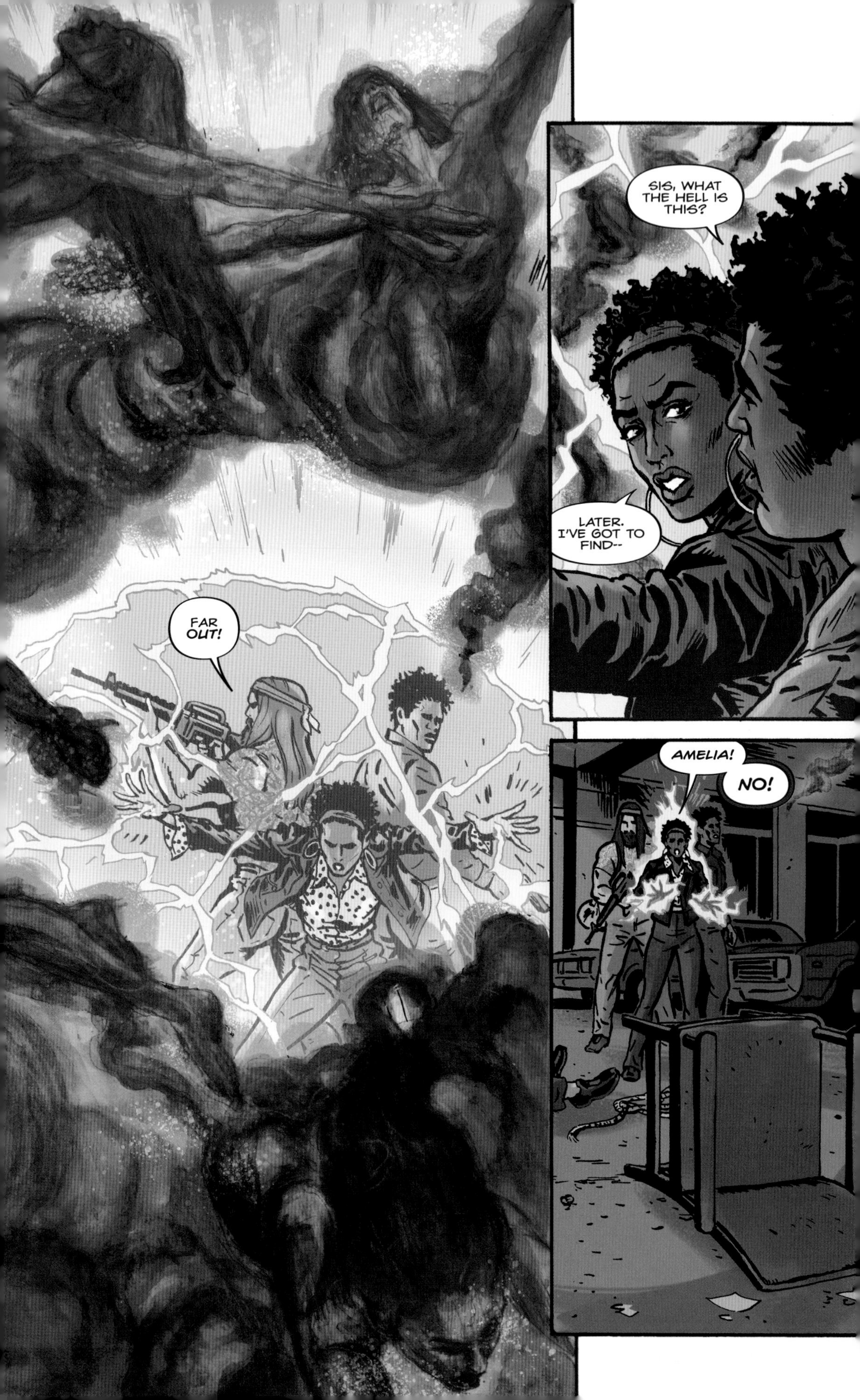
FAR OUT!
SIS, WHAT THE HELL IS THIS?
LATER. I'VE GOT TO FIND--
AMELIA!
NO!

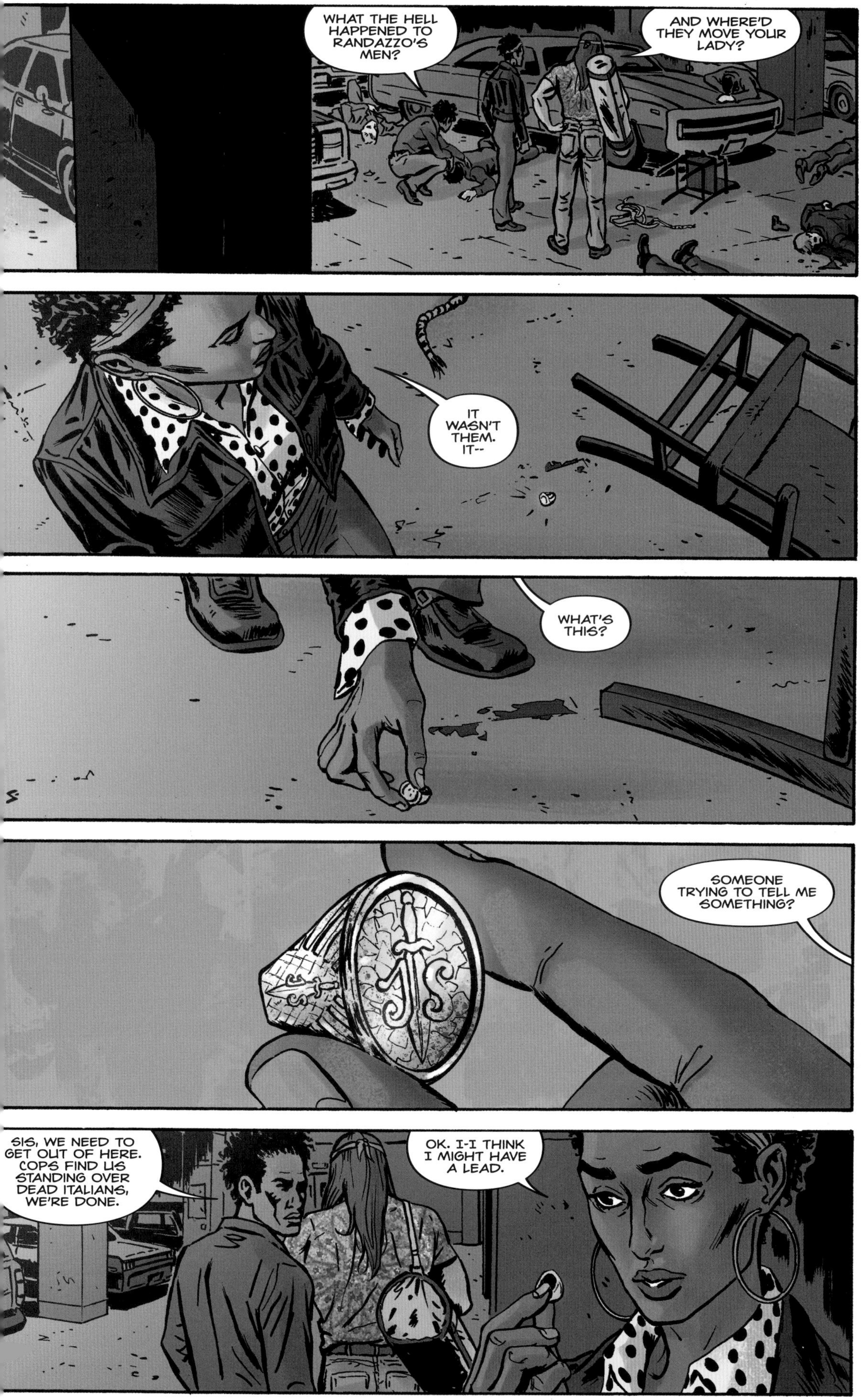
WHAT THE HELL HAPPENED TO RANDAZZO'S MEN?
AND WHERE'D THEY MOVE YOUR LADY?
IT WASN'T THEM. IT--
WHAT'S THIS?
SOMEONE TRYING TO TELL ME SOMETHING?
SIS, WE NEED TO GET OUT OF HERE. COPS FIND US STANDING OVER DEAD ITALIANS, WE'RE DONE.
OK. I-I THINK I MIGHT HAVE A LEAD.

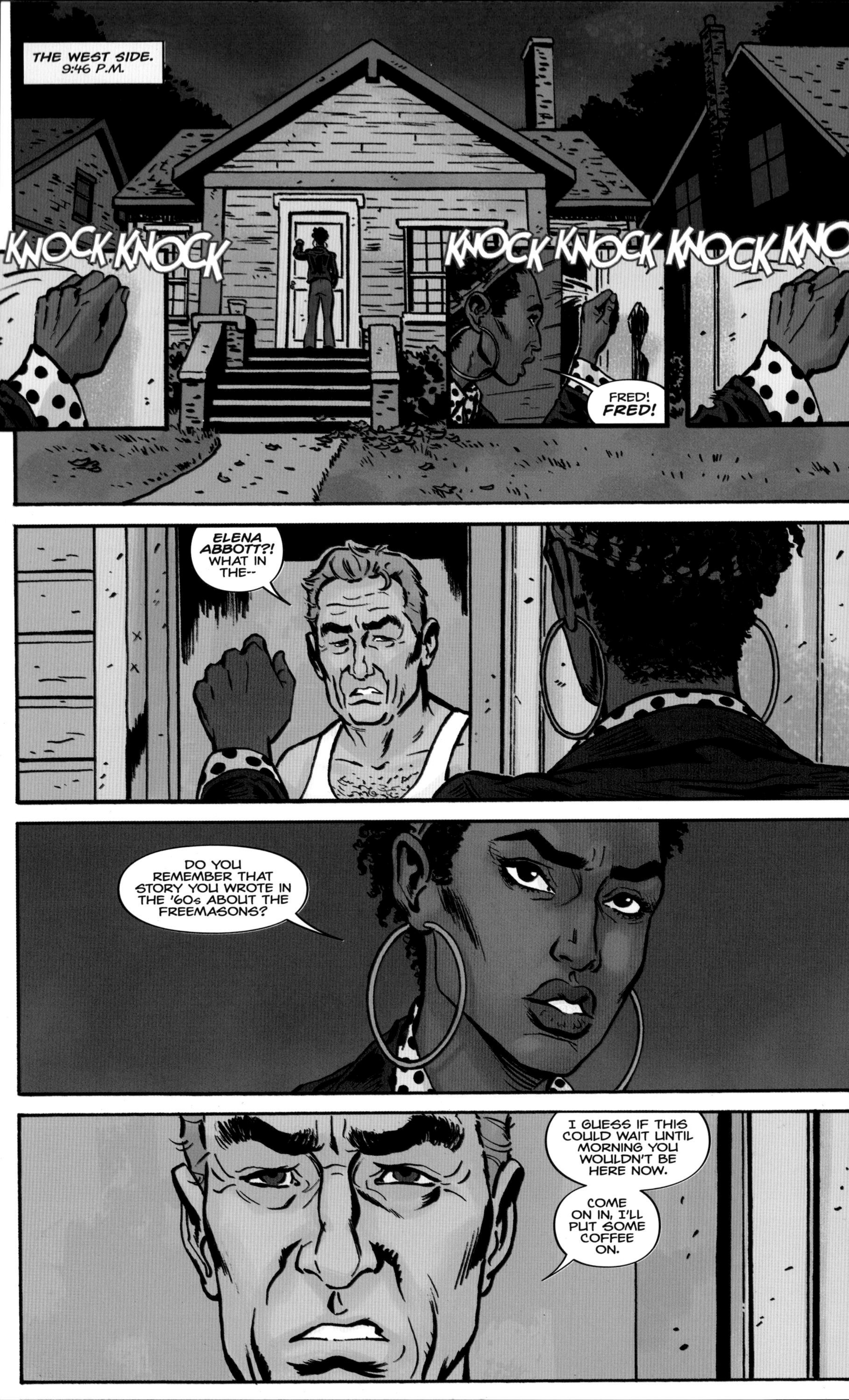
THE WEST SIDE. 9:46 P.M.
KNOCK KNOCK
KNOCK KNOCK KNOCK KNO
FRED! FRED!
ELENA ABBOTT?! WHAT IN THE--
DO YOU REMEMBER THAT STORY YOU WROTE IN THE '60s ABOUT THE FREEMASONS?
I GUESS IF THIS COULD WAIT UNTIL MORNING YOU WOULDN'T BE HERE NOW.
COME ON IN, I'LL PUT SOME COFFEE ON.

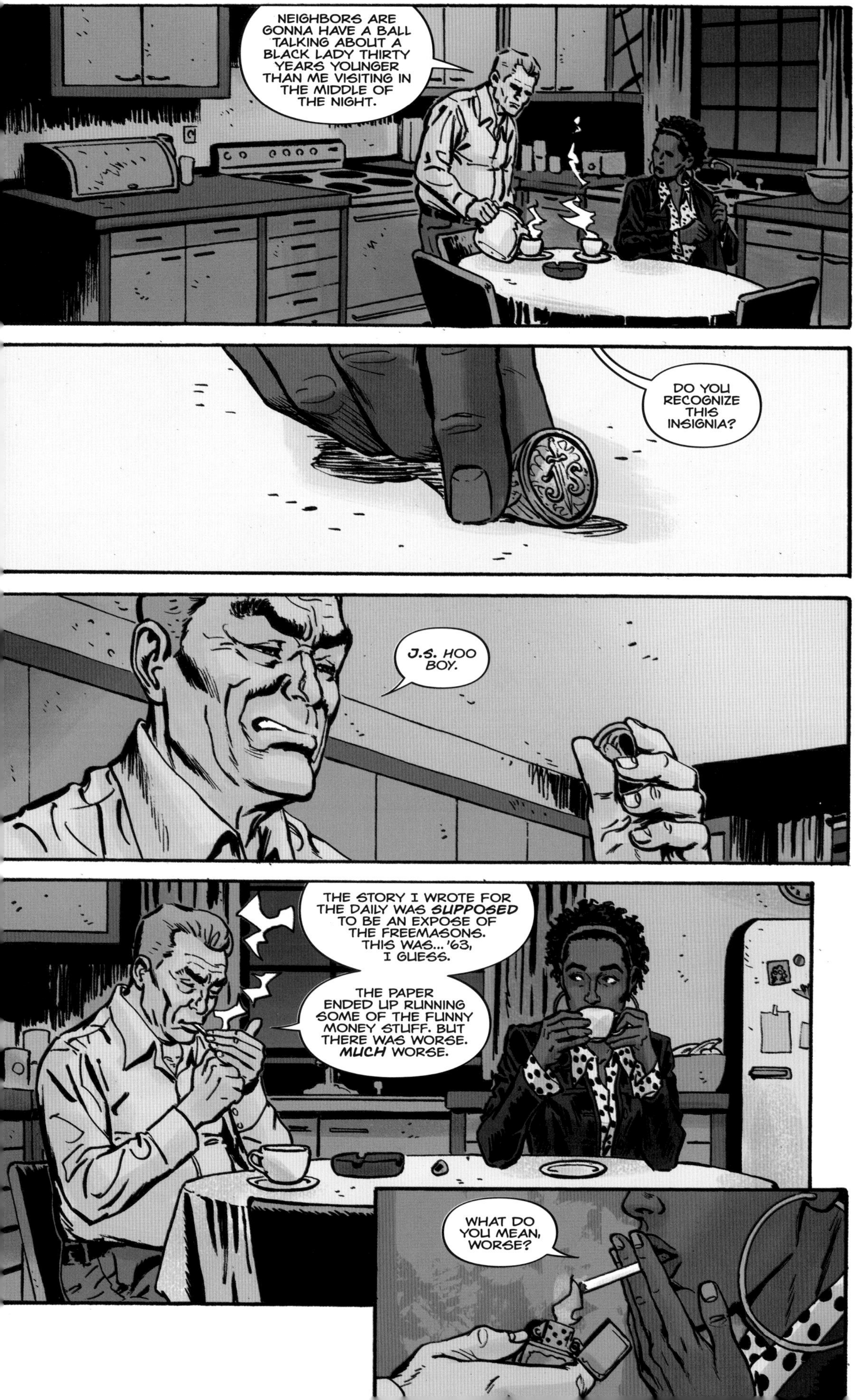
NEIGHBORS ARE GONNA HAVE A BALL TALKING ABOUT A BLACK LADY THIRTY YEARS YOUNGER THAN ME VISITING IN THE MIDDLE OF THE NIGHT.
DO YOU RECOGNIZE THIS INSIGNIA?
J.S. HOO BOY.
THE STORY I WROTE FOR THE DAILY WAS *SUPPOSED* TO BE AN EXPOSE OF THE FREEMASONS. THIS WAS... '63, I GUESS.
THE PAPER ENDED UP RUNNING SOME OF THE FUNNY MONEY STUFF. BUT THERE WAS WORSE. ***MUCH*** WORSE.
WHAT DO YOU MEAN, WORSE?

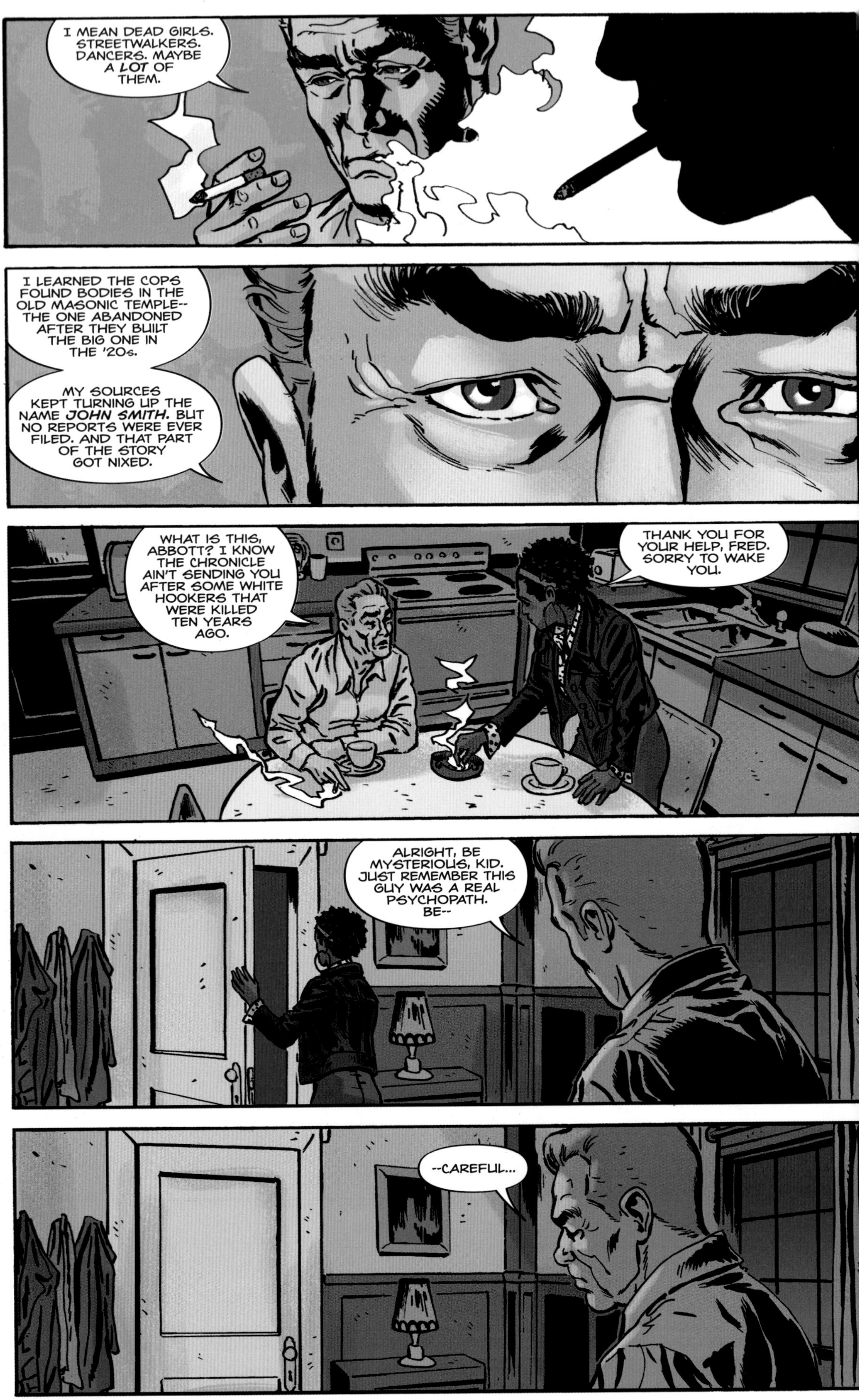
I MEAN DEAD GIRLS. STREETWALKERS. DANCERS. MAYBE A *LOT* OF THEM.
I LEARNED THE COPS FOUND BODIES IN THE OLD MASONIC TEMPLE-- THE ONE ABANDONED AFTER THEY BUILT THE BIG ONE IN THE '20s.
MY SOURCES KEPT TURNING UP THE NAME **JOHN SMITH.** BUT NO REPORTS WERE EVER FILED. AND THAT PART OF THE STORY GOT NIXED.
WHAT IS THIS, ABBOTT? I KNOW THE CHRONICLE AIN'T SENDING YOU AFTER SOME WHITE HOOKERS THAT WERE KILLED TEN YEARS AGO.
THANK YOU FOR YOUR HELP, FRED. SORRY TO WAKE YOU.
ALRIGHT, BE MYSTERIOUS, KID. JUST REMEMBER THIS GUY WAS A REAL PSYCHOPATH. BE--
--CAREFUL...

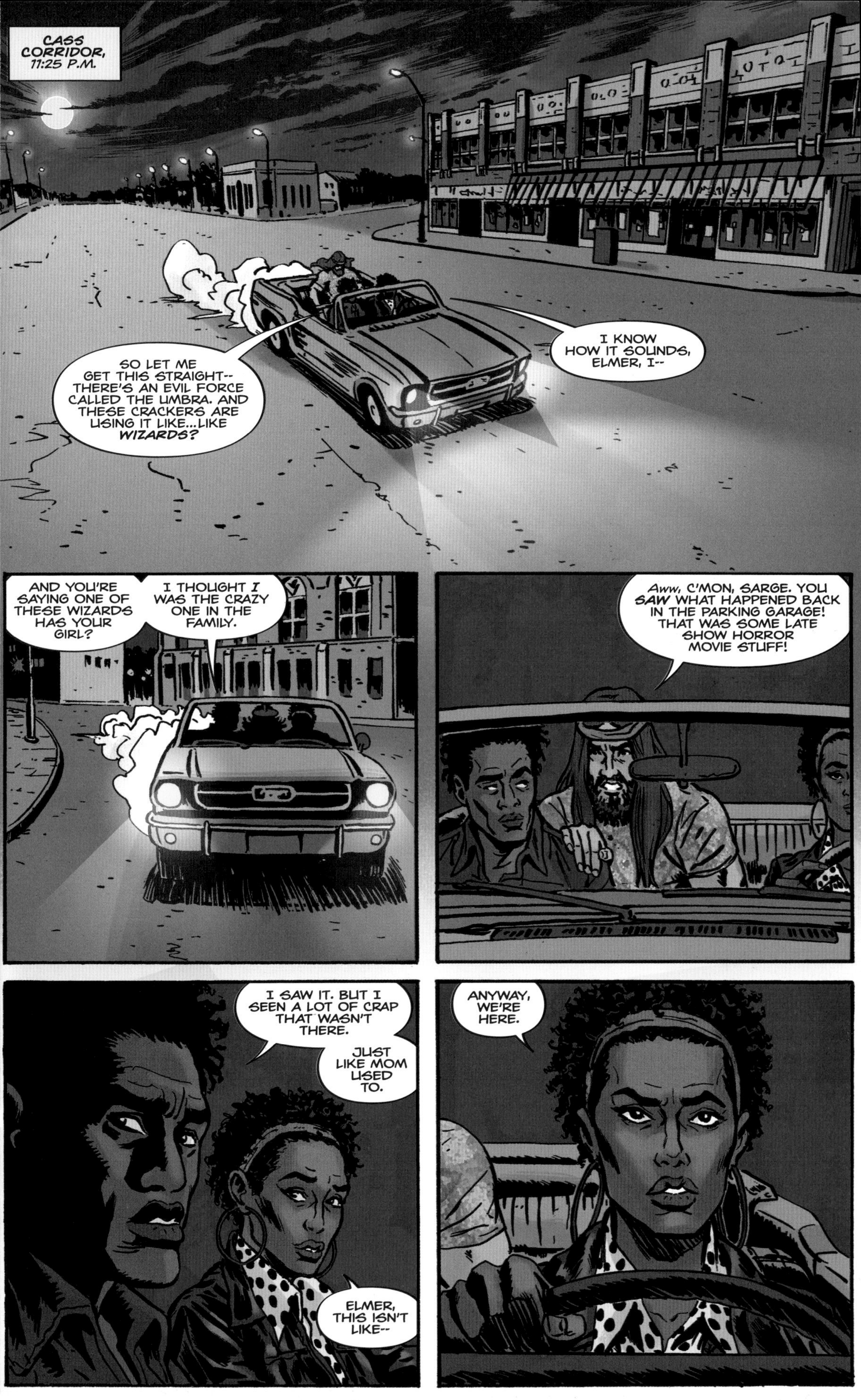
CASS CORRIDOR, 11:25 P.M.
SO LET ME GET THIS STRAIGHT-- THERE'S AN EVIL FORCE CALLED THE UMBRA. AND THESE CRACKERS ARE USING IT LIKE...LIKE WIZARDS?
I KNOW HOW IT SOUNDS, ELMER, I--
AND YOU'RE SAYING ONE OF THESE WIZARDS HAS YOUR GIRL?
I THOUGHT I WAS THE CRAZY ONE IN THE FAMILY.
Aww, C'MON, SARGE. YOU SAW WHAT HAPPENED BACK IN THE PARKING GARAGE! THAT WAS SOME LATE SHOW HORROR MOVIE STUFF!
I SAW IT. BUT I SEEN A LOT OF CRAP THAT WASN'T THERE.
JUST LIKE MOM USED TO.
ELMER, THIS ISN'T LIKE--
ANYWAY, WE'RE HERE.

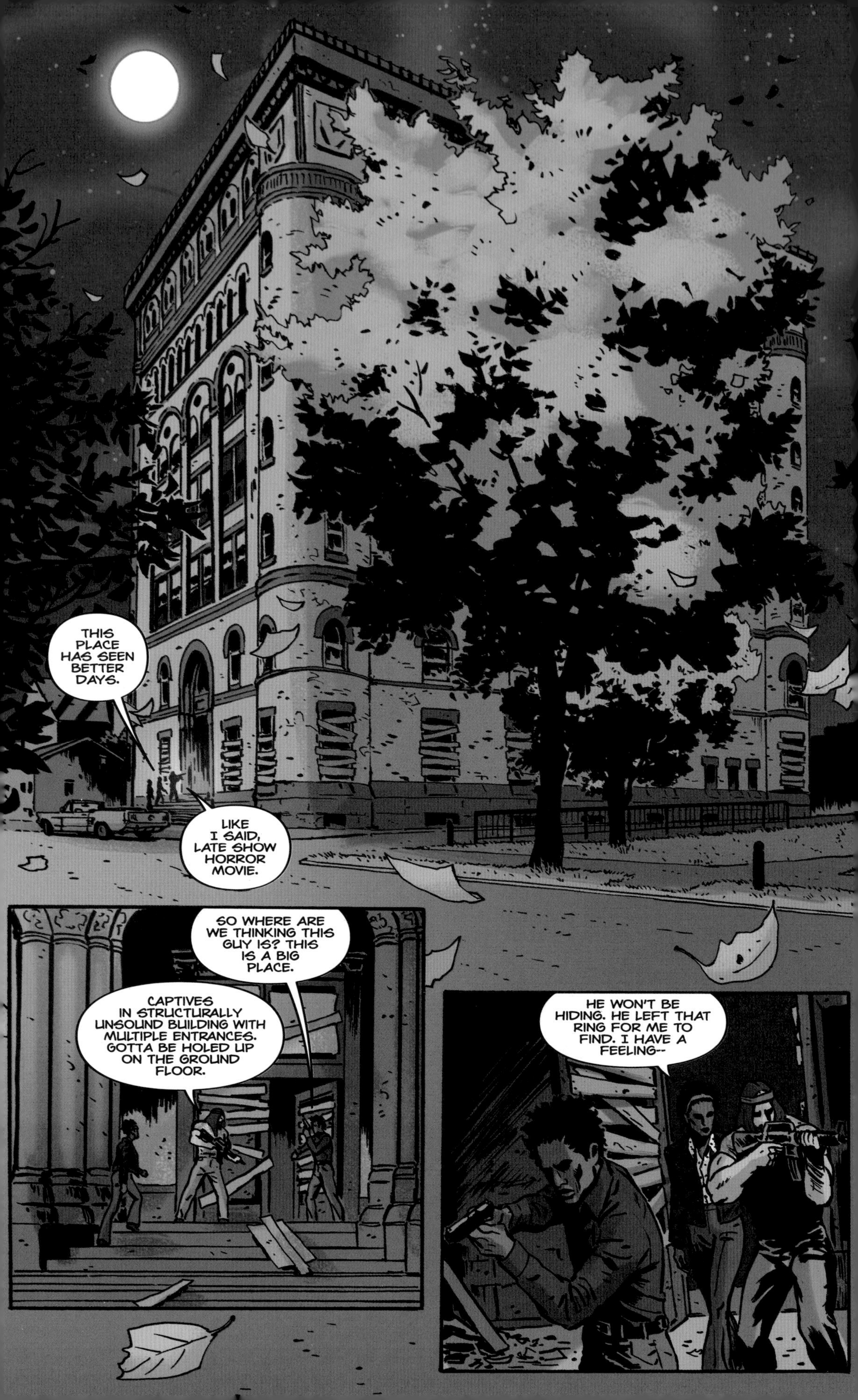
THIS PLACE HAS SEEN BETTER DAYS.
LIKE I SAID, LATE SHOW HORROR MOVIE.
SO WHERE ARE WE THINKING THIS GUY IS? THIS IS A BIG PLACE.
CAPTIVES IN STRUCTURALLY UNSOUND BUILDING WITH MULTIPLE ENTRANCES. GOTTA BE HOLED UP ON THE GROUND FLOOR.
HE WON'T BE HIDING. HE LEFT THAT RING FOR ME TO FIND. I HAVE A FEELING--

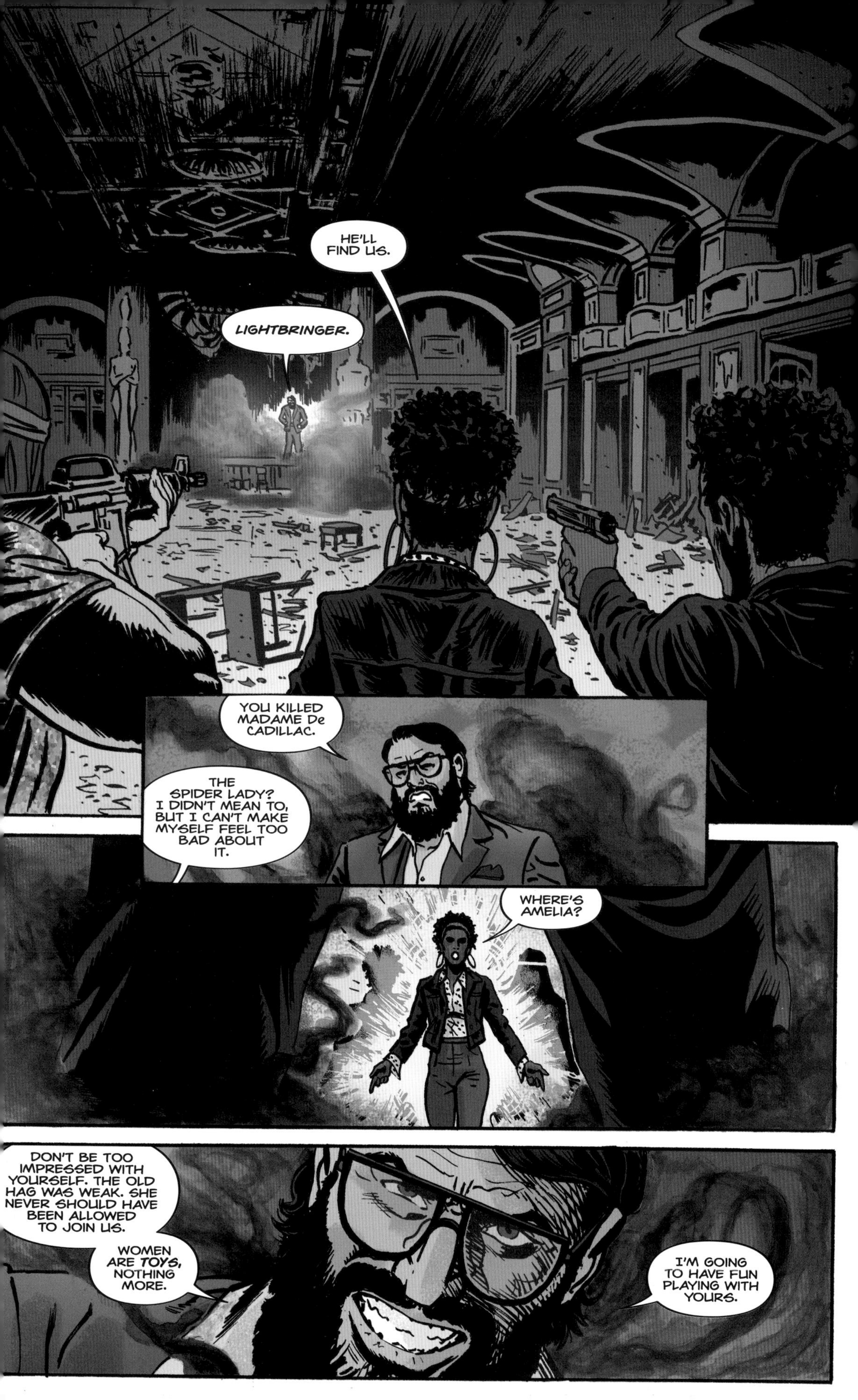
HE'LL FIND US.
LIGHTBRINGER.
YOU KILLED MADAME De CADILLAC.
THE SPIDER LADY? I DIDN'T MEAN TO, BUT I CAN'T MAKE MYSELF FEEL TOO BAD ABOUT IT.
WHERE'S AMELIA?
DON'T BE TOO IMPRESSED WITH YOURSELF. THE OLD HAG WAS WEAK. SHE NEVER SHOULD HAVE BEEN ALLOWED TO JOIN US.
WOMEN ARE TOYS, NOTHING MORE.
I'M GOING TO HAVE FUN PLAYING WITH YOURS.

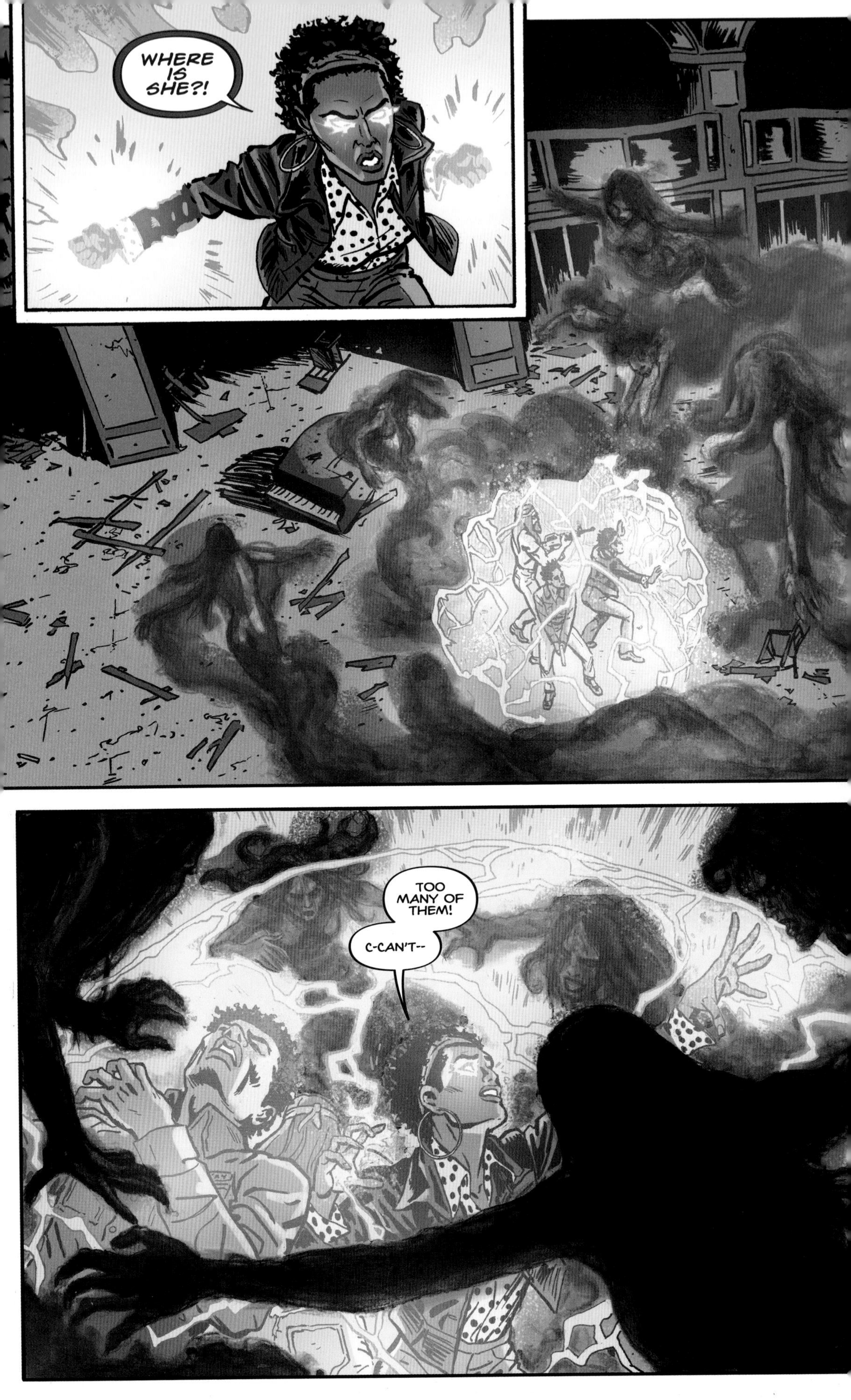
WHERE IS SHE?!
TOO MANY OF THEM!
C-CAN'T--

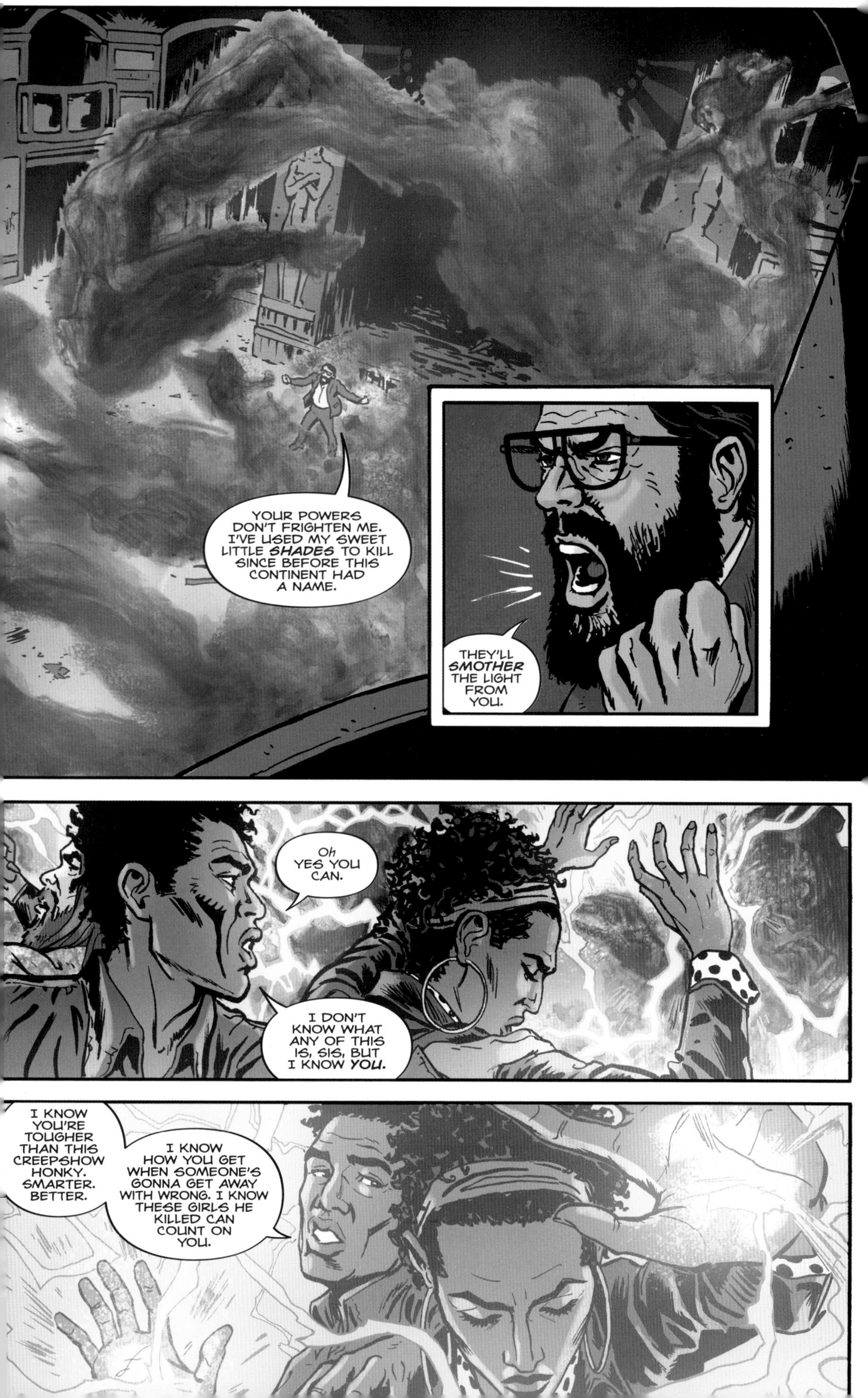
YOUR POWERS DON'T FRIGHTEN ME. I'VE USED MY SWEET LITTLE SHADES TO KILL SINCE BEFORE THIS CONTINENT HAD A NAME.
THEY'LL SMOTHER THE LIGHT FROM YOU.
Oh YES YOU CAN.
I DON'T KNOW WHAT ANY OF THIS IS, SIS, BUT I KNOW YOU.
I KNOW YOU'RE TOUGHER THAN THIS CREEPSHOW HONKY. SMARTER. BETTER.
I KNOW HOW YOU GET WHEN SOMEONE'S GONNA GET AWAY WITH WRONG. I KNOW THESE GIRLS HE KILLED CAN COUNT ON YOU.

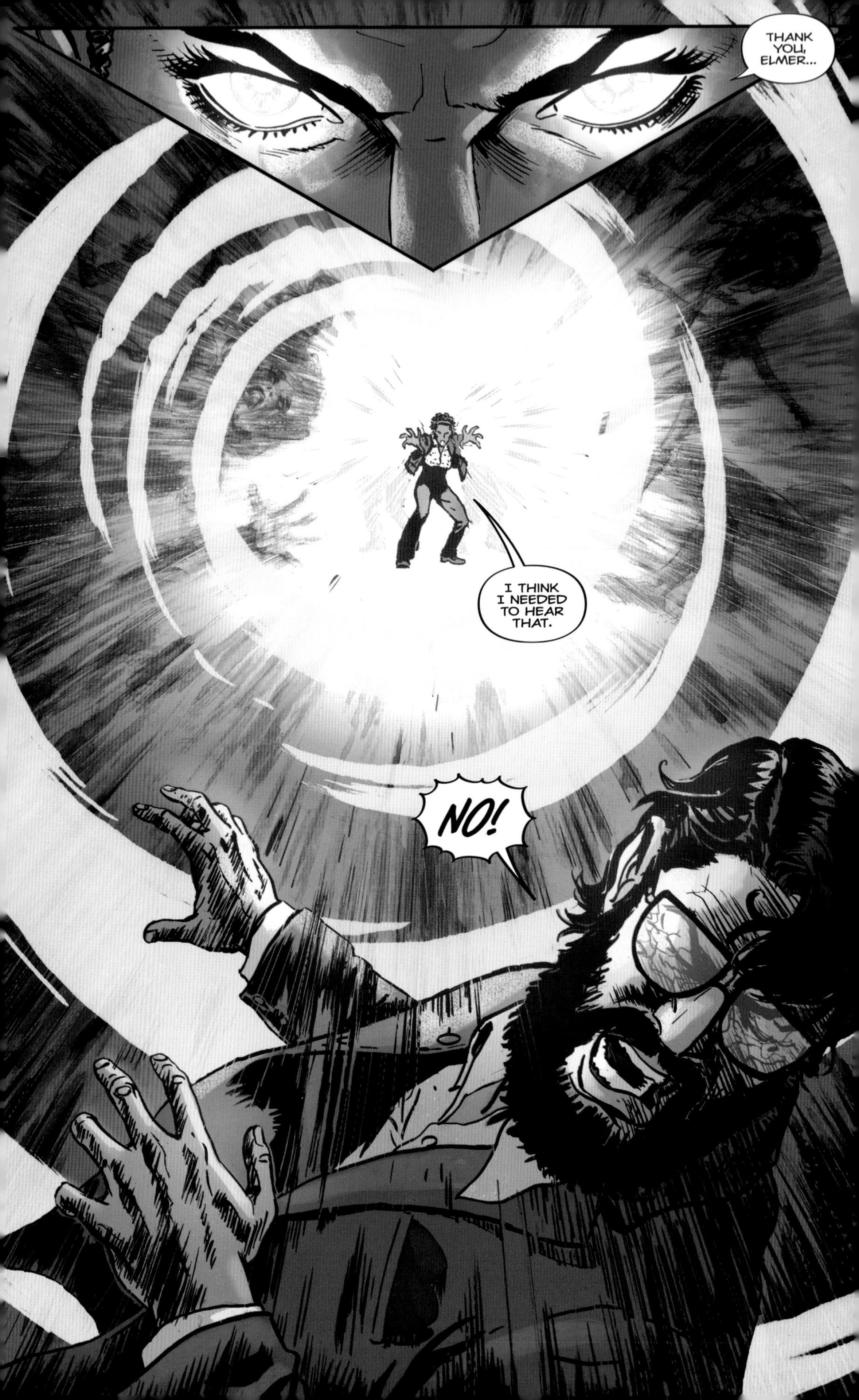
THANK YOU, ELMER...
I THINK I NEEDED TO HEAR THAT.
NO!

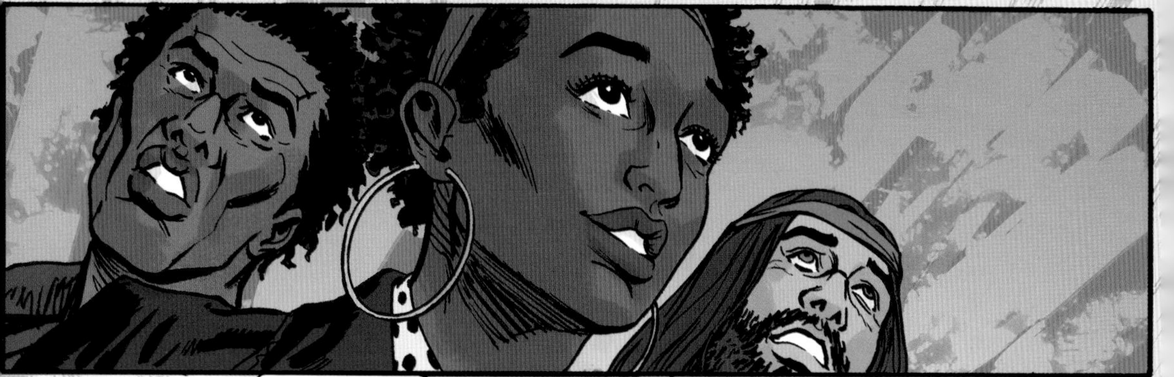

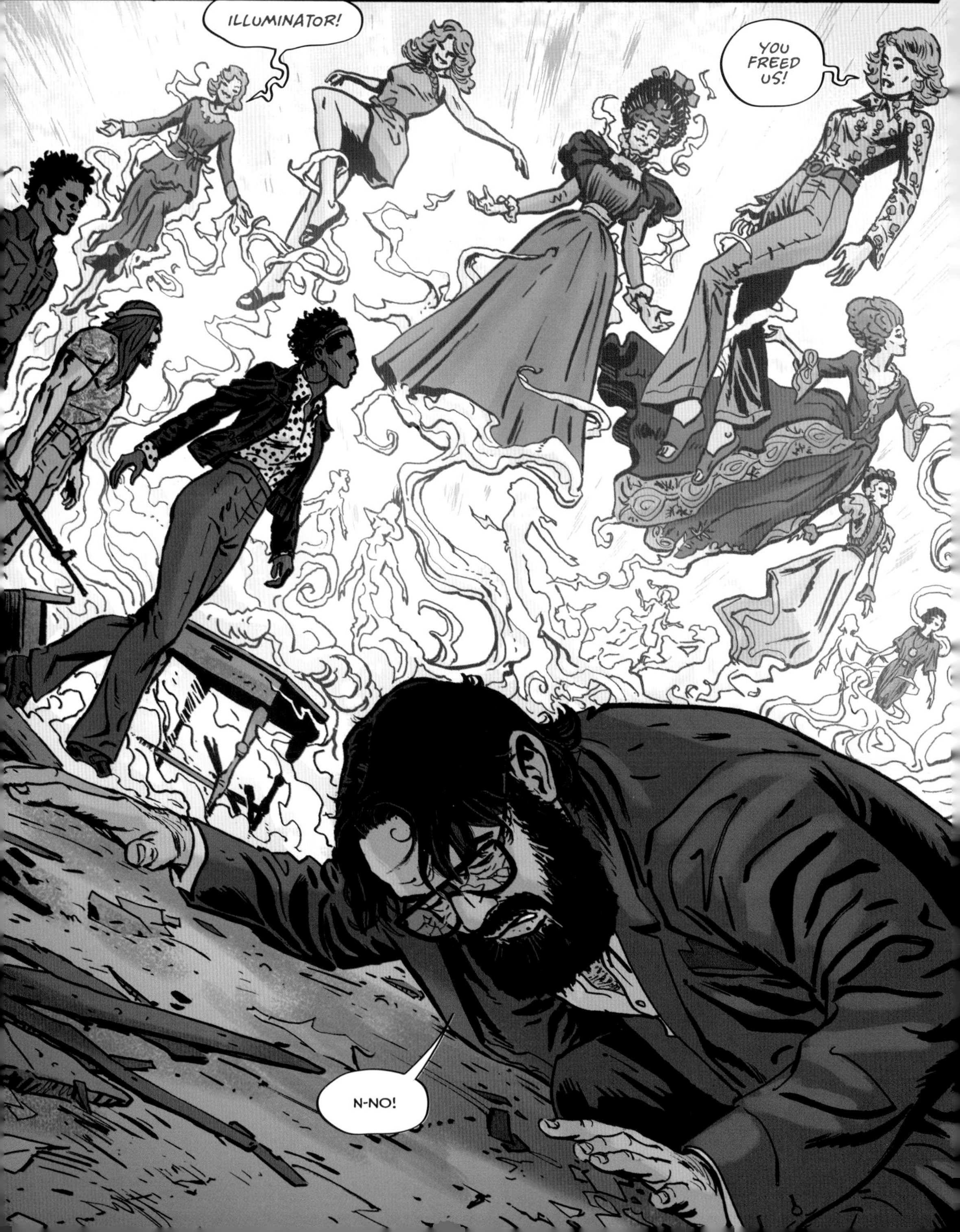
ILLUMINATOR!
YOU FREED US!
N-NO!

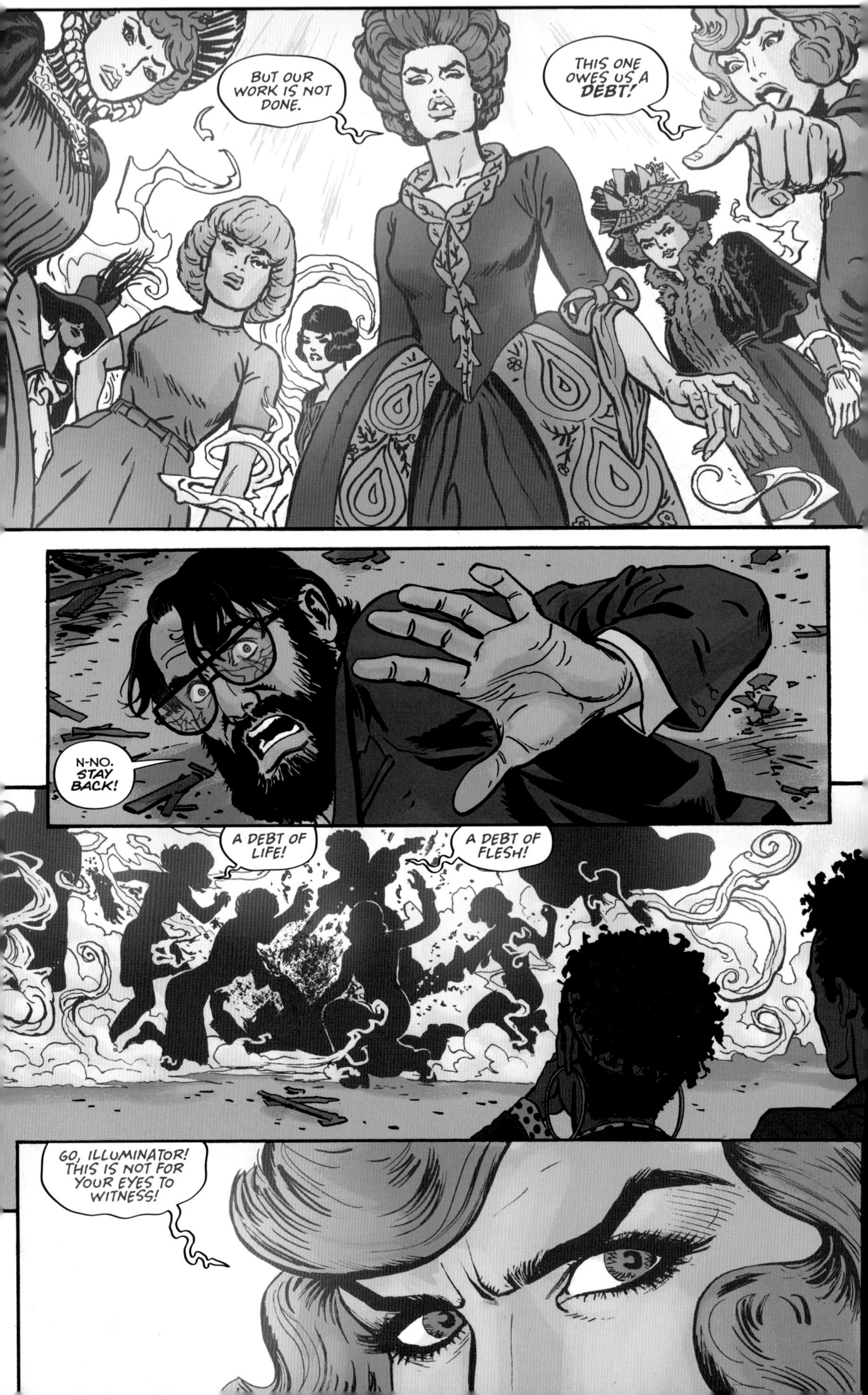
BUT OUR WORK IS NOT DONE.
THIS ONE OWES US A DEBT!
N-NO. STAY BACK!
A DEBT OF LIFE!
A DEBT OF FLESH!
GO, ILLUMINATOR! THIS IS NOT FOR YOUR EYES TO WITNESS!

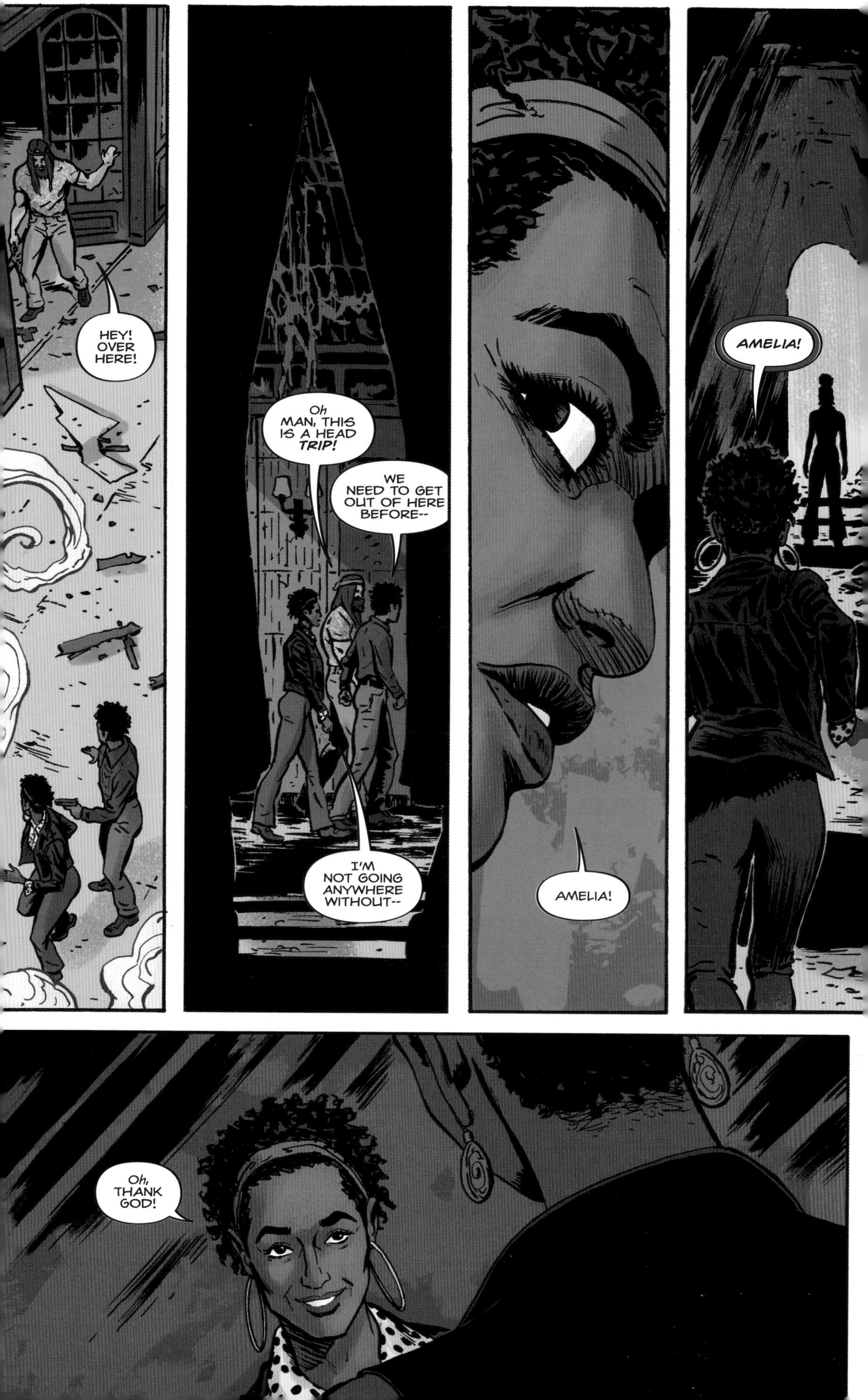
HEY! OVER HERE!
Oh MAN, THIS IS A HEAD TRIP!
WE NEED TO GET OUT OF HERE BEFORE--
I'M NOT GOING ANYWHERE WITHOUT--
AMELIA!
AMELIA!
Oh, THANK GOD!

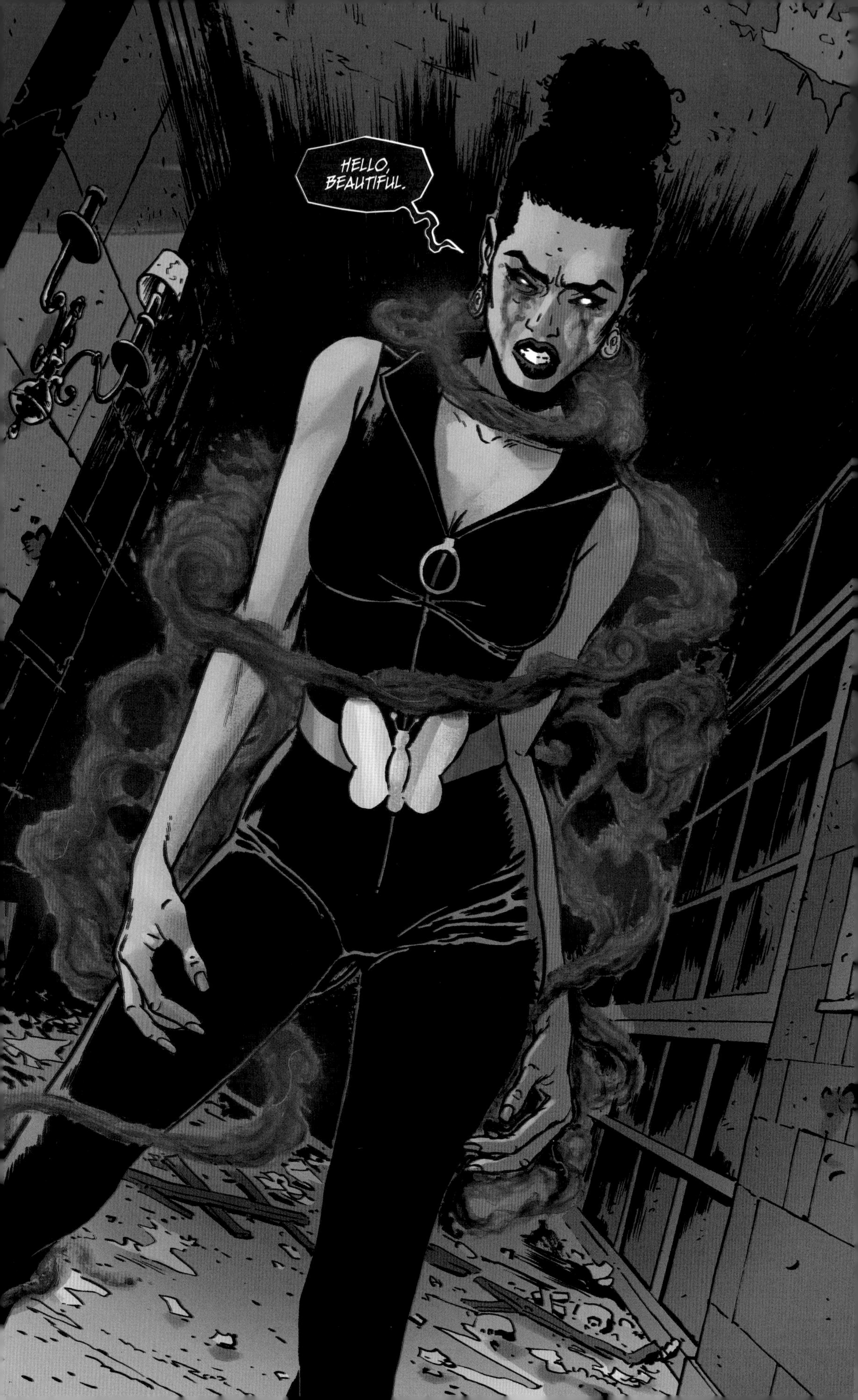
HELLO, BEAUTIFUL.

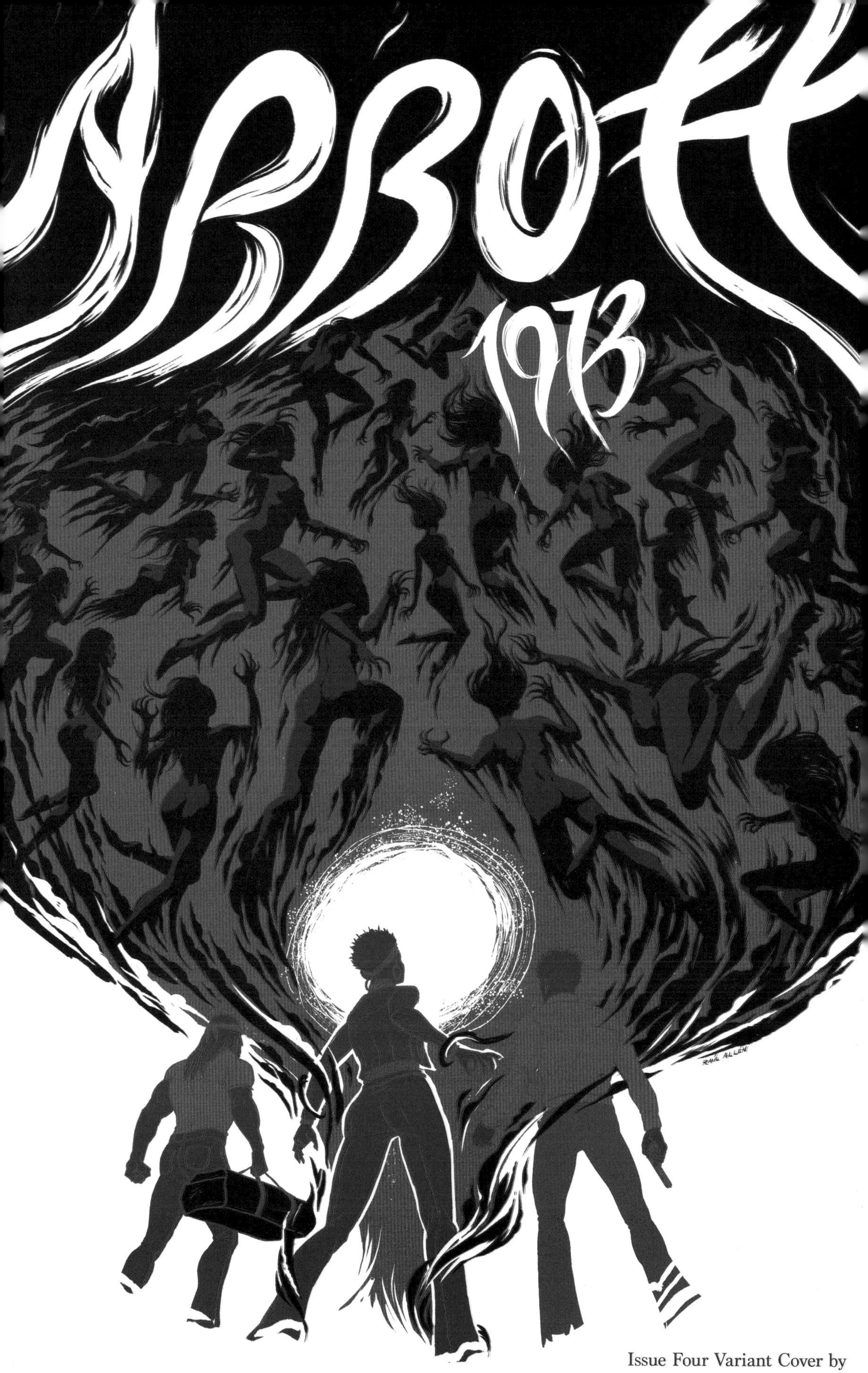
ABBOTT
1973
RAÚL ALLÉN

Issue Four Variant Cover by
Raúl Allén

CHAPTER FIVE

Issue Five Cover by Taj Tenfold

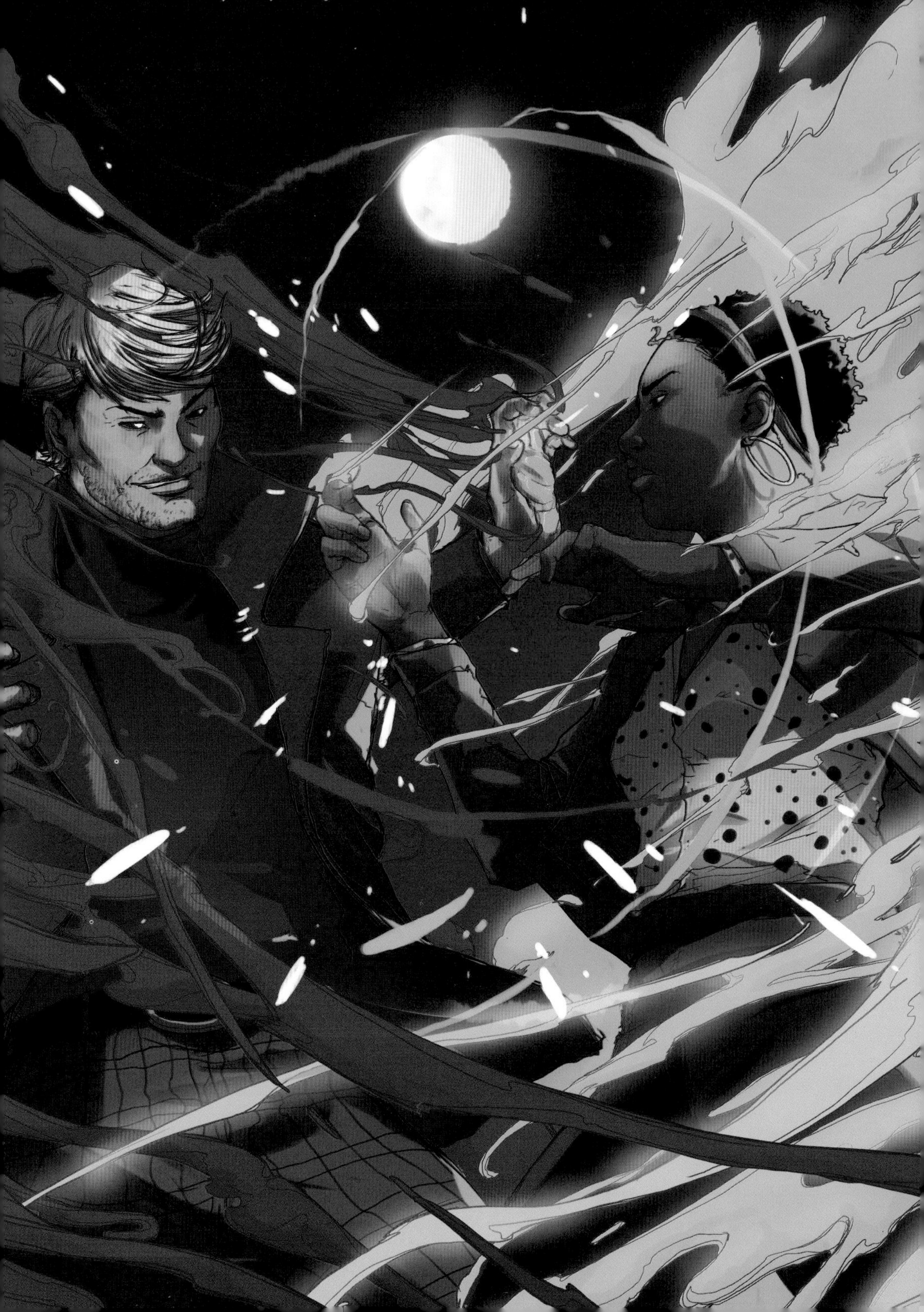

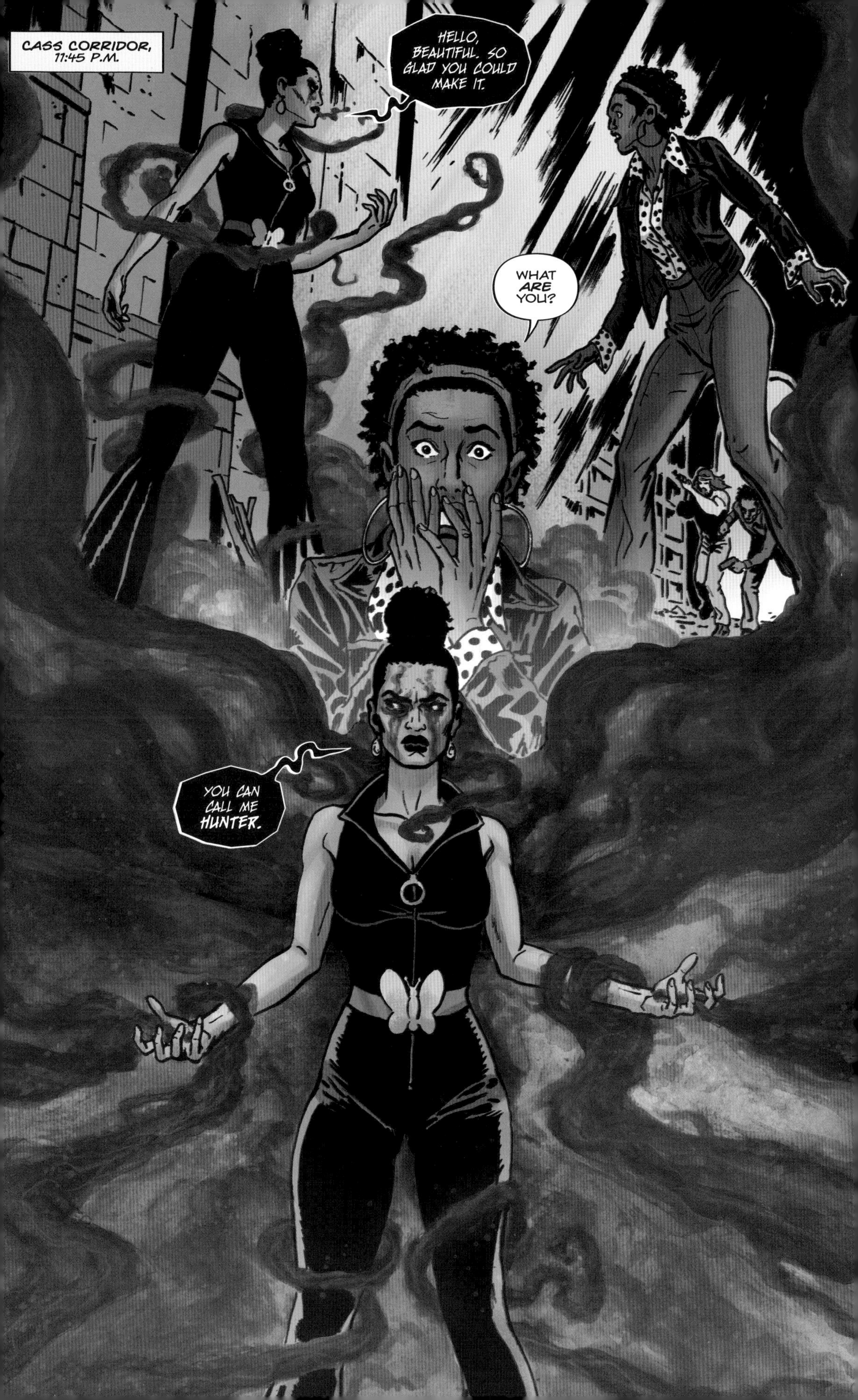
CASS CORRIDOR, 11:45 P.M.
HELLO, BEAUTIFUL. SO GLAD YOU COULD MAKE IT.
WHAT ARE YOU?
YOU CAN CALL ME HUNTER.

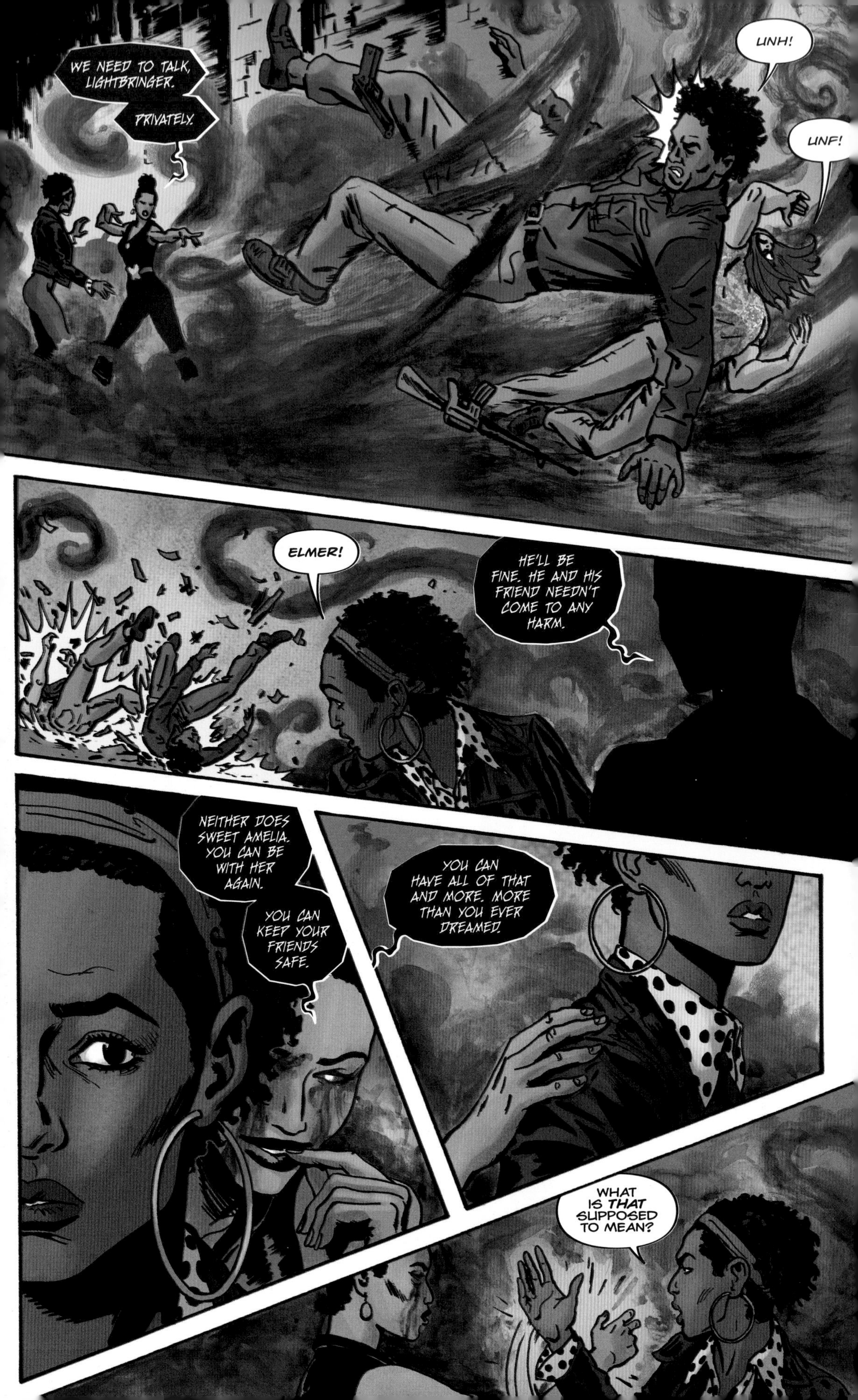
WE NEED TO TALK, LIGHTBRINGER.
PRIVATELY.
UNH!
UNF!
ELMER!
HE'LL BE FINE. HE AND HIS FRIEND NEEDN'T COME TO ANY HARM.
NEITHER DOES SWEET AMELIA. YOU CAN BE WITH HER AGAIN.
YOU CAN KEEP YOUR FRIENDS SAFE.
YOU CAN HAVE ALL OF THAT AND MORE. MORE THAN YOU EVER DREAMED.
WHAT IS THAT SUPPOSED TO MEAN?

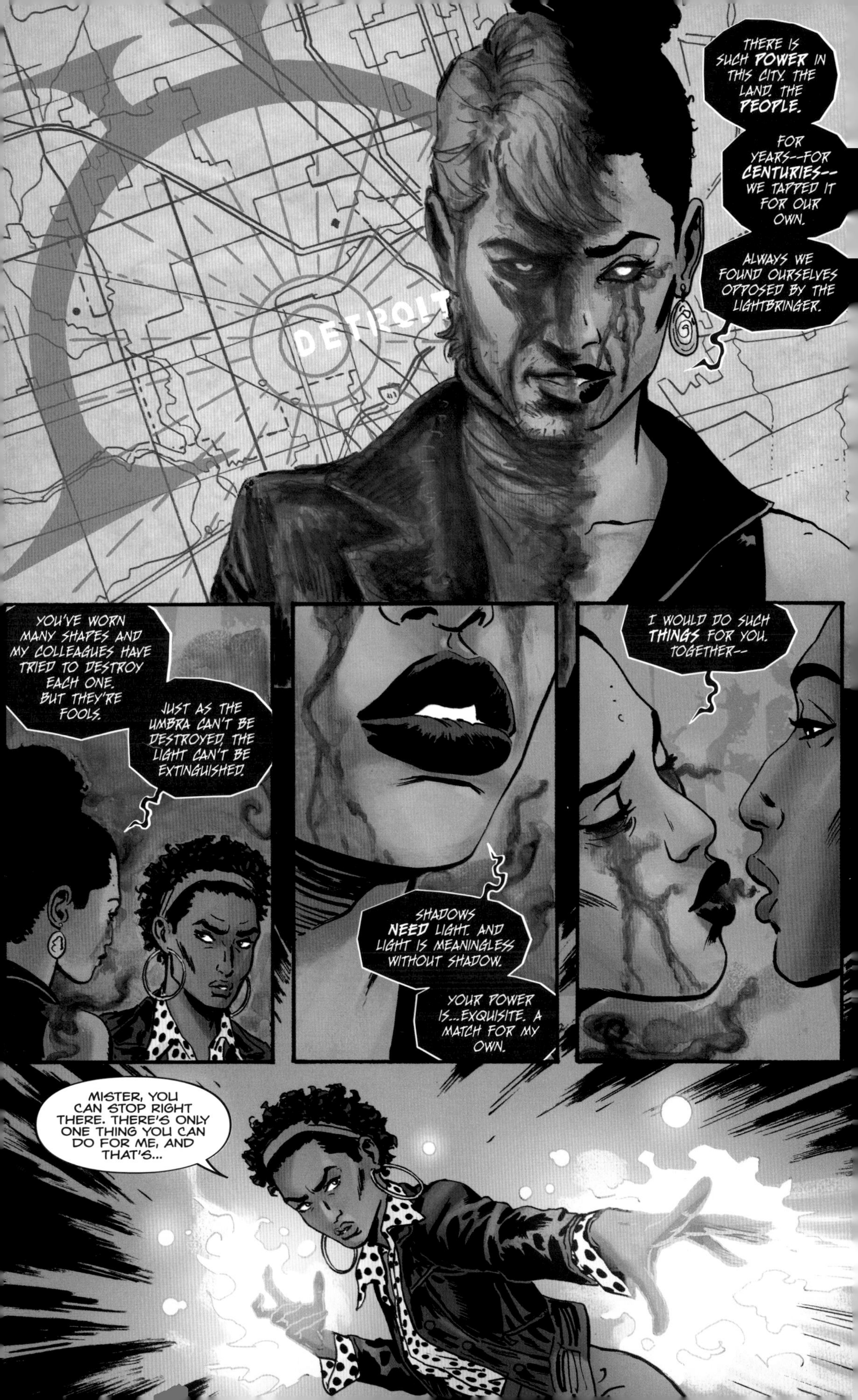
DETROIT
THERE IS SUCH POWER IN THIS CITY. THE LAND. THE PEOPLE.
FOR YEARS--FOR CENTURIES--WE TAPPED IT FOR OUR OWN.
ALWAYS WE FOUND OURSELVES OPPOSED BY THE LIGHTBRINGER.
YOU'VE WORN MANY SHAPES AND MY COLLEAGUES HAVE TRIED TO DESTROY EACH ONE. BUT THEY'RE FOOLS.
JUST AS THE UMBRA CAN'T BE DESTROYED, THE LIGHT CAN'T BE EXTINGUISHED.
SHADOWS NEED LIGHT. AND LIGHT IS MEANINGLESS WITHOUT SHADOW.
YOUR POWER IS...EXQUISITE. A MATCH FOR MY OWN.
I WOULD DO SUCH THINGS FOR YOU. TOGETHER--
MISTER, YOU CAN STOP RIGHT THERE. THERE'S ONLY ONE THING YOU CAN DO FOR ME, AND THAT'S...

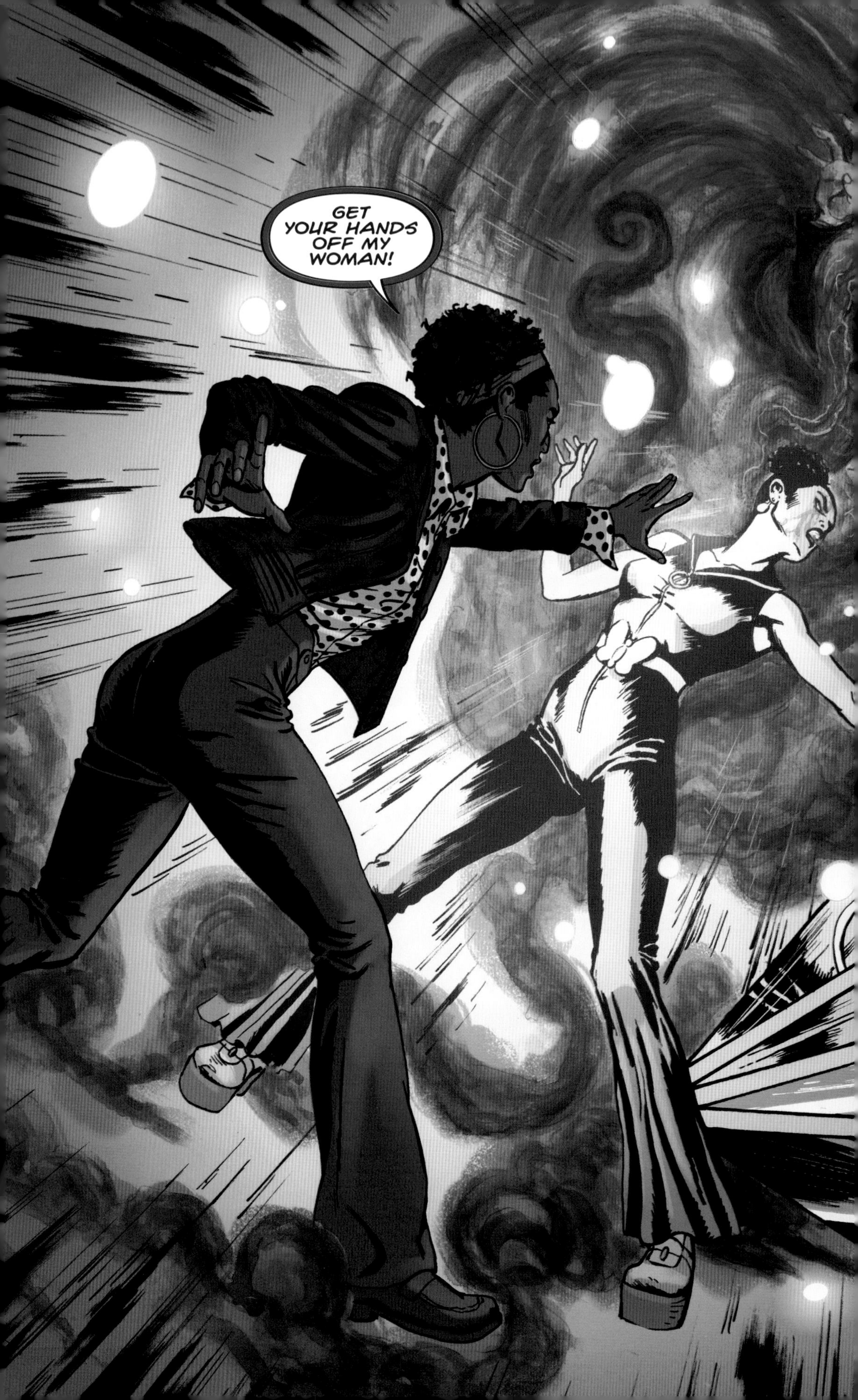
GET YOUR HANDS OFF MY WOMAN!

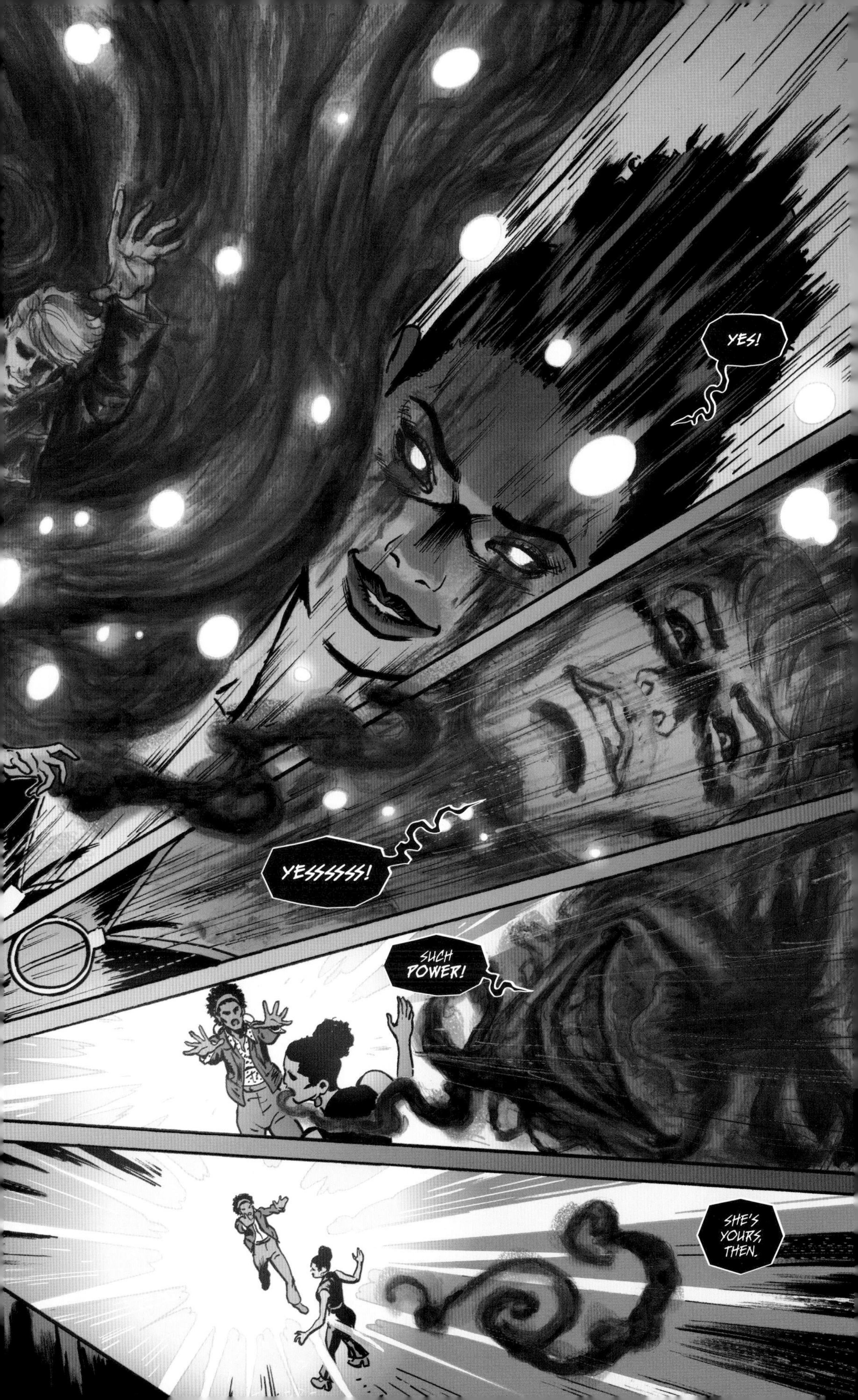
YES!
YESSSSSS!
SUCH POWER!
SHE'S YOURS, THEN.

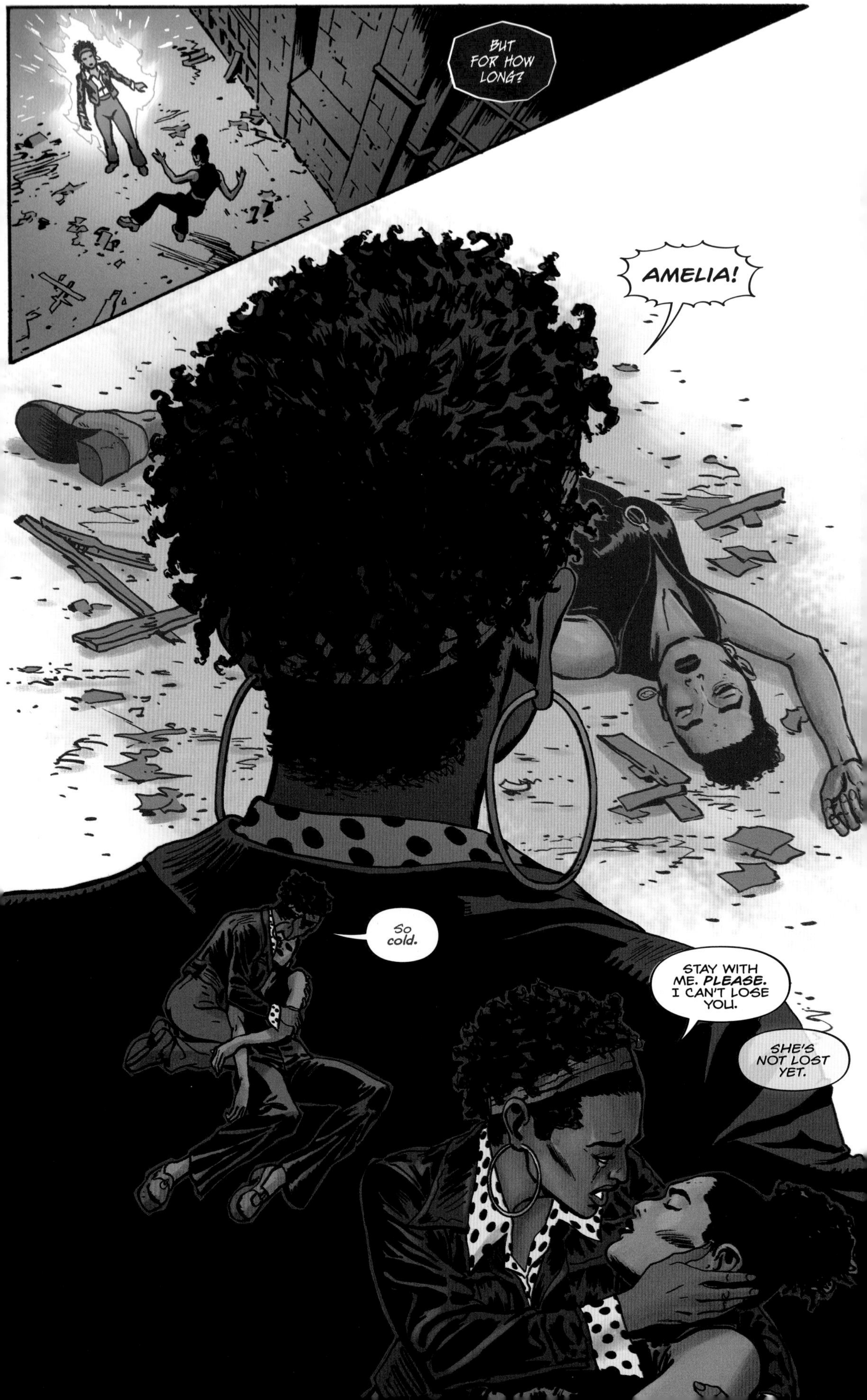
BUT FOR HOW LONG?
AMELIA!
So cold.
STAY WITH ME. PLEASE. I CAN'T LOSE YOU.
SHE'S NOT LOST YET.

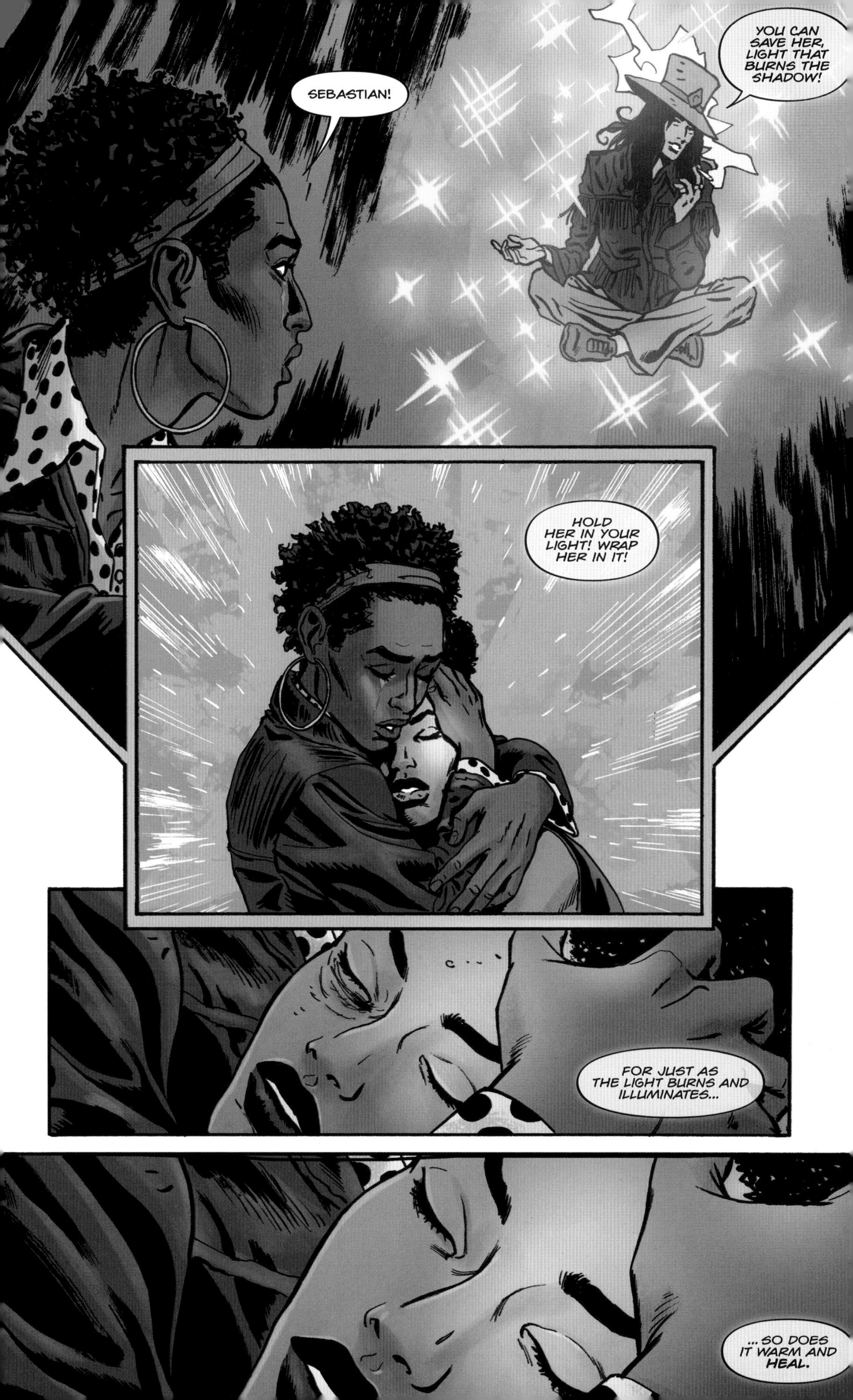
SEBASTIAN!
YOU CAN SAVE HER, LIGHT THAT BURNS THE SHADOW!
HOLD HER IN YOUR LIGHT! WRAP HER IN IT!
C...
FOR JUST AS THE LIGHT BURNS AND ILLUMINATES...
...SO DOES IT WARM AND HEAL.

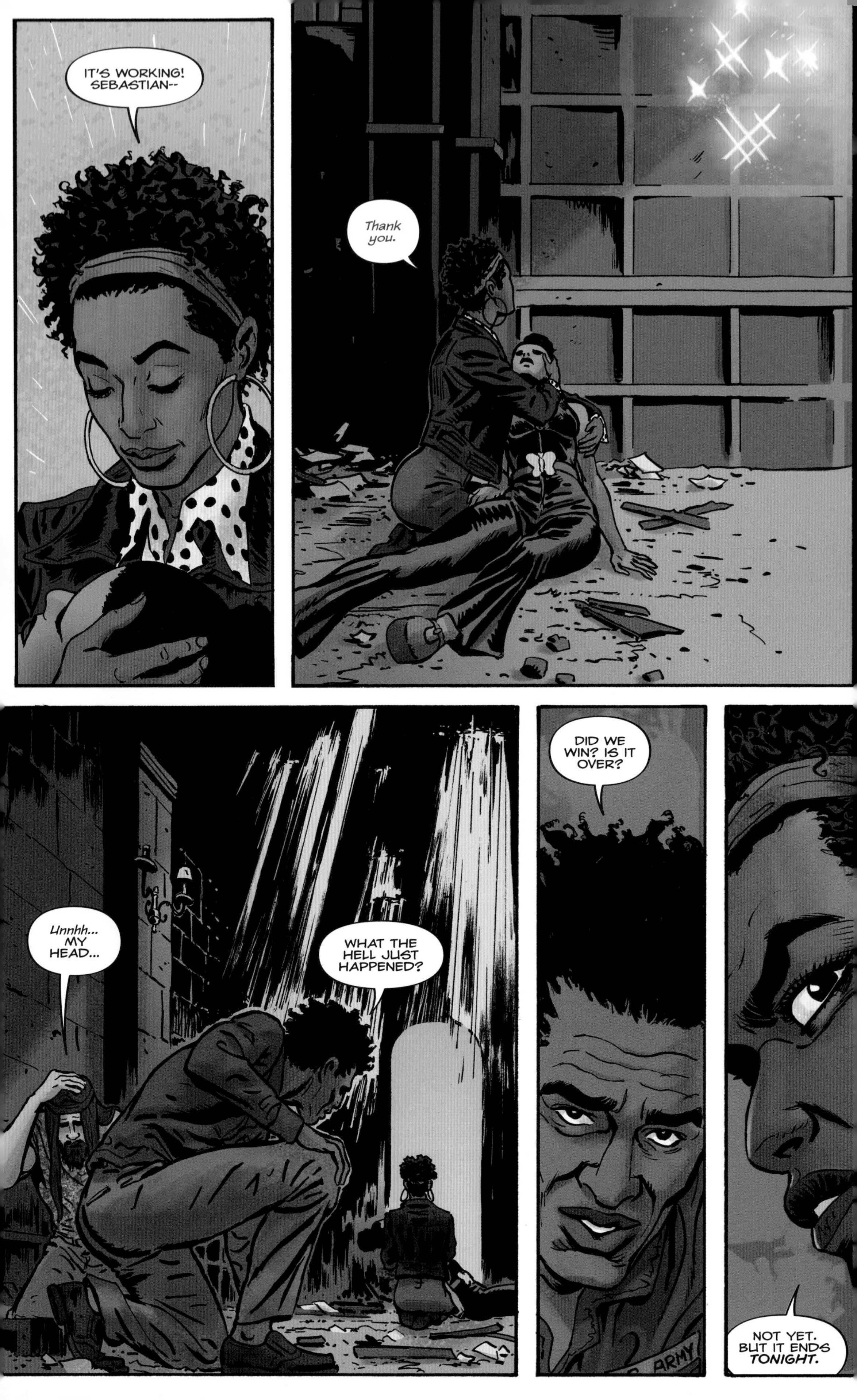
IT'S WORKING! SEBASTIAN--
Thank you.
Unnhh... MY HEAD...
WHAT THE HELL JUST HAPPENED?
DID WE WIN? IS IT OVER?
NOT YET. BUT IT ENDS *TONIGHT.*
ARMY

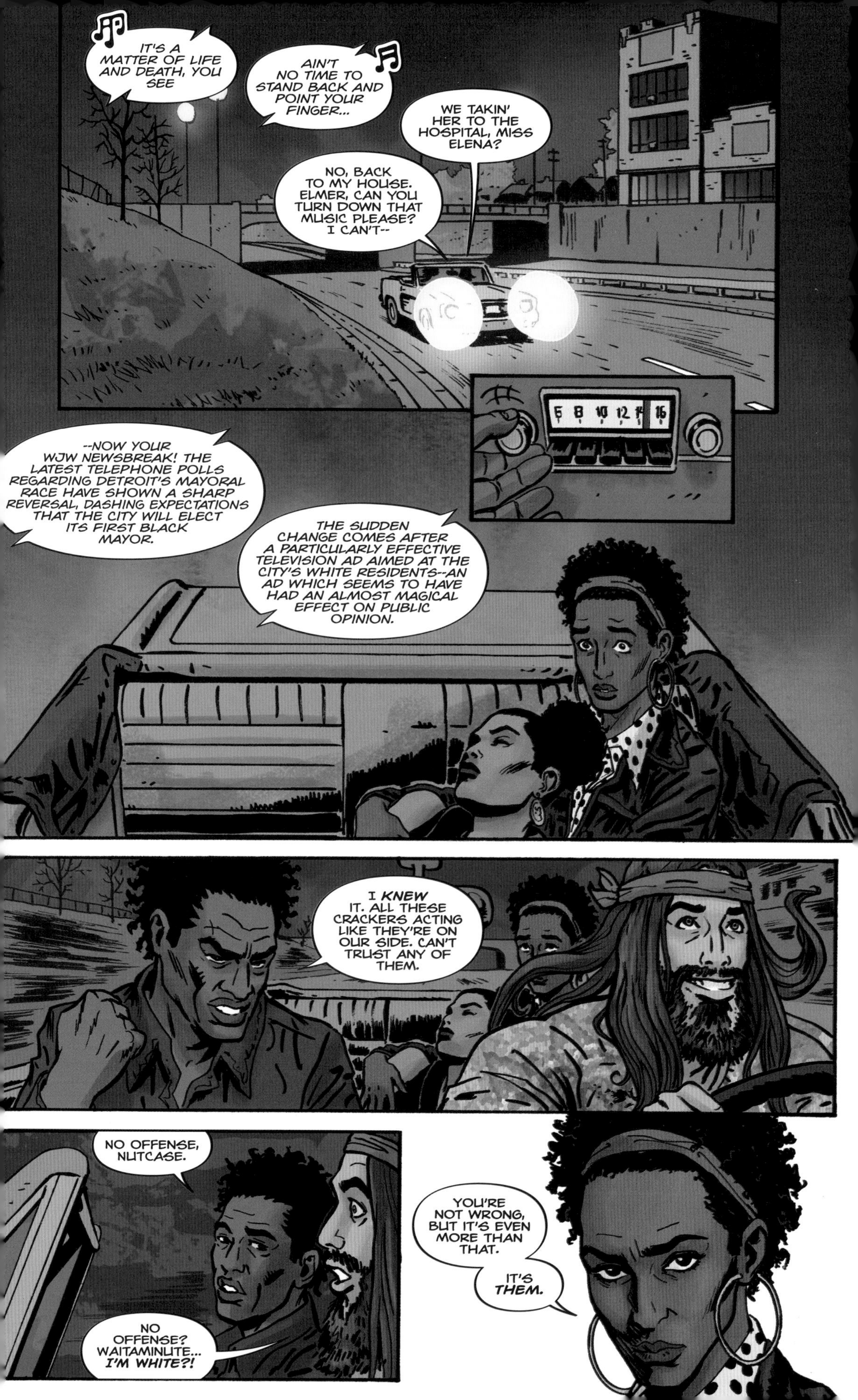
IT'S A MATTER OF LIFE AND DEATH, YOU SEE
AIN'T NO TIME TO STAND BACK AND POINT YOUR FINGER...
WE TAKIN' HER TO THE HOSPITAL, MISS ELENA?
NO, BACK TO MY HOUSE. ELMER, CAN YOU TURN DOWN THAT MUSIC PLEASE? I CAN'T--
--NOW YOUR WJW NEWSBREAK! THE LATEST TELEPHONE POLLS REGARDING DETROIT'S MAYORAL RACE HAVE SHOWN A SHARP REVERSAL, DASHING EXPECTATIONS THAT THE CITY WILL ELECT ITS FIRST BLACK MAYOR.
THE SUDDEN CHANGE COMES AFTER A PARTICULARLY EFFECTIVE TELEVISION AD AIMED AT THE CITY'S WHITE RESIDENTS--AN AD WHICH SEEMS TO HAVE HAD AN ALMOST MAGICAL EFFECT ON PUBLIC OPINION.
I *KNEW* IT. ALL THESE CRACKERS ACTING LIKE THEY'RE ON OUR SIDE. CAN'T TRUST ANY OF THEM.
NO OFFENSE, NUTCASE.
NO OFFENSE? WAITAMINUTE... *I'M WHITE?!*
YOU'RE NOT WRONG, BUT IT'S EVEN MORE THAN THAT.
IT'S *THEM.*

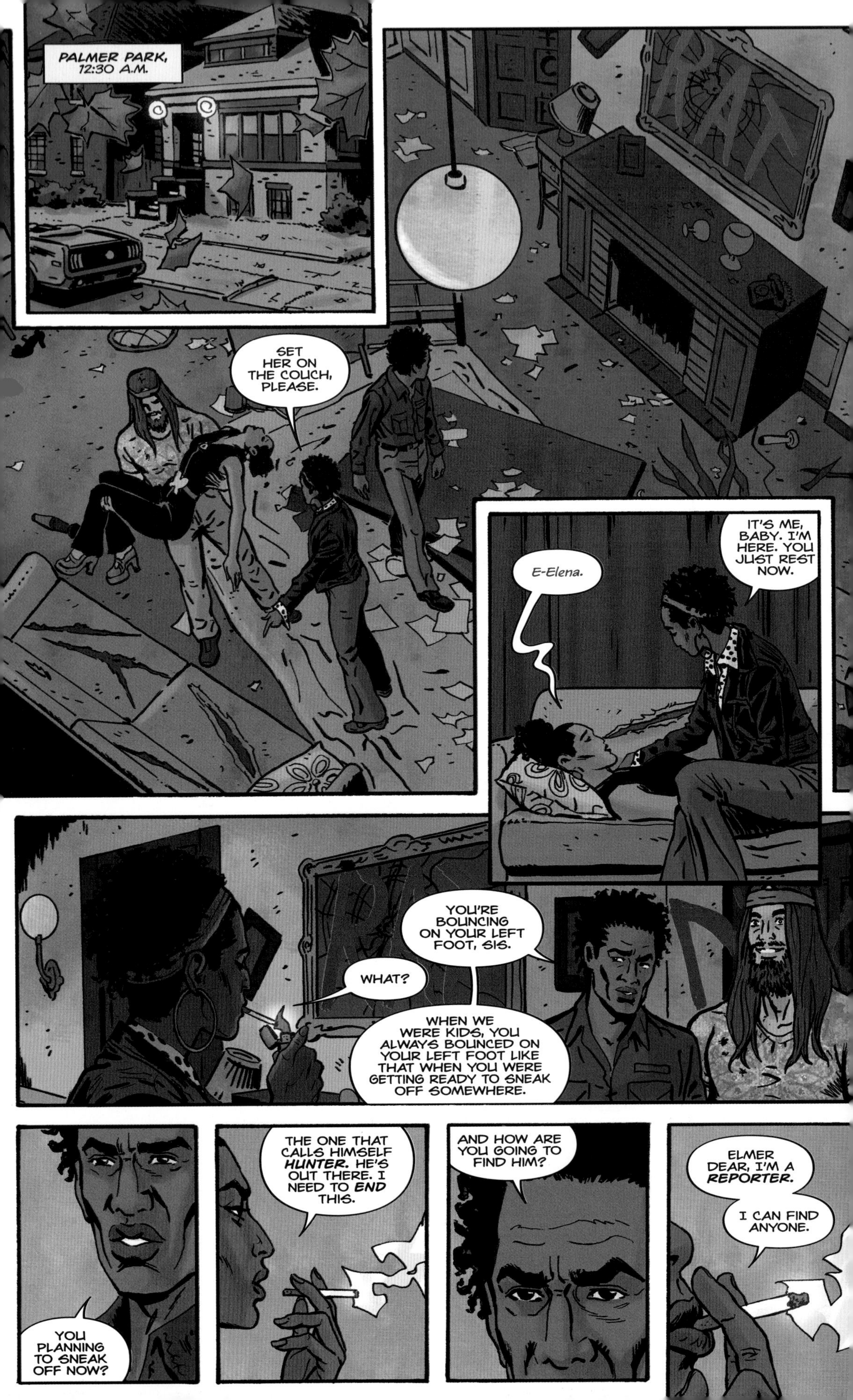

PALMER PARK, 12:30 A.M.
RAT
SET HER ON THE COUCH, PLEASE.
E-Elena.
IT'S ME, BABY. I'M HERE. YOU JUST REST NOW.
YOU'RE BOUNCING ON YOUR LEFT FOOT, SIS.
WHAT?
WHEN WE WERE KIDS, YOU ALWAYS BOUNCED ON YOUR LEFT FOOT LIKE THAT WHEN YOU WERE GETTING READY TO SNEAK OFF SOMEWHERE.
YOU PLANNING TO SNEAK OFF NOW?
THE ONE THAT CALLS HIMSELF **HUNTER.** HE'S OUT THERE. I NEED TO **END** THIS.
AND HOW ARE YOU GOING TO FIND HIM?
ELMER DEAR, I'M A **REPORTER.**
I CAN FIND ANYONE.

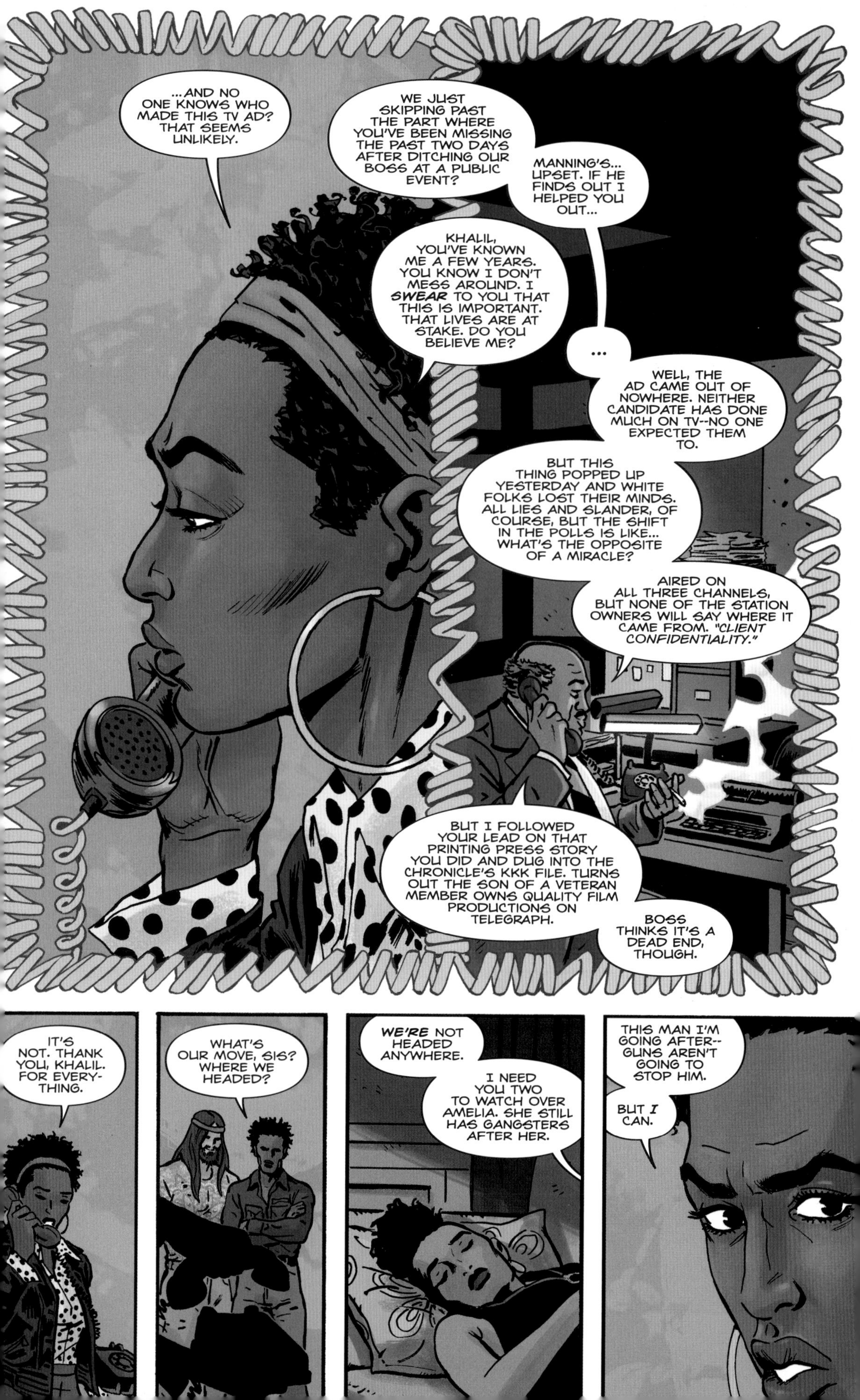
...AND NO ONE KNOWS WHO MADE THIS TV AD? THAT SEEMS UNLIKELY.
WE JUST SKIPPING PAST THE PART WHERE YOU'VE BEEN MISSING THE PAST TWO DAYS AFTER DITCHING OUR BOSS AT A PUBLIC EVENT?
MANNING'S... UPSET. IF HE FINDS OUT I HELPED YOU OUT...
KHALIL, YOU'VE KNOWN ME A FEW YEARS. YOU KNOW I DON'T MESS AROUND. I *SWEAR* TO YOU THAT THIS IS IMPORTANT. THAT LIVES ARE AT STAKE. DO YOU BELIEVE ME?
...
WELL, THE AD CAME OUT OF NOWHERE. NEITHER CANDIDATE HAS DONE MUCH ON TV--NO ONE EXPECTED THEM TO.
BUT THIS THING POPPED UP YESTERDAY AND WHITE FOLKS LOST THEIR MINDS. ALL LIES AND SLANDER, OF COURSE, BUT THE SHIFT IN THE POLLS IS LIKE... WHAT'S THE OPPOSITE OF A MIRACLE?
AIRED ON ALL THREE CHANNELS, BUT NONE OF THE STATION OWNERS WILL SAY WHERE IT CAME FROM. *"CLIENT CONFIDENTIALITY."*
BUT I FOLLOWED YOUR LEAD ON THAT PRINTING PRESS STORY YOU DID AND DUG INTO THE CHRONICLE'S KKK FILE. TURNS OUT THE SON OF A VETERAN MEMBER OWNS QUALITY FILM PRODUCTIONS ON TELEGRAPH.
BOSS THINKS IT'S A DEAD END, THOUGH.
IT'S NOT. THANK YOU, KHALIL. FOR EVERY-THING.
WHAT'S OUR MOVE, SIS? WHERE WE HEADED?
WE'RE NOT HEADED ANYWHERE.
I NEED YOU TWO TO WATCH OVER AMELIA. SHE STILL HAS GANGSTERS AFTER HER.
THIS MAN I'M GOING AFTER--GUNS AREN'T GOING TO STOP HIM.
BUT *I* CAN.

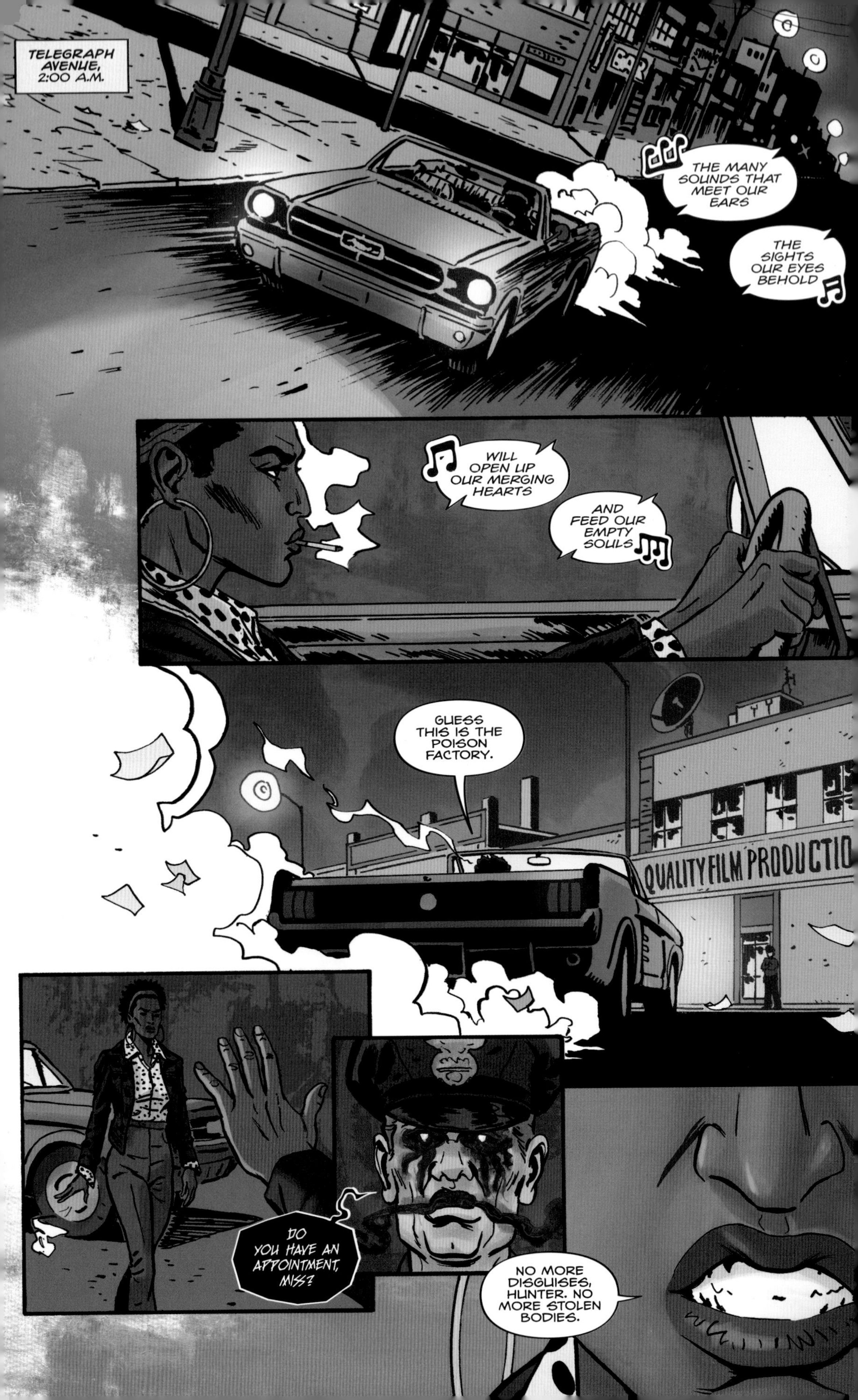
TELEGRAPH AVENUE, 2:00 A.M.
THE MANY SOUNDS THAT MEET OUR EARS
THE SIGHTS OUR EYES BEHOLD
WILL OPEN UP OUR MERGING HEARTS
AND FEED OUR EMPTY SOULS
GUESS THIS IS THE POISON FACTORY.
QUALITY FILM PRODUCTIO
DO YOU HAVE AN APPOINTMENT, MISS?
NO MORE DISGUISES, HUNTER. NO MORE STOLEN BODIES.

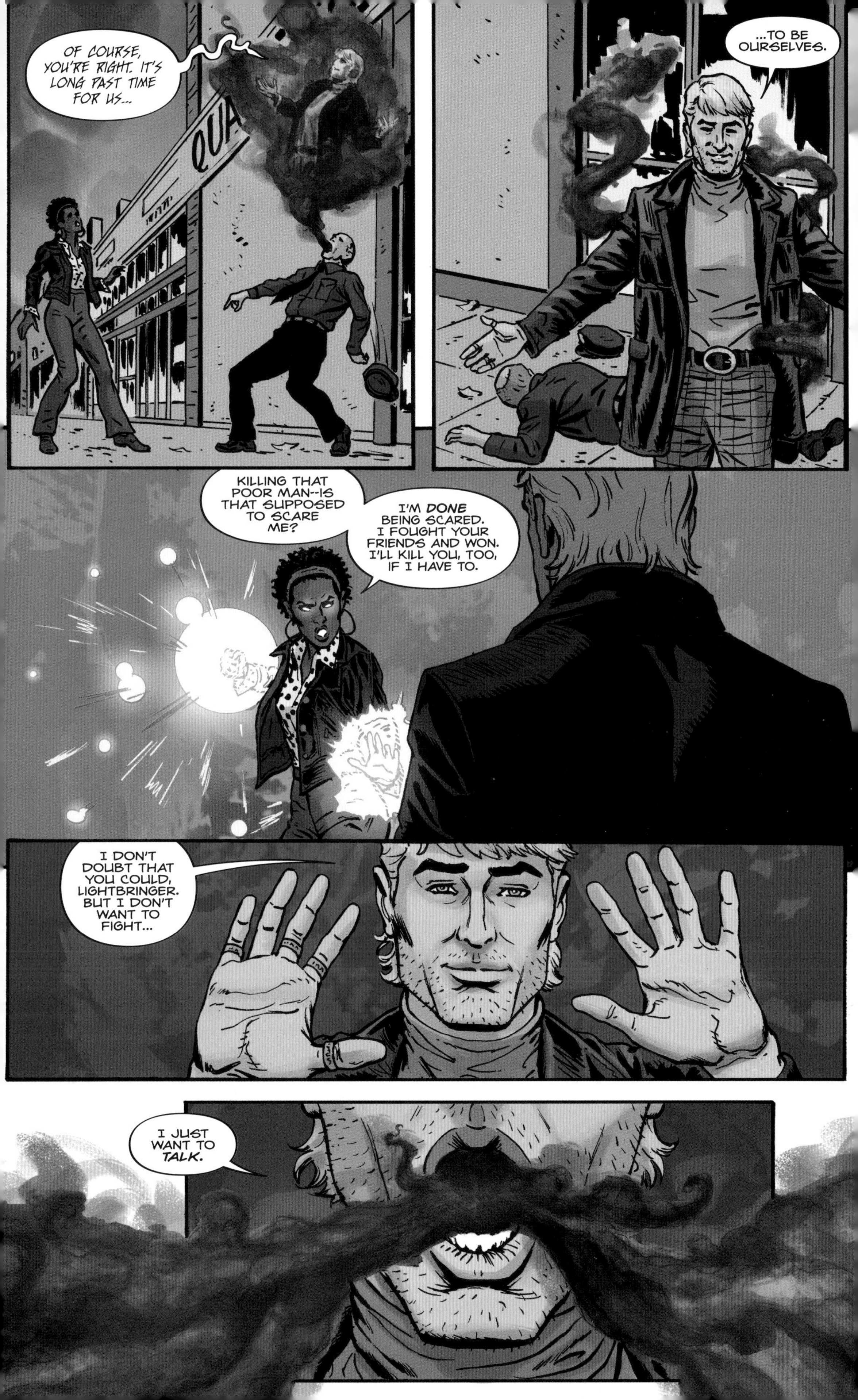

OF COURSE, YOU'RE RIGHT. IT'S LONG PAST TIME FOR US...
...TO BE OURSELVES.
KILLING THAT POOR MAN--IS THAT SUPPOSED TO SCARE ME?
I'M DONE BEING SCARED. I FOUGHT YOUR FRIENDS AND WON. I'LL KILL YOU, TOO, IF I HAVE TO.
I DON'T DOUBT THAT YOU COULD, LIGHTBRINGER. BUT I DON'T WANT TO FIGHT...
I JUST WANT TO TALK.

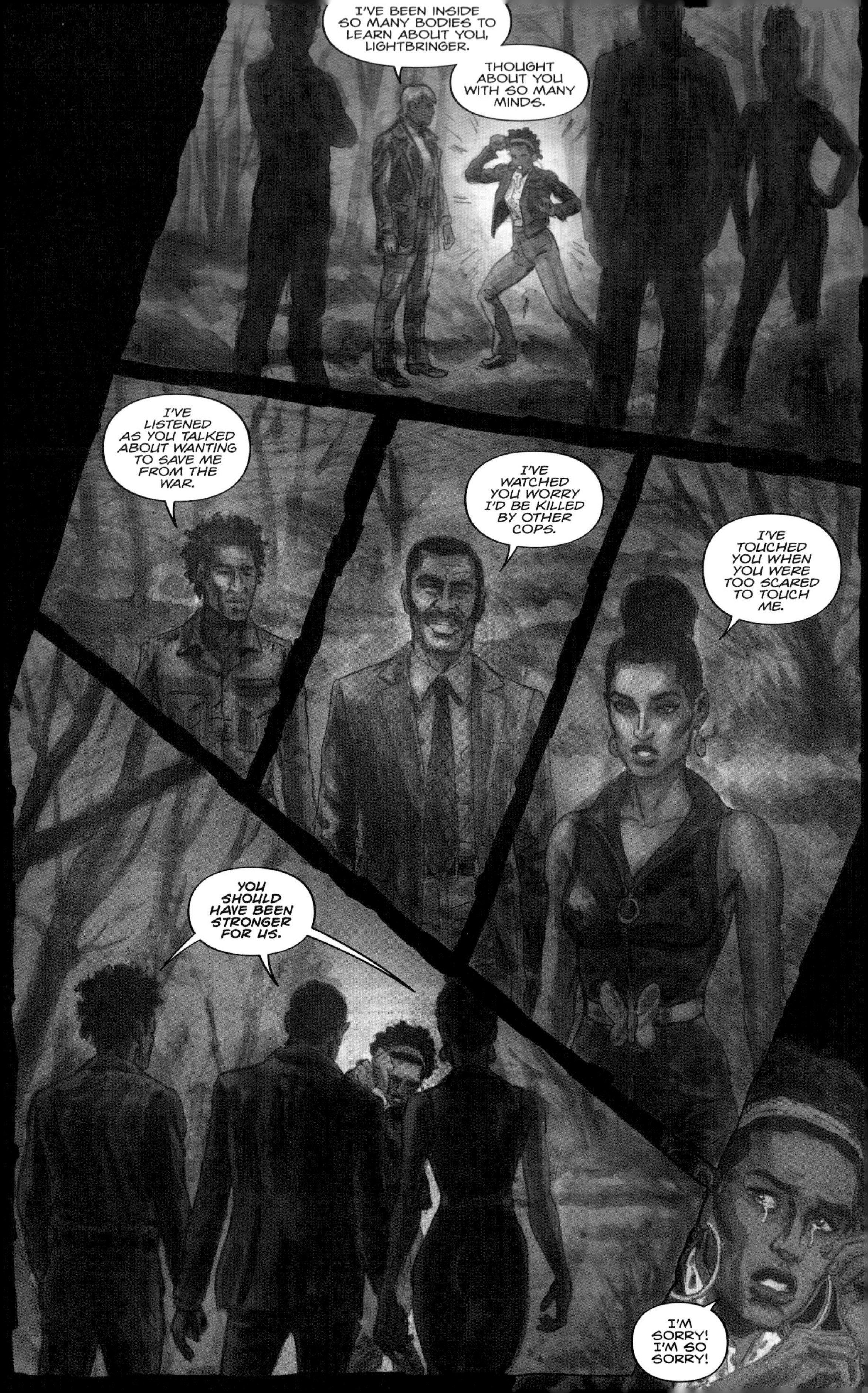
I'VE BEEN INSIDE SO MANY BODIES TO LEARN ABOUT YOU, LIGHTBRINGER.
THOUGHT ABOUT YOU WITH SO MANY MINDS.
I'VE LISTENED AS YOU TALKED ABOUT WANTING TO SAVE ME FROM THE WAR.
I'VE WATCHED YOU WORRY I'D BE KILLED BY OTHER COPS.
I'VE TOUCHED YOU WHEN YOU WERE TOO SCARED TO TOUCH ME.
YOU SHOULD HAVE BEEN STRONGER FOR US.
I'M SORRY! I'M SO SORRY!

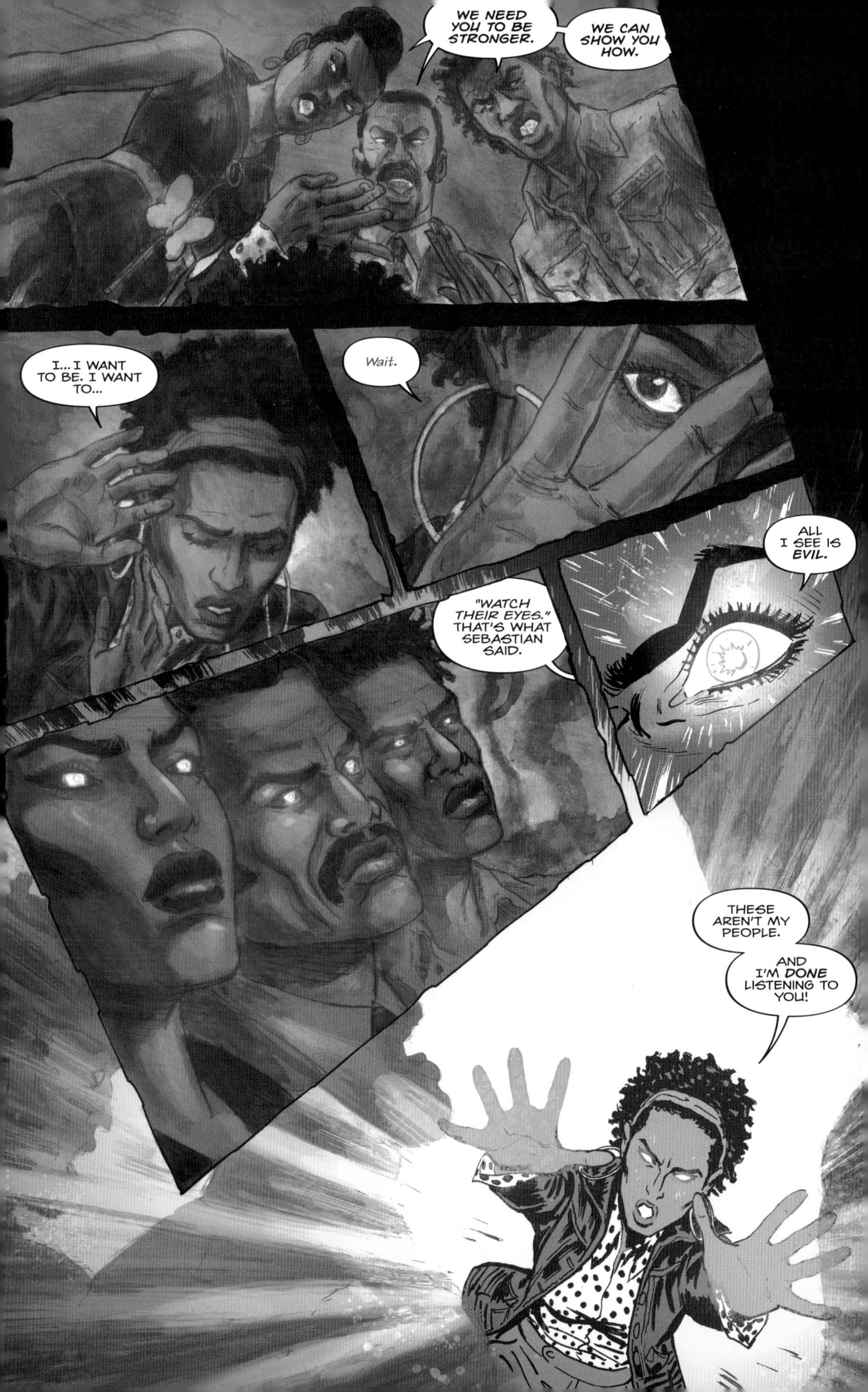
WE NEED YOU TO BE STRONGER.
WE CAN SHOW YOU HOW.
I... I WANT TO BE. I WANT TO...
Wait.
ALL I SEE IS EVIL.
"WATCH THEIR EYES." THAT'S WHAT SEBASTIAN SAID.
THESE AREN'T MY PEOPLE.
AND I'M DONE LISTENING TO YOU!

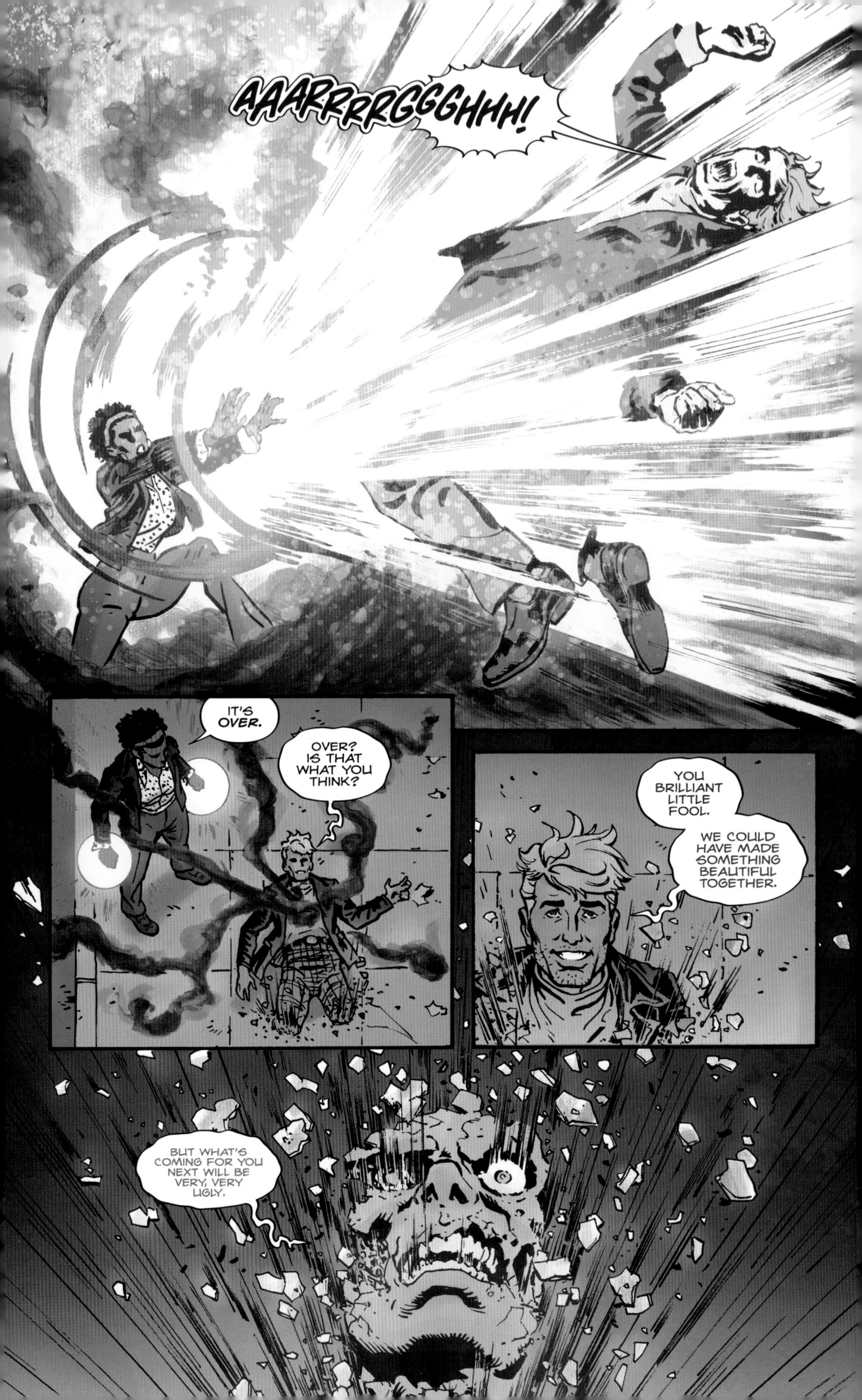
AAARRRRRGGGHHH!
IT'S OVER.
OVER? IS THAT WHAT YOU THINK?
YOU BRILLIANT LITTLE FOOL.
WE COULD HAVE MADE SOMETHING BEAUTIFUL TOGETHER.
BUT WHAT'S COMING FOR YOU NEXT WILL BE VERY, VERY UGLY.

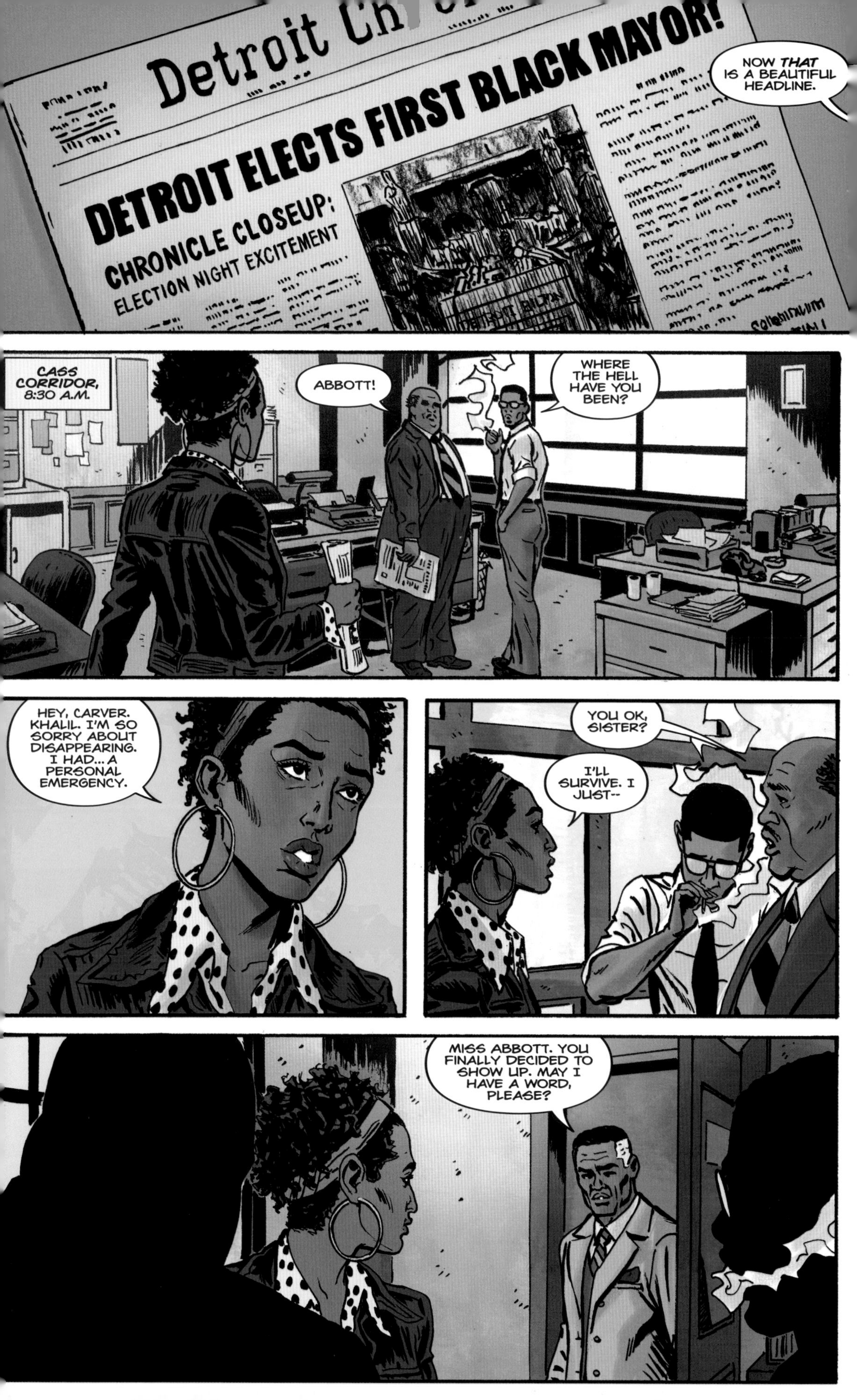
Detroit Ch
DETROIT ELECTS FIRST BLACK MAYOR!
CHRONICLE CLOSEUP:
ELECTION NIGHT EXCITEMENT
NOW THAT IS A BEAUTIFUL HEADLINE.
CASS CORRIDOR, 8:30 A.M.
ABBOTT!
WHERE THE HELL HAVE YOU BEEN?
HEY, CARVER. KHALIL. I'M SO SORRY ABOUT DISAPPEARING. I HAD... A PERSONAL EMERGENCY.
YOU OK, SISTER?
I'LL SURVIVE. I JUST--
MISS ABBOTT. YOU FINALLY DECIDED TO SHOW UP. MAY I HAVE A WORD, PLEASE?

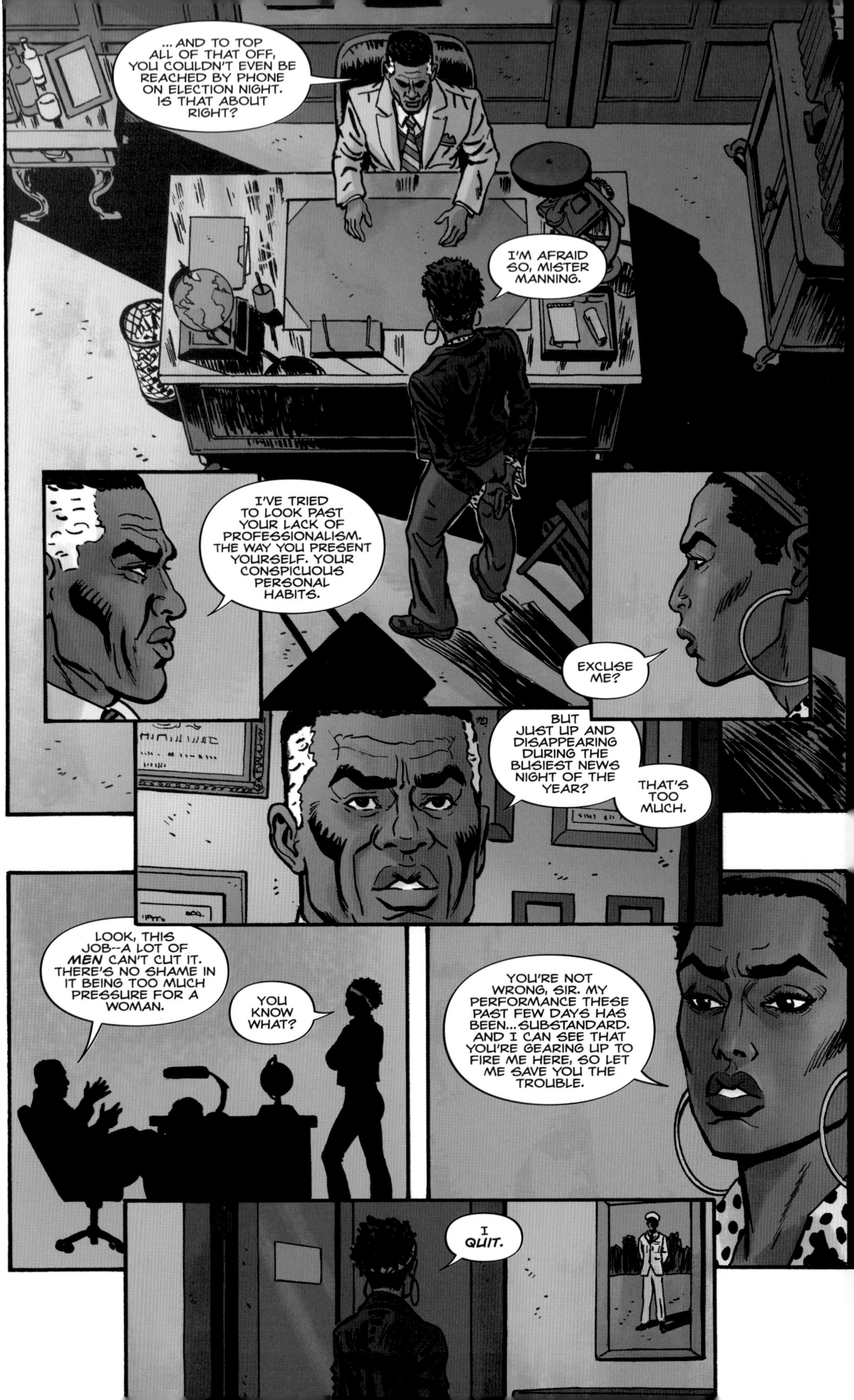
...AND TO TOP ALL OF THAT OFF, YOU COULDN'T EVEN BE REACHED BY PHONE ON ELECTION NIGHT. IS THAT ABOUT RIGHT?
I'M AFRAID SO, MISTER MANNING.
I'VE TRIED TO LOOK PAST YOUR LACK OF PROFESSIONALISM. THE WAY YOU PRESENT YOURSELF. YOUR CONSPICUOUS PERSONAL HABITS.
EXCUSE ME?
BUT JUST UP AND DISAPPEARING DURING THE BUSIEST NEWS NIGHT OF THE YEAR?
THAT'S TOO MUCH.
LOOK, THIS JOB--A LOT OF MEN CAN'T CUT IT. THERE'S NO SHAME IN IT BEING TOO MUCH PRESSURE FOR A WOMAN.
YOU KNOW WHAT?
YOU'RE NOT WRONG, SIR. MY PERFORMANCE THESE PAST FEW DAYS HAS BEEN...SUBSTANDARD. AND I CAN SEE THAT YOU'RE GEARING UP TO FIRE ME HERE, SO LET ME SAVE YOU THE TROUBLE.
I QUIT.

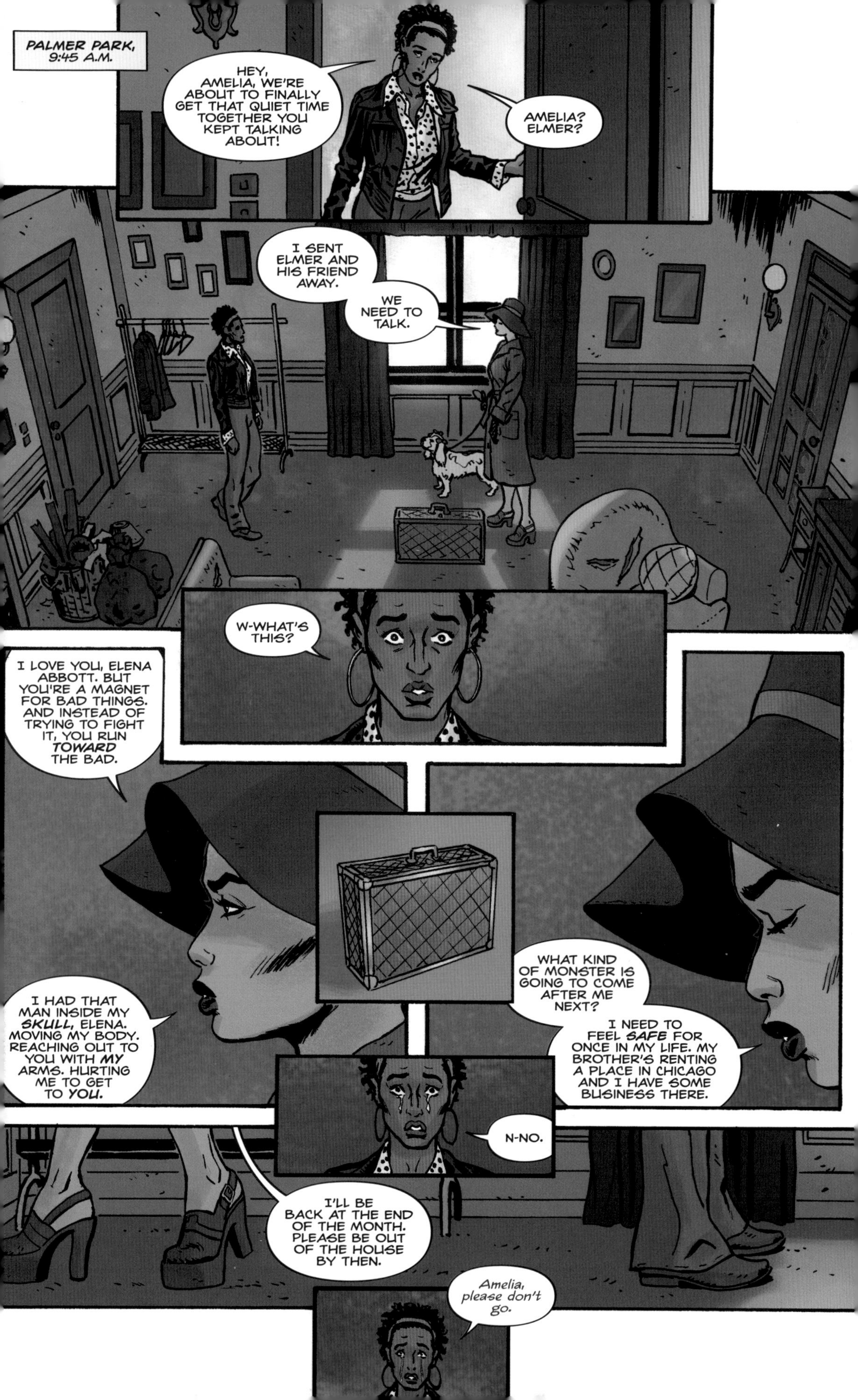
PALMER PARK, 9:45 A.M.
HEY, AMELIA, WE'RE ABOUT TO FINALLY GET THAT QUIET TIME TOGETHER YOU KEPT TALKING ABOUT!
AMELIA? ELMER?
I SENT ELMER AND HIS FRIEND AWAY.
WE NEED TO TALK.
W-WHAT'S THIS?
I LOVE YOU, ELENA ABBOTT. BUT YOU'RE A MAGNET FOR BAD THINGS. AND INSTEAD OF TRYING TO FIGHT IT, YOU RUN TOWARD THE BAD.
I HAD THAT MAN INSIDE MY SKULL, ELENA. MOVING MY BODY. REACHING OUT TO YOU WITH MY ARMS. HURTING ME TO GET TO YOU.
WHAT KIND OF MONSTER IS GOING TO COME AFTER ME NEXT?
I NEED TO FEEL SAFE FOR ONCE IN MY LIFE. MY BROTHER'S RENTING A PLACE IN CHICAGO AND I HAVE SOME BUSINESS THERE.
N-NO.
I'LL BE BACK AT THE END OF THE MONTH. PLEASE BE OUT OF THE HOUSE BY THEN.
Amelia, please don't go.

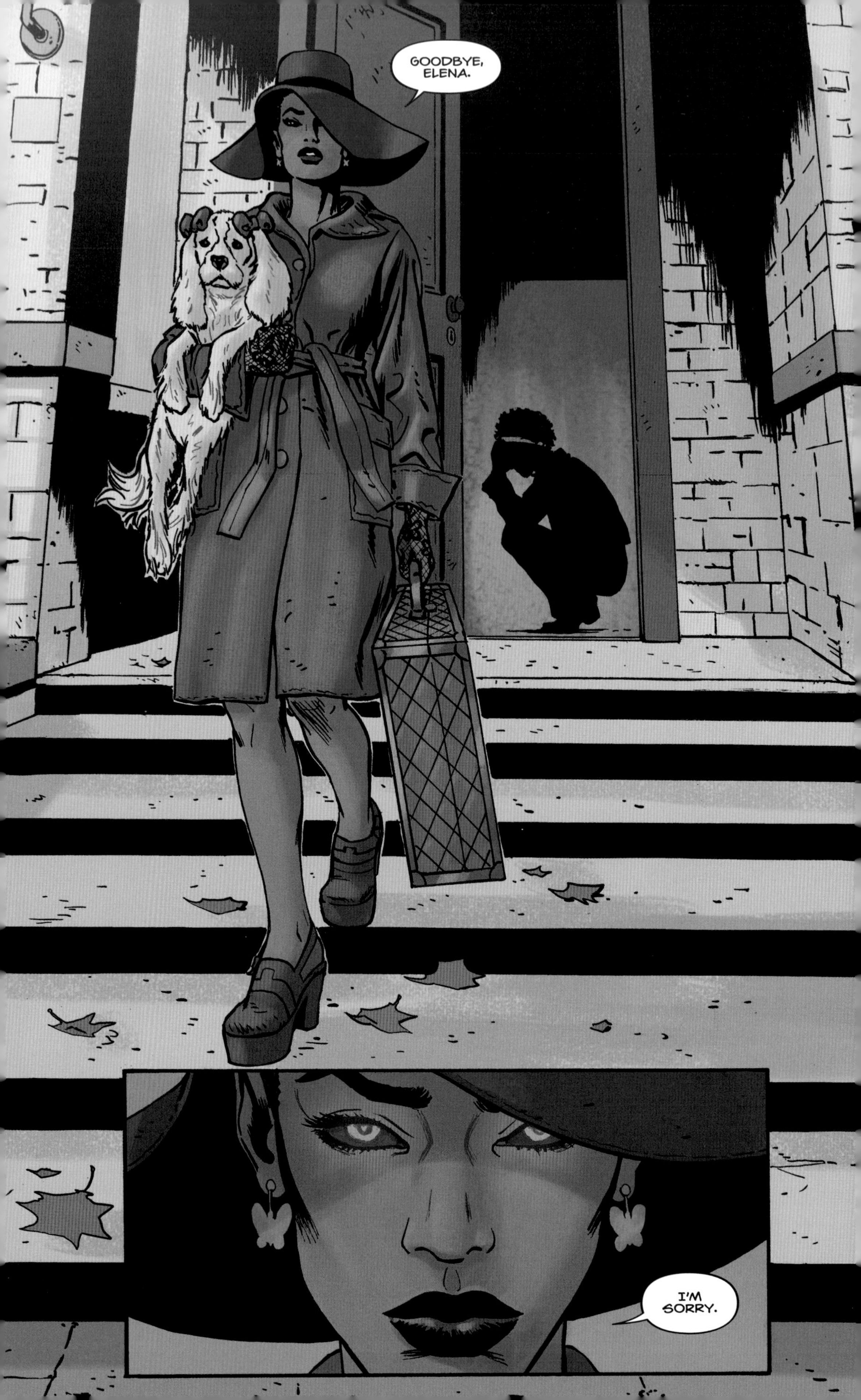
GOODBYE, ELENA.
I'M SORRY.

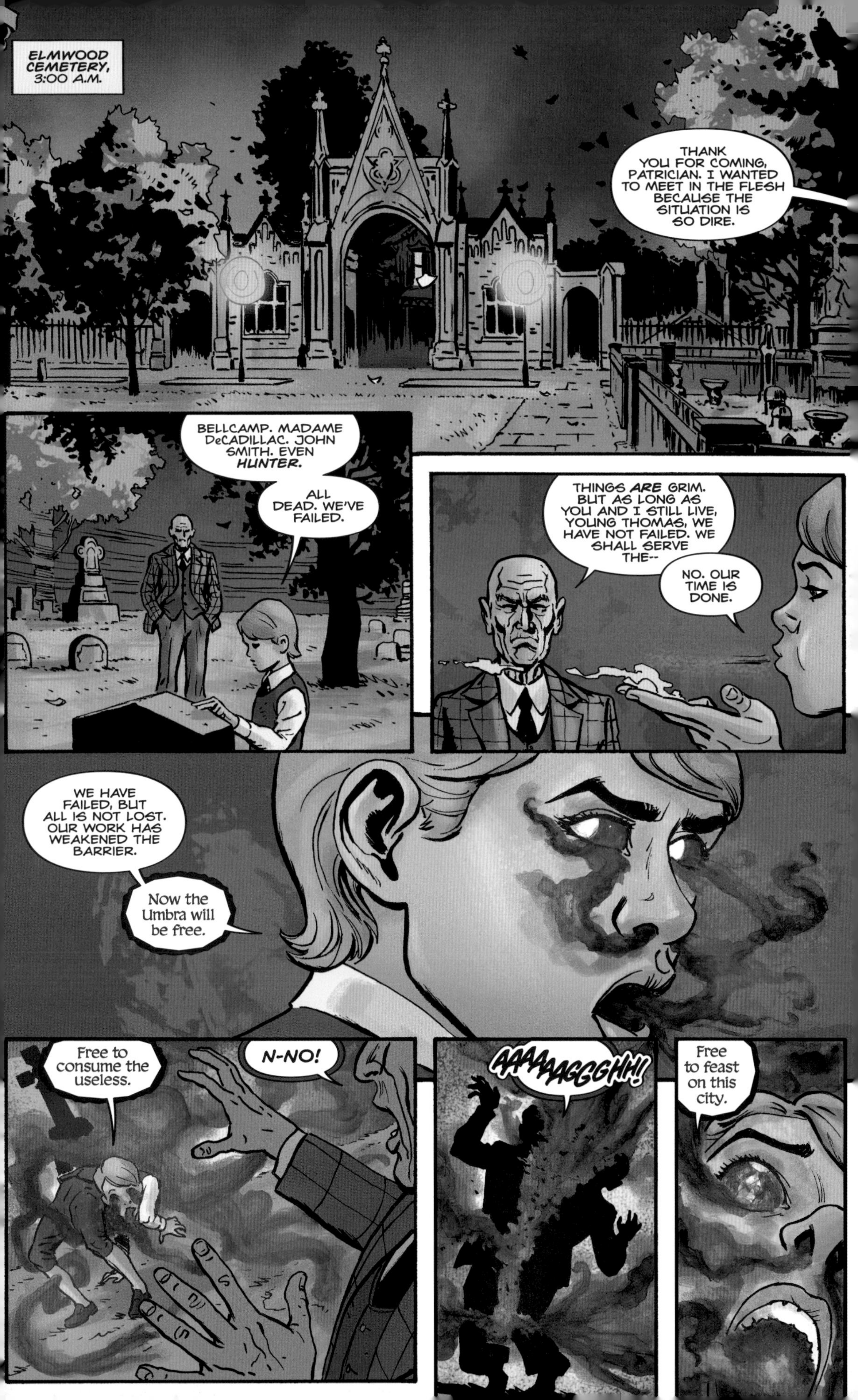
ELMWOOD CEMETERY, 3:00 A.M.
THANK YOU FOR COMING, PATRICIAN. I WANTED TO MEET IN THE FLESH BECAUSE THE SITUATION IS SO DIRE.
BELLCAMP. MADAME DeCADILLAC. JOHN SMITH. EVEN HUNTER.
ALL DEAD. WE'VE FAILED.
THINGS ARE GRIM. BUT AS LONG AS YOU AND I STILL LIVE, YOUNG THOMAS, WE HAVE NOT FAILED. WE SHALL SERVE THE--
NO. OUR TIME IS DONE.
WE HAVE FAILED, BUT ALL IS NOT LOST. OUR WORK HAS WEAKENED THE BARRIER.
Now the Umbra will be free.
Free to consume the useless.
N-NO!
AAAAAAGGGHH!
Free to feast on this city.

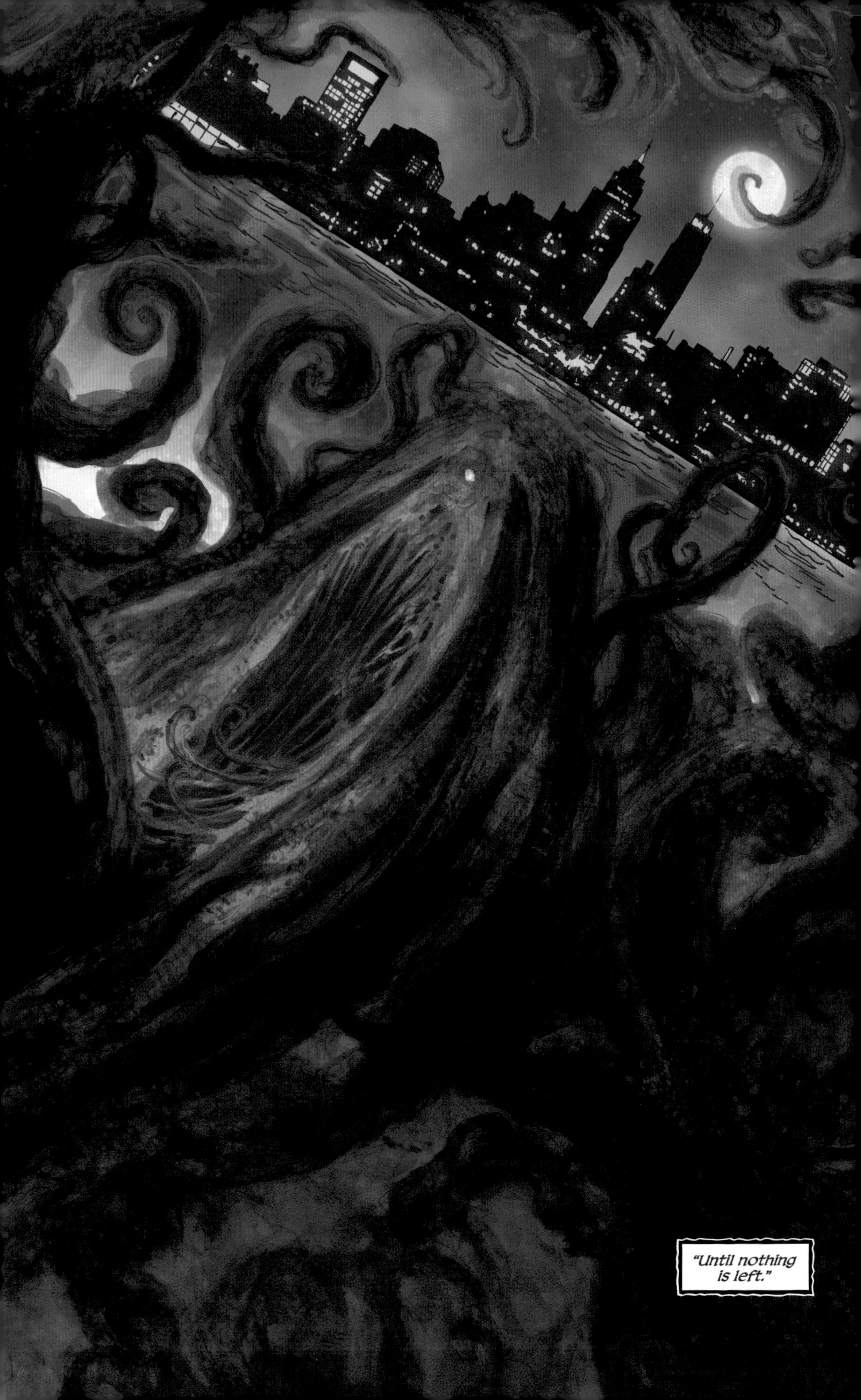
"Until nothing is left."

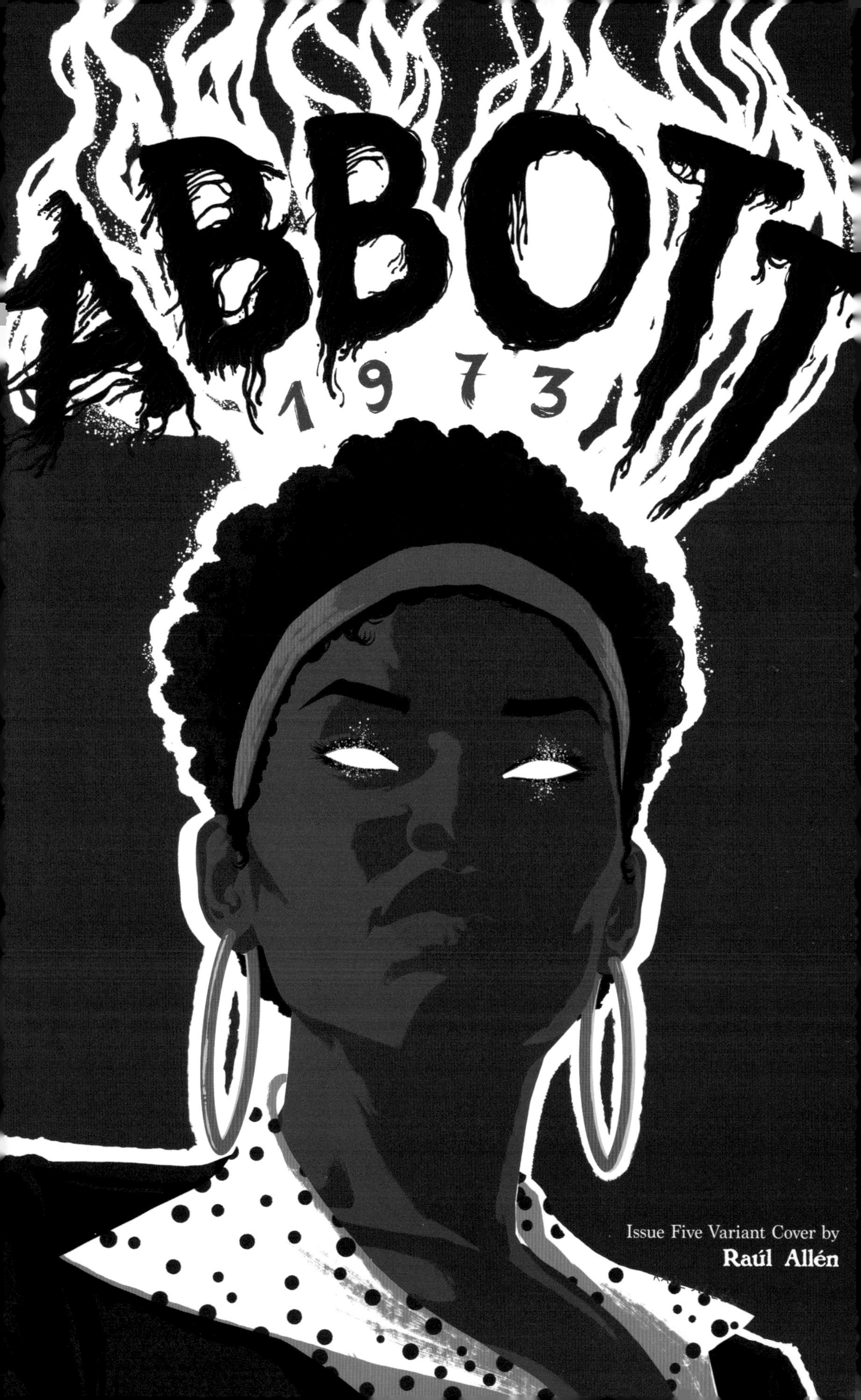
ABBOTT
1973
Issue Five Variant Cover by
Raúl Allén

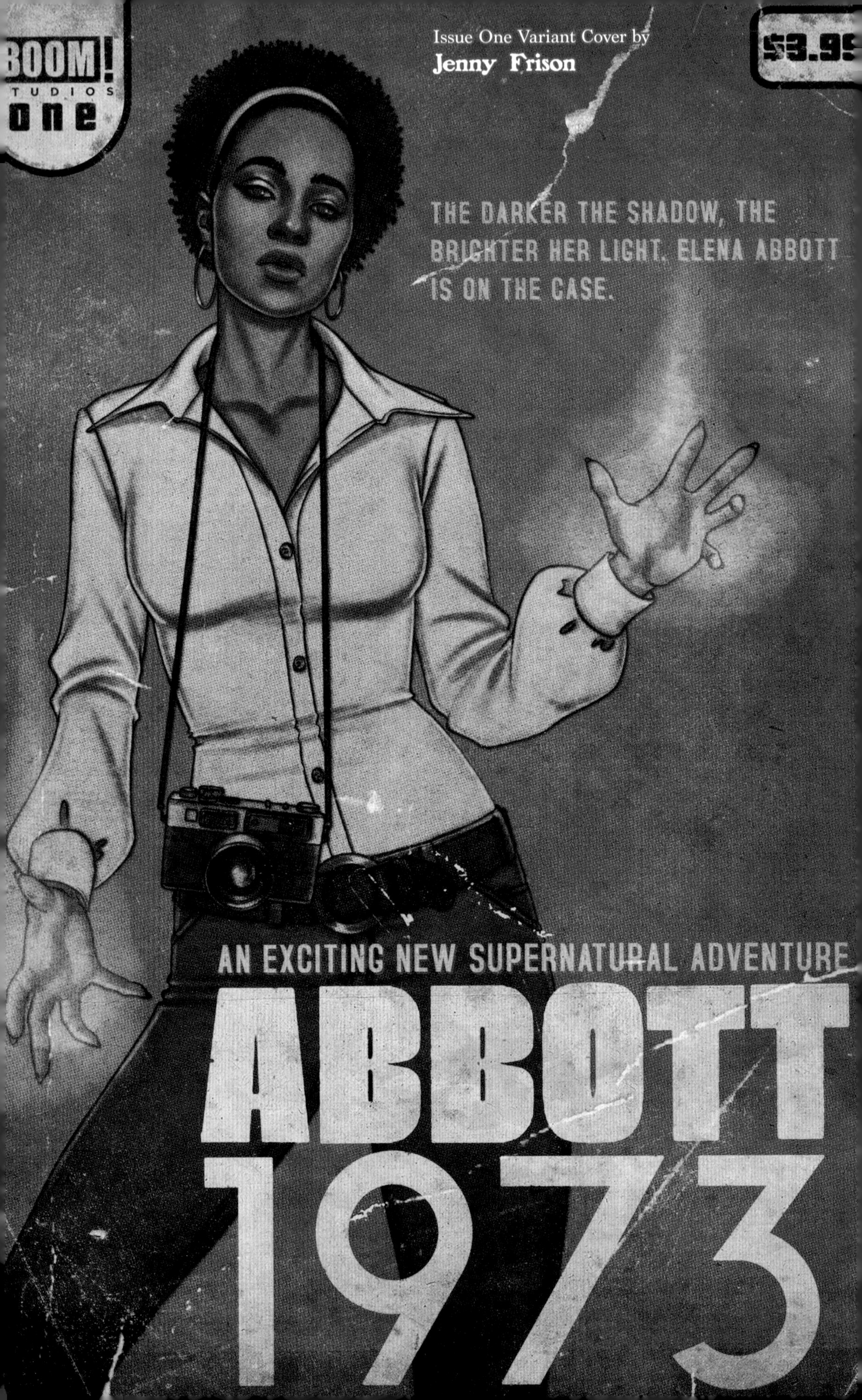
Issue One Variant Cover by
Jenny Frison
THE DARKER THE SHADOW, THE BRIGHTER HER LIGHT. ELENA ABBOTT IS ON THE CASE.
AN EXCITING NEW SUPERNATURAL ADVENTURE
ABBOTT
1973

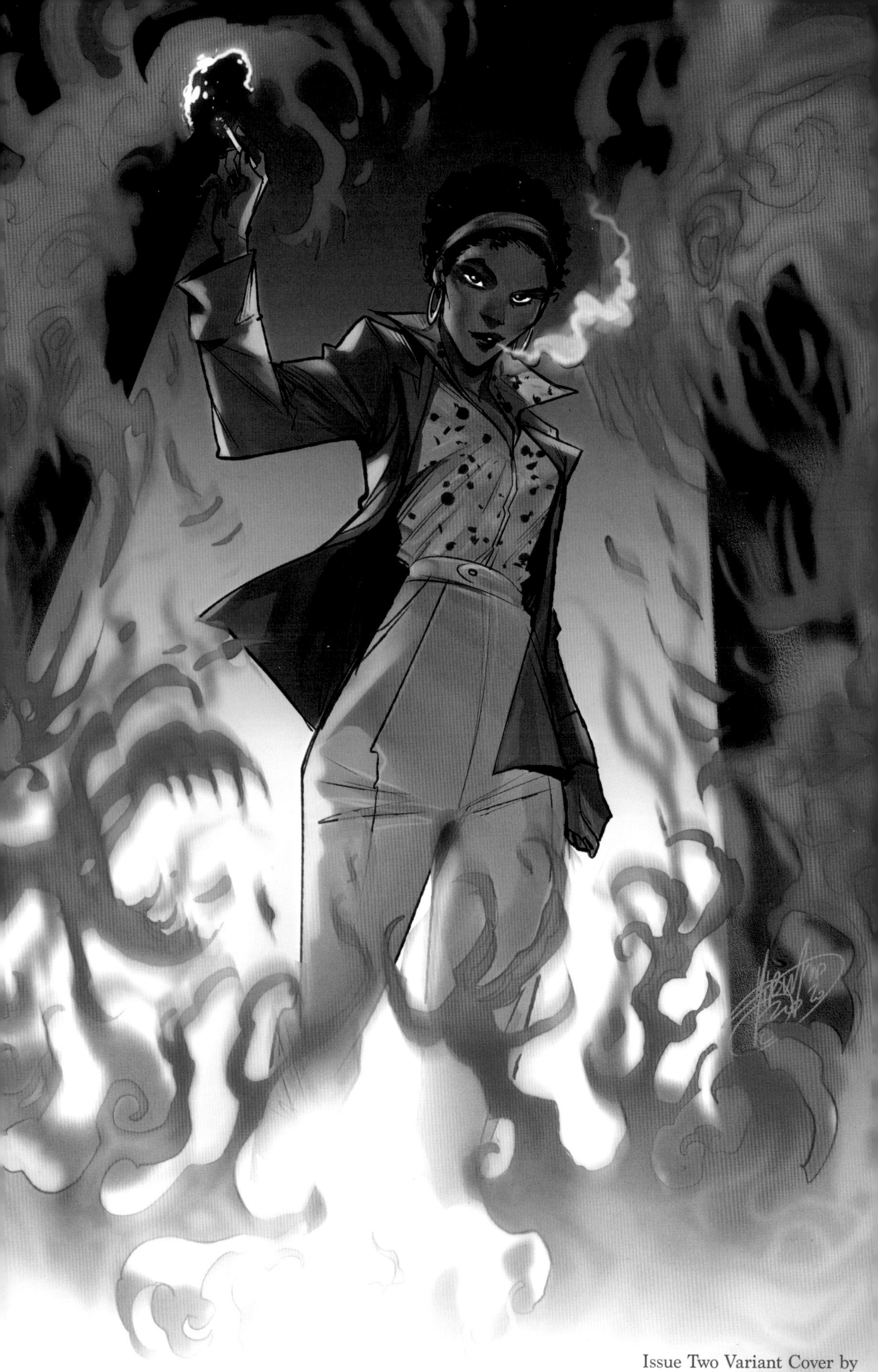

Issue Two Variant Cover by
Mirka Andolfo

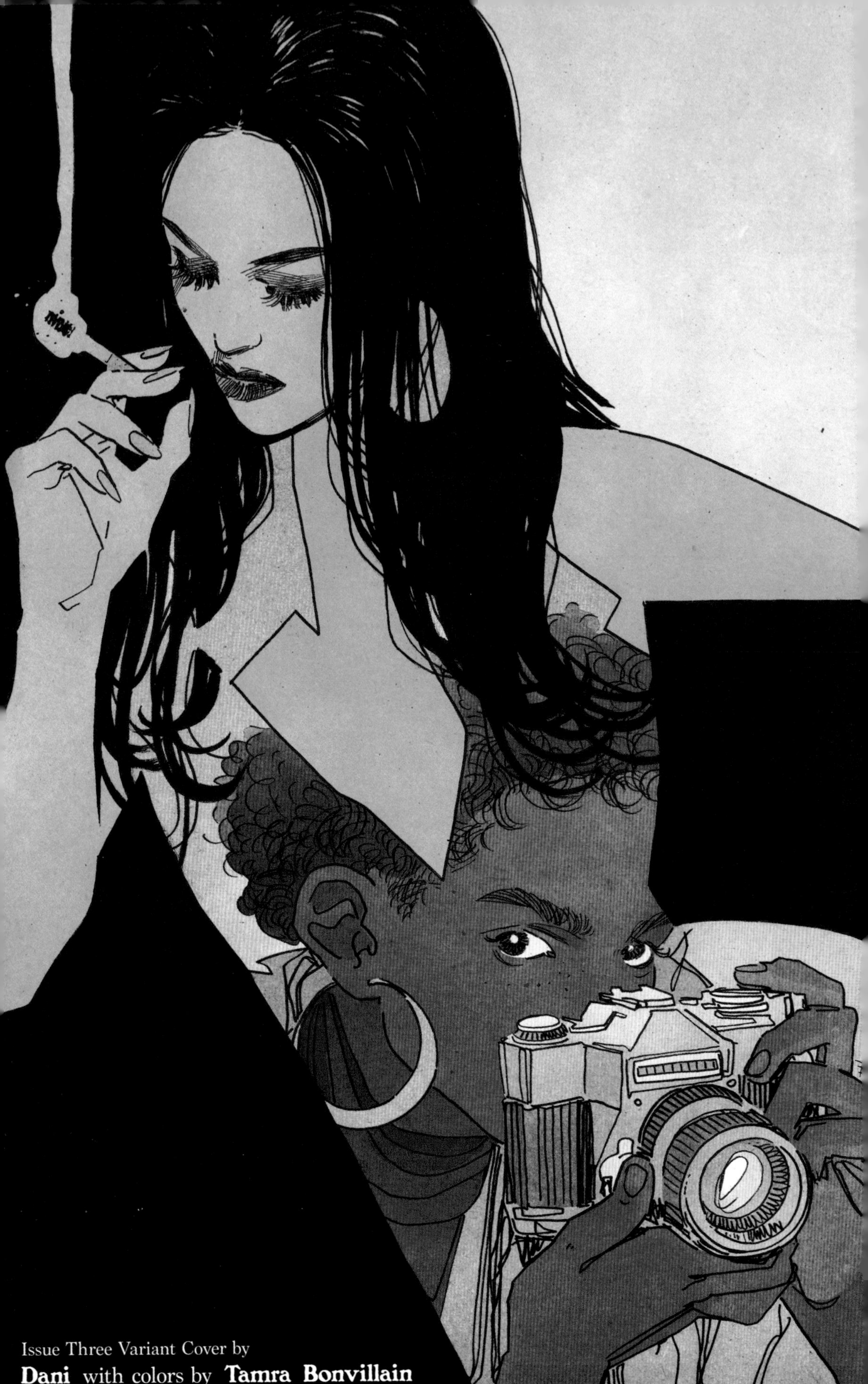

Issue Three Variant Cover by
Dani with colors by **Tamra Bonvillain**

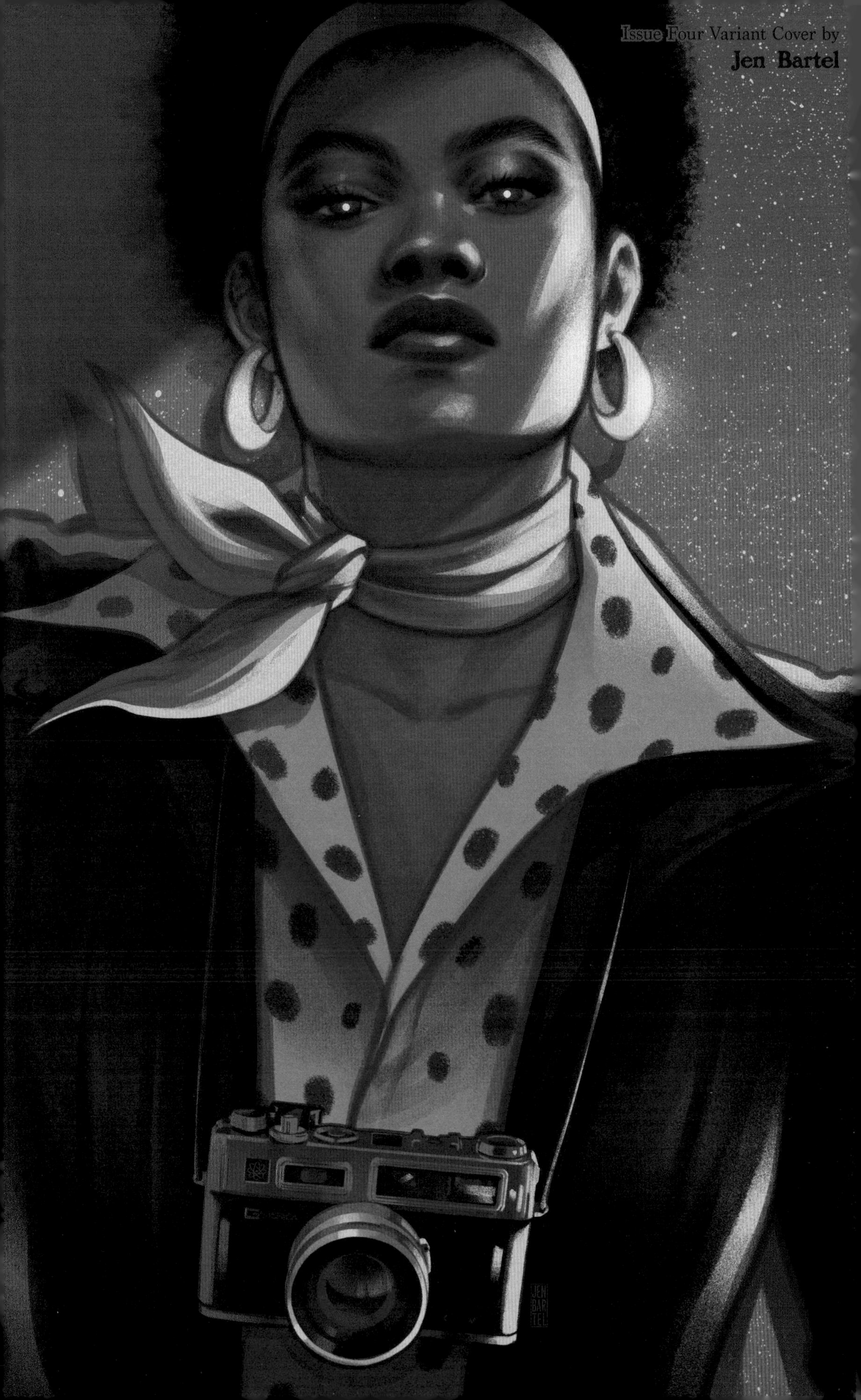
JEN BARTEL

Issue Four Variant Cover by
Jen Bartel

Issue Five Variant Cover by
Tula Lotay

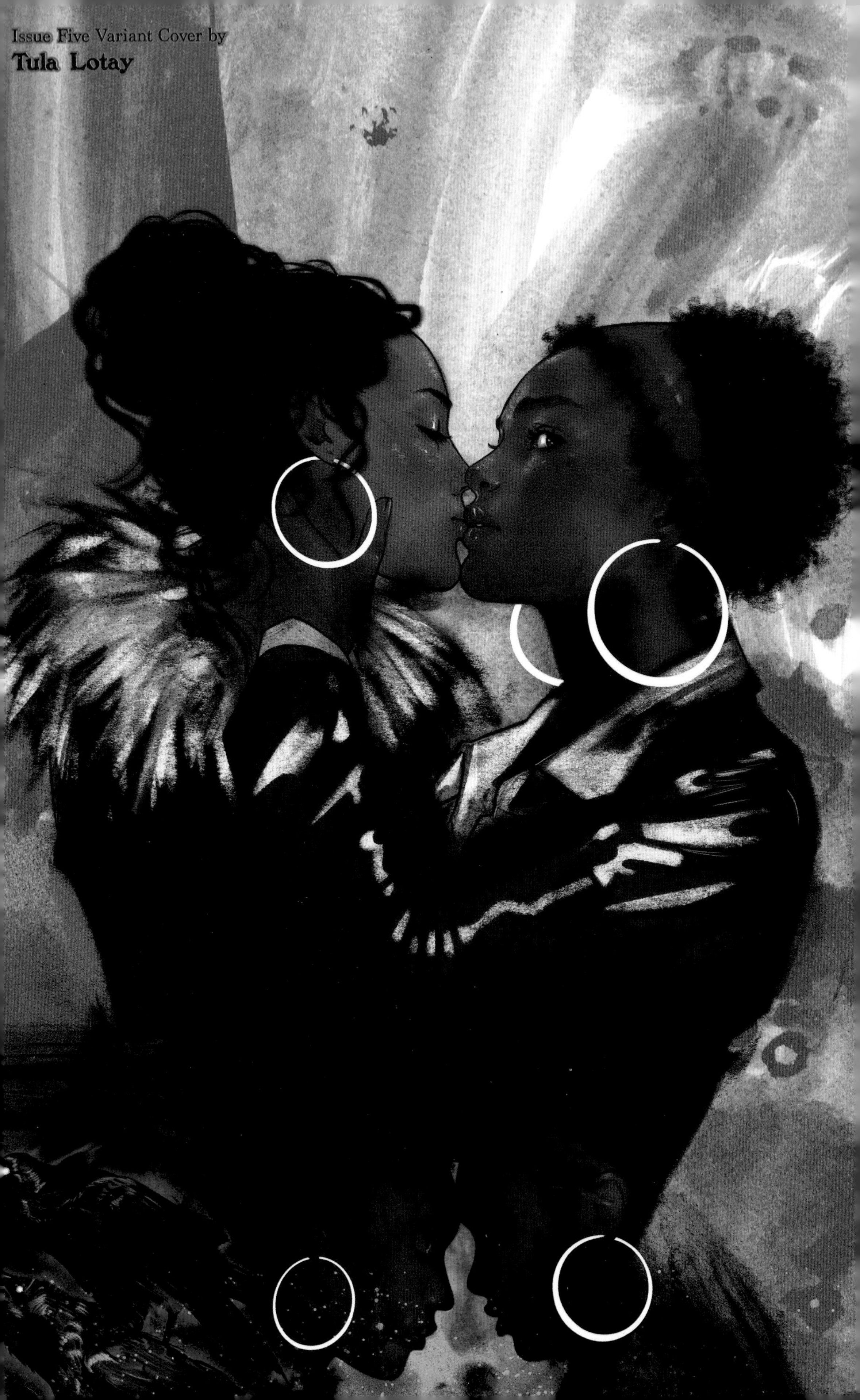